WALKING
by
FAITH

---

*A Daily Devotional
Guide*

by
James R. Thompson
and
Elmer C. Brown

•••

Avalon Valley Press
Graham, North Carolina
1998

WALKING *by* FAITH

Copyright © 1998
Elmer C. Brown

All rights reserved. No part of this book may be reproduced without permission from the publisher, except for the inclusion of brief quotations in a review or article; nor may any part of this book be reproduced, stored in a retrieval system or copied by mechanical photocopying, recording or other means, without express written permission from the publisher.

All references in this book are from the
King James Version of the Bible.

Published by:

Avalon Valley Press
P. O. Box 1186
Graham, NC 27253
(336) 226-4695

Library of Congress Card Catalog Number 97-94843
ISBN: 0-9661986-0-3

Printed in the U. S. A. by:
Morris Publishing
3212 East Highway 30 • Kearney, NE 68847
1-800-650-7888

Table of Contents

Foreword.. 5

Chapter One - January................................... 7

Chapter Two - February................................ 39

Chapter Three - March.................................. 69

Chapter Four - April..................................... 101

Chapter Five - May...................................... 133

Chapter Six - June....................................... 164

Chapter Seven - July.................................... 197

Chapter Eight - August................................. 227

Chapter Nine - September............................ 259

Chapter Ten - October................................. 293

Chapter Eleven - November.......................... 322

Chapter Twelve - December......................... 357

Do You Need to Be Saved?........................... 389

Suggestions for Devotions............................ 390

Topical Index... 391

How to Order Additional Books..................... 395

Acknowledgements

We wish to thank the firm of Cobb Ezekiel Brown and Company, P. A., Certified Public Accountants, of Graham, North Carolina, for allowing us to use their computer equipment in preparing the manuscript for this book. We also wish to thank Gerry Brown for her encouragement and valuable assistance during the months that were required to compile and proof the manuscript.

•••

Dedication

Pastor James R. Thompson's expressed desire was to be a faithful minister of Christ. In Genesis 2:18 we read: "And the Lord God said, It is not good that the man should be alone; I will make him a help meet for him." The Lord certainly fulfilled His promise for Pastor Thompson in the person of Audrey B. Thompson, who has been a faithful minister's wife down through the years. It is because of her faithfulness as a wife that this volume is lovingly dedicated to Audrey B. Thompson. Her devotion to her husband has been an inspiration to those of us who have known and loved her for many years.

Foreword

In 1961 our young family began attending South Elm Street Baptist Church, in Greensboro, North Carolina. It was not a large church, having a Sunday School attendance of between two and three hundred people. We had just about decided that this was the church we wanted to become a member of when the pastor accepted the call to another church. We then decided to wait and see what the new pastor would be like before we joined the church.

James R. Thompson was soon called to be the pastor of the church. He was from the eastern part of the state. We immediately fell in love with the new pastor and his wife, Audrey, so we joined the church shortly after they came.

Pastor Thompson was a graduate of Bob Jones University and he also received a doctor's degree from Luther Rice Seminary. He served as pastor of Livingston Baptist Church, in Delco, North Carolina, for eight years, before coming to South Elm Street Baptist Church, in Greensboro, North Carolina, in 1961.

Pastor Thompson believed strongly in "the Book, the Blood, and the Blessed Hope." He set out right away to teach powerful Biblical principles to his church. What he did permanently instilled in our family and in many other families the great principles of the Bible. Our family (my wife, our son and daughter, and I) grew under his ministry until 1976, when for business reasons we moved out of the area.

One of the things Pastor Thompson always stressed to his church was the importance of daily Bible reading and daily devotionals. At one time our church was preparing a monthly daily devotional guide for our church family, with the articles being written by some of the men of the church.

Pastor Thompson retired in 1984, after twenty-three years as pastor of South Elm Street Baptist Church. After that he served in several different churches as interim pastor, until declining health in 1991 prevented him from doing so any longer. Then, on January 1, 1996, Pastor Thompson went to meet the One whom he had served so faithfully.

It was only after his passing that I discovered that Pastor Thompson had written a number of daily devotionals with the intention of publishing them, but his declining health had prevented him from doing so. After reading some of these devotionals I sensed the need to pick up where Pastor Thompson had left off and to get his project finished. I believe it is important that others share the insights into Christian living with which this humble pastor was blessed.

Pastor Thompson is remembered as a faithful minister of Christ. He was faithful in a way unlike anyone else I have ever known. It is our prayer and sincere belief that, as you faithfully study your Bible and meditate on the content of these devotionals, you also will become the faithful follower of Christ that you have been called to be.

Elmer C. Brown
Titus 2:13
November, 1997

Chapter One

••

January

••

Verse to Memorize

Psalm 119:11

"Thy word have I hid in mine heart, that I might not sin against thee."

January 1 -- Psalm 89:15-17
The Smile of God's Countenance

The Lord called me to be a pastor. By nature I am a peace loving pastor. I do not like trouble in the church. When there is trouble, someone is bound to be angry with the pastor. Even though I do not expect everyone to always agree with me, I want to do all that I can to keep peace in the church. It is my desire to be loved by "my people." I want their smile upon my work and me.

However, it is more important to me to have God's smile upon my work and me. Although I never expect to be named among the great in this world, I do want to be named among the faithful of God's preachers.

Paul, in writing to the Colossians, said, "Epaphras our dear fellowservant, who is for you a faithful minister of Christ" (Col. 1:7). What better thing could be said about a pastor! Preachers are remembered for different things. Some are remembered by the jokes they tell; some are remembered by the buildings they build; and some are remembered by the friendliness they show. All of these are good and have their place, but I hope to be remembered as a faithful minister of the Lord Jesus Christ.

Yes, I want the smile of God's countenance upon my ministry and me. I want the inward calm, peace, and rest of faith that comes only as one has a consciousness of faithfulness to God and of the smile of God. I want to hear Him say one day, "Well done, thou good and faithful servant."

THOUGHT: Pardon and purity in Christ give real heaven in the soul.

January 2 -- Psalm 42:1-3
A Built-in Desire

Every person is religious in one way or another. There is that inner desire to relate to a higher power. We know that higher power as our Lord Jesus Christ. Only the Christian knows this.

In Acts 10 we see that Cornelius had this inner desire. The Bible says that Cornelius was a devout man who feared God and who prayed unto God always. As a result of this desire and this seeking after God, Cornelius was given the Word of God. Cornelius and his household were saved as the result of receiving the Word of God.

We find this desire in the lives of people of the world. Often people will fast for long periods of time really seeking for something that they do not understand. I have just recently heard someone speak of "meditation." This is a way of saying that success, money, popularity, and all that the world has to offer are not the answer.

What is the answer? It is not meditation! A make-believe thing will not fulfill the longing of the human soul. There is only one way to satisfy the hungry heart and that is by putting faith in the Lord Jesus Christ.

The Lord Jesus Christ said, "But seek ye first the kingdom of God, and his righteousness; and all these things shall be added unto you" (Matt. 6:33).

Receive Him by faith, and then walk with Him by faith. "Blessed are they which do hunger and thirst after righteousness: for they shall be filled" (Matt. 5:6).

THOUGHT: The hunger of the soul is satisfied only by the Son of God.

January 3 -- I Corinthians 4:1-2
The Young Christian and Stewardship

Stewardship is often mistakenly believed to refer only to tithing. We mean by this that many people think only of tithing their income as related to stewardship. This is entirely wrong. Stewardship is applicable to many realms of our life. Someone has suggested four tests for discipleship, these being: (1) take up your cross (Luke 14:26-27); (2) obedience (John 8:31); (3) brotherly love (John 13:35); and (4) fruit bearing (John 15:8). We could very well substitute the word stewardship for discipleship.

Another suggestion that I would offer under the topic of stewardship is that you search the scriptures regularly. Read Acts 17:11.

It is my firm belief that a person should be a good steward toward his church in the following matters.

1. Prayer. We can never pray too much for our church, its pastor, and its leaders. We will spend some time discussing prayer in other devotionals. We are urged to pray in Romans 10:1, I Timothy 2:1-8, and James 4:1-3. God has told us to pray for our heart's desire. Surely one desire of our heart is to pray for the church to which God has led us.

2. Presence. We will also discuss the importance of church attendance. We should be faithful stewards in this area. To begin with, we should be a member of a church that stands for and preaches the truth of God's Word. Then we should be in every service possible in order to receive the teaching of the scriptures. Read Malachi 3:16 and Psalm 122:1. Our church needs us to be there in every service if we can.

Our study of stewardship will continue next time.

THOUGHT: We bring honor to the Lord by being in our place in church.

January 4 -- Psalm 4:3-4
The Young Christian and Stewardship

We continue our study of stewardship.

3. Reverence. Many times there is a great lack of reverence in church. Many times it has been my sad experience to have to call down some people who were disturbing the service by talking, laughing, passing notes, or doing other things that were distracting. We need to learn something of the sacredness that should exist when a group of His children gathers for the purpose of publicly worshipping Him. The closer we are to God, the more we love Him and the more we try to please Him. God will speak to us in quietness, holiness, and reverence.

4. Talents and abilities. What talents and abilities do you have? Many people would be quick to say that they have few, if any. I am convinced that more talent is wasted than is developed. Most of us would be surprised if we just knew what we were capable of doing with the help of the Lord. He would show us so much that we could do if we would yield to Him. Read Romans 12:1-2. Many people are held back by a barrier called inferiority complex. In other words, they have no confidence in themselves and they feel that everyone else can do a thing better than they can. As a result of this, they are embarrassed to get up before a group of people and are afraid to try anything. How does a person overcome this problem? First, ask if the Lord would want you, as His child, to perform a certain service. Second, ask if there is any reason why this should not be done and why you should not do it. Third, if God wants you to do it, He will give you what it takes to get it done. Read Philippians 4:13-19 and Matthew 18:24-35.

THOUGHT: Talents can be useful in the Lord's work if you don't bury them.

January 5 -- Luke 9:51-56
Steadfastly

The life of Jesus had been one of helping others. For the past three and more years He had been up and down that little country preaching, teaching and healing. Now He is nearing the end of His life upon this earth.

He had told the disciples that He must go to Jerusalem and that there He would be betrayed into the hands of man and would die. He also told them that He would rise again on the third day. He had "steadfastly set his face to go to Jerusalem."

He knew the cup that He was to drink. He knew about your sins and mine and He knew that He was to bear them. He knew about the ill treatment that He was to suffer. He knew that His own people would turn against Him and that He would be betrayed by one of His own. He also knew that all of this was in the plan of the Father.

Dear friend, what does it matter whether we suffer or not in this life, if it is a part of God's plan? What does it really matter if we are persecuted if it is to conform us to the image of God's Son?

Let us be quick to say, "Here am I, send me" (Isaiah 6:8). Let us be firm in the way that we follow the Lord's direction for our life. Just as Jesus "set his face to go to Jerusalem," let us also be steadfast in seeking, finding, and following the Father's will for our lives.

THOUGHT: To be rich in God is better than to be rich in this world's goods.

January 6 -- Matthew 10:29-31
Hallelujah Chorus

Do you ever become despondent? Do you ever feel left alone? Do you ever feel that nobody loves you and that nobody is concerned about you?

We all probably face times of discouragement and even despondency and despair. This is simply human nature, and as long as we are in the flesh, these things will come upon us from time to time.

We should understand this. It is no sin to become discouraged, but it is a sin for a Christian to remain discouraged. Why? This is true because Jesus Christ is our peace and contentment and we should rely upon Him to carry us through these things.

These verses just thrill my heart and soul. The woods and fields are just filled with sparrows. You can see them everywhere. Yet, God knows about each of them and He is concerned when even one of them falls to the ground in death.

How many hairs do you suppose are on your head? Think about the more than four billion people on earth today. God has every hair on every head numbered. He knows about each of them, even those that have fallen out of our head.

Since God is concerned about the sparrows and since He has numbered the hairs of our head, isn't the real hallelujah chorus the fact that He is concerned about us more than for all of those things?

THOUGHT: If you don't want the bitter fruit of sin, stay out of the devil's orchard.

January 7 -- I Corinthians 16:1-4
Our Giving Ought to Be Punctual

Paul tells the people at Corinth that they should make their gifts on the first day of the week. The principle he is enforcing here is punctuality. They are not to be taking God's gifts from the "bottom of the stack" but from the top.

One man, who was regular in attendance, always came in the church office on Sunday morning with the same statement. As he took his pocketbook from his pocket, he said, "Well, let me see if there is anything left." Usually he found that there was little or nothing left.

God is not pleased with that kind of stewardship. He has supplied our needs and, for most of us, He has given us far beyond our needs. The rent is paid, the car payment is made, the furniture payment is made, and food is put on the table. All of this is done because of God's faithfulness to us. Are we then going to leave thinking of Him and giving to carry on His work until last?

When a person receives his pay for the week, he should take out God's tithe and offerings and put them in a special place so that they will not be used with his other money. The tithes and offerings are not ours to spend but they are God's.

When we go to church on the Lord's day, we should make our gift to Him through the church. I personally do not believe that it all should be given at one time. We will perhaps have more to say about this in a later devotional, but we should make immediate gifts in obedience to His Word. Let us remember to be punctual in our giving to the Lord's work.

THOUGHT: God's tithe comes first.

January 8 -- I Corinthians 16:1-4
Christian Giving

If God's people were faithful tithers, the pastor would never have to preach on financial stewardship. Perhaps far fewer than fifty percent of church members tithe. They miss the joy of obedience and the blessing of God.

In I Corinthians 15, Paul talks about the resurrection. He speaks of the resurrection of Jesus Christ and of the saints. He talks about our new body and our final victory and the immortality reached by each child of God. In view of this, he calls for our steadfastness in serving the Lord and moves from that mountain peak directly to the "collection." Paul thought that our faithfulness in Christian giving was important.

Because of skimpy giving of the members, most churches have to spend skimpily for literature, facilities, furniture, missions, and really in every area of their activities.

The Bible teaches faithfulness in Christian giving. Prayer is mentioned some five hundred times in the Bible and faith is mentioned less than that, but material possessions are mentioned over a thousand times.

Our Lord had much to say about our financial obligation to the ministry of the Word of God. It is said that Jesus preached more on material possessions than on any other subject. Sixteen of his twenty-eight parables have to do with the material things.

It takes money for the church of the living God to operate. God intended that the church operate on the tithes and offerings of His people.

THOUGHT: No man can outgive God.

January 9 -- I Corinthians 16:1-4
Our Giving Ought to Be Provisional

The term "provisional" is being used in this case to mean changeable or adapted to prevailing needs. We will discuss this matter in more detail.

Paul said, "Upon the first day of the week, let every one of you lay by him in store." We must give some thought and prayer to the matter of our gifts through our church. We should work out a system that best suits the program of our church. This has been of real concern to me and I have worked out a system that seems to be practical. I want to share that with you.

Friday is my pay day. As soon as possible after receiving my pay, I go to the bank and make a deposit. I have determined how much of each check is the Lord's. This is a fixed figure. Each week this amount is "laid by me in store." I do not keep it with my money. Then on Sunday I make out an envelope for each member of my family and each of us has an offering to give.

Here is what I believe is an important matter that I want to share with you. I never give all of "the Lord's money" on any given Sunday. I always keep back a portion of it and when we have revival or other special services, I always have money in "the Lord's treasury" to give at that time. For example, if my gifts were thirty dollars per week, I would give twenty seven dollars each week and have three dollars left each week. This amount would be used for special offerings. Of course, at three dollars per week, this would amount to one hundred and fifty-six dollars per year.

THOUGHT: Don't give until it hurts; keep on giving until it stops hurting.

January 10 -- I Corinthians 16:1-4
Our Giving Ought to Be Personal

Paul said, "Upon the first day of the week let every one of you lay by him in store." This is simple language and it is easily understood. Paul is saying that whether there are four or six or ten members in your family, let all of them make an offering to the Lord.

The smallest and youngest member of the family ought to have an envelope to put into the offering on the Lord's day. As these youngsters grow up bringing their offerings to the church, they will continue to do so in later life.

Speaking of the individual, Paul says, "Every man according as he purposeth in his heart, so let him give, not grudgingly, or of necessity: for God loveth a cheerful giver" (II Cor. 9:7).

Again, speaking of faithfulness in giving, Paul says, "Therefore, as ye abound in every thing, in faith, and utterance, and knowledge, and in all diligence, and in your love to us, see that ye abound in this grace also" (II Cor. 8:7).

Where there are children in the home, the father ought to see that each of them has an offering as they go to Sunday School and the preaching service. They should be taught that their family is a tithing family and that there is a gift for each one to give.

THOUGHT: God loves and wants to receive your obedience rather than your sacrifice.

January 11 -- II Corinthians 9:6-11
Our Giving Ought to Be with Pleasure

This is a precious passage of scripture. We could not adequately expound on it here and our purpose is only to mention certain challenging thoughts.

Paul tells us that if we give sparingly we will receive sparingly. This is simple language and it is plain enough for us to understand.

We are told that we should not give grudgingly or of necessity. This means that I should not give wishing that I did not have to and with a deep desire to keep the money for myself. It means that I should give feeling that I am constrained to give in order to have my part in the church and in obedience to God.

My giving should be with a note of joy and with a cheerful heart, knowing that I am having a part in proclaiming the gospel to the ends of the earth.

We must answer the question, "Do I love God and His church and His program of reaching the world with the gospel?" Once we do that, we will have no further trouble with giving grudgingly and of necessity, but we will give cheerfully.

In verse 8 of our reading today, Paul explains the ability of God to make all grace abound to us. We should realize our own unfaithfulness to God and we should pray fervently for His leadership in every area of our life and for our cheerful fellowship.

God says, "Every man...as God hath prospered him...cheerfully."

THOUGHT: We can expect to receive from God what He gets from us.

January 12 -- Deuteronomy 16:17
Our Giving Ought to Be Proportional

The Apostle Paul said, "Upon the first day of the week let every one of you lay by him in store as God hath prospered him" (I Cor. 16:2).

We do not find instructions in the Bible that a person with one hundred dollars a week income should give ten dollars to the ministry of the gospel and that a person with five hundred dollars a week income should give one hundred dollars. We do find the instructions that each person, whether he has a small or large income, should tithe and make offerings above the tithe.

A tithe is ten percent. If a person receives one hundred dollars, the tithe is ten dollars. If a person receives five hundred dollars, the tithe is fifty dollars. Any person with reasonable understanding would say that offerings above the tithe should be larger from the person who receives five hundred dollars than from the person who receives one hundred dollars.

The Bible says that a person is to give "as God hath prospered him." The Bible also says, "For if there be first a willing mind, it is accepted according to that a man hath, and not according to that he hath not" (II Cor. 8:12).

Those people who love God and desire to be faithful to Him will have no real problem in making their gifts proportionate to "as God hath prospered him."

THOUGHT: God is first, then our gifts.

January 13 -- John 5:24
Do You Have a Favorite Verse?

As a young fellow of nine years of age, I responded to an invitation to receive Jesus Christ as personal Savior. I did not know what to do but I did know that I wanted to be saved. I told the pastor that I wanted to be saved. He said, "That is fine, young fellow. Come back next Sunday and we will baptize you and you will be a member of the church."

As I said, I did not know what to do but I did know that I needed salvation, not baptism. No one gave me any instructions. I did not go back for baptism and it was thirteen years later before anyone told me how to be saved.

A preacher, who later became my first pastor, sat down one night with the Word of God and pointed me to a saving knowledge of Jesus Christ. That was many years ago and I am still rejoicing in Jesus Christ.

John 5:24 is the basic verse my pastor used that night. I have loved it ever since. Its message is so simple. Jesus is speaking to "you" individually. His Word is that Jesus died on Calvary's cross to pay your sin debt. He says that if you believe that, you "have everlasting life and shall not come into condemnation" and you are "passed from death unto life."

When one receives Jesus Christ as personal Savior, he receives a new possession, a new provision, and a new position. Have you received Him? Do you have these things?

THOUGHT: Salvation is not by what you do, but by whom you receive.

January 14 -- John 3:1-16
The Love of God

The most inexpressible thought that ever came to the mind of man is the fact that God loves him. There is nothing in man to attract the love of God. Man can do nothing to merit the love of God. Man is completely hopeless and helpless apart from the love of God.

Many of us have memorized John 3:16. We can say it without thinking. We know the words but do we really know the meaning? We got it, but did it get us?

If man would come to an understanding of the words "God so loved the world" and apply himself in the context of God's expression of Himself (that is, "God so loved me"), we would have a different world today.

We would see international turmoil cleared away as each country would be interested in how it could help the other, rather than how it could exploit the other.

We would see great changes in national affairs, as persons in government would see everyone as a brother or sister and not just as another source of revenue.

We would see wars coming to an end and greed becoming unacceptable. We would see fears being abated and sin being conquered. We would see doubt being dissipated by faith and worry being overcome by joy. We would see heartache being replaced by the conscious presence of our Savior. Oh, how I wish that day could come!

THOUGHT: The love of God is greater far than any pen and tongue can tell.

January 15 -- John 3:16
I Am Confident

A four year old boy asked for his third lollipop of the day. However, his mother told him no. Soon, the little fellow was missing. His mother began looking for him and she finally located him about a block from home. He had his pajamas stuffed in a paper bag.

His mother asked, "Tommy, where are you going?"

"I am running away from home," was the reply.

She then asked, "Why?"

"Mama does not love me," he said. "She would not let me have a lollipop."

The mother had to explain that it was because of her love that she would not let him have the third lollipop. Two lollipops a day are enough for any four year old and more would just produce more cavities in his teeth.

This is like many of us today. If we do not get what we want, when we want it, and as much as we want, we feel that God does not love us and that He is withholding good things from us. The Bible says, "But God commendeth his love toward us, in that, while we were yet sinners, Christ died for us" (Rom. 5:8). The Bible also says, "I have loved thee with an everlasting love" (Jer. 31:3).

Yes, I am confident that God loves everyone and we can say with John, "We love him, because he first loved us" (I John 4:19). In Philippians 1:6 Paul says, "Being confident of this very thing, that he which hath begun a good work in you will perform it until the day of Jesus Christ."

THOUGHT: Love lifted me.

January 16 -- II Timothy 3:15-16
I Am Convinced

I do not believe that man would have ever written a book like the Bible. I am convinced that the Bible is the Word of God. I do not believe that the Bible just *contains* the Word of God but I believe that the Bible *is* the Word of God.

No man would have written a book that was to be the basis of a way of life and that was to put forth the principles of that way of life and then have given the unfavorable reports on some of its principal characters as the Bible has done.

The Bible tells about Abraham hearing the call of God, leaving his country, and going into the land of Canaan. It tells of his faith in God. It says that he "believed God, and it was counted unto him for righteousness" (Rom. 4:3). The Bible also tells of Abraham disobeying God and going down into Egypt. Furthermore, it tells of his plotting with Sarai and lying to Pharaoh of Egypt, saying that she was not his wife but that she was his sister. The Bible gives a true report, whether it be a good report or a bad one.

When man gives a report about a friend, he is inclined to tell all the good things but he mentions none of the bad things that he knows about him. When man gives a report about his enemy, he is inclined to tell all the bad things but he mentions none of the good things.

When the Bible reports about an individual, it gives the truth, whether it be good or whether it be bad. Yes, I am convinced that the Bible is the Word of God.

THOUGHT: True faith takes God at His Word.

January 17 -- I Corinthians 15:1-5
It Is Confirmed

Very lengthy discussions and debates have been held on the subject of whether Christ died for all people or for just a few of them. Many books have been written and many sermons have been preached on that subject.

The question is sometimes asked, "Brother, are you one of the elect?"

An old Negro preacher once answered this question by saying, "Yes, I know I am one of the elect. The devil voted against me, God voted for me, I broke the tie by voting for me, and I am elected."

Who are the elect? This question has been asked for years and will continue to be asked and debated for years to come. The best place to get the answer is in the Word of God.

Romans 10:13 says, "Whosoever shall call upon the name of the Lord shall be saved." John 1:11-12 says, "He came unto his own, and his own received him not; but as many as received him, to them gave he power to become the sons of God, even to them that believe on his name." The Bible also tells us, "Whosoever will, let him take the water of life freely" (Rev. 22:17).

These scriptures pretty well confirm that Christ died for us all. The "whosoever will" the Bible refers to are those who actually are saved.

The best thing to do is to receive Him now, if you have not done so. Praise Him for salvation if you have already received Him.

THOUGHT: The death of Christ is sufficient for all, but it is efficient only for those who receive Him.

January 18 -- Romans 3:19-23
I Have Concluded

It is generally believed, whether it is admitted or not, that whether people go to heaven or hell depends upon how good they live in this life.

Someone says, "He was such a quiet man. He was good to his wife and family and he was a good neighbor. You just never see a better person. I know that he must have been good enough to go to heaven."

No, that is not the way one gets to heaven. Our scripture reading for today tells us that all have sinned and come short of the glory of God. Anyone who comes short of the glory of God is "dead in trespasses and sins." One who is dead in trespasses and sins is a sinner. Therefore, he is lost and is in need of a savior.

In the last half of Romans chapter 1 and again in chapter 3, we are given a good description of a sinner. He is said to be without excuse and he is described as being unprofitable. This is a person who needs to be saved.

The Bible says, "The wages of sin is death; but the gift of God is eternal life through Jesus Christ our Lord" (Rom. 6:23). The Bible concludes that all are under sin, all are dead in trespasses and sins, all are in need of a savior, and none are able to save themselves. The good news that is given to us by the Bible is that salvation is available to every person who is willing to put his faith in the Lord Jesus Christ.

What have you concluded? Have you decided to put your faith in Him?

THOUGHT: Sin damns; Christ saves.

January 19 -- Matthew 16:13-18
Three Things about the Church

We have heard an abundance of criticism about the church in recent years. Some people think that God has finished with the church and that He has turned, or is turning, to movements outside the church. This thinking is not acceptable and I want us to look at three things that are right about the church today.

The church has the right master. Peter was exactly right when he said, "We believe and are sure that thou art the Christ, the Son of the living God" (John 6:69). Paul says that we are to grow in our knowledge of Him so that we will be no longer tossed to and fro by every kind of doctrine. Christ is certainly the right Master.

The church has the right message. Our message is the Word of God. Our message speaks of the deity of Jesus Christ, His virgin birth, salvation by faith, and redemption through His substitutionary death on Calvary's cross. The message speaks of a real and personal devil, of the depravity of man, of man's ruin by sin, and of his only hope being in Jesus Christ. This is the right message.

The church has the right mission. The mission of the church is to reach the lost with the gospel and to feed the saved upon the Word of God. It is also to share the Savior with the world and to fellowship together as we serve our Lord. This is our mission.

THOUGHT: The purpose of the Christian is to glorify the Father in the Son.

January 20 -- Isaiah 53: 5-6
Substitute

Recently I ordered three books from a book store in another state. When the books arrived, there was one book that I had ordered and a note saying that two books had been substituted for the other two that I had ordered. This meant, of course, that they did not send the other two books that I ordered, but that they had sent two more books in their place.

This reminded me of what the Lord Jesus Christ did for us on the cross.

The Bible says, "The soul that sinneth, it shall die" (Ezek. 18:4). None of us should ever be guilty of saying that we have not sinned. Each one of us would surely be condemned to death by this verse and we would have no way of escaping this terrible sentence.

Jesus Christ saw the predicament that we faced and He went to the cross and died in our place. Peter said, "Who his own self bare our sins in his own body on the tree, that we, being dead to sins, should live unto righteousness: by whose stripes ye were healed" (I Pet 2:24).

Paul said, "For he hath made him to be sin for us, who knew no sin; that we might be made the righteousness of God in him" (II Cor. 5:21).

Jesus Christ is our Substitute--our only Substitute.

THOUGHT: He became what I was that I might become what He is.

January 21 -- John 4:33-38
Stop-Look-Listen

I grew up by the railroad tracks out in the country. In those days, there were signs at all railroad crossings that said, "Stop-Look-Listen." We were to make sure that there was no train coming before we crossed the railroad tracks.

We have signs given to us in the Word of God to direct us in the will of God. We find one of these signs in John 4:35.

The Lord Jesus Christ says that we are not to wait for a period of time and then plan to go out to reach the lost with the Word of God. He says that the harvest is ready now, not that it will be ready four months from now. We are to lift up our eyes and look on the fields around us for they are ready now to be harvested.

We are doing so little today to carry out the directions of our Lord in taking the gospel to the ends of the earth. People are dying in sin every day because no one has brought the gospel to them.

We are told of over a billion people in China, over five hundred million people in India, and millions upon millions of people in Africa, South America and the Pacific Islands. There are hundreds of tribes that have never heard the gospel and there are hundreds of tribes that have no written Word in their own native languages.

We need to heed the words of Jesus Christ and lift up our eyes and look on the fields. What will you do about His command to you?

THOUGHT: We must go ourselves or we must send a substitute instead.

January 22 -- Matthew 9:35-38
Slums and Ghettos

Many cities across America have areas of utter poverty and filth. People who live in small towns or rural areas and who never get into the cities do not realize what an unsightly appearance some of these places present.

Some years ago I was in another country and visited some of the larger cities there. In one of the cities I went into a massive ghetto in which thousands of people lived. It was sickening to see the utter congestion, confusion and filth. The people lived in little shacks. Sometimes ten people would live in one room about twelve feet square. I was angered that anyone should have to call this his own home. There were hundreds of these little huts that were all jammed up together. They all looked alike and they had just a narrow trail winding around between them.

It made me think of the words of Jesus in today's scripture reading. Until we can have enough vision to look past the poverty and the physical filth and see that the spiritual need is far beyond the physical need, we will accomplish very little in missions work.

Jesus saw these people as depraved in heart, apart from God, deceived by man, and destined for hell. How do we see them? How we see them will determine what we do to try to reach them.

THOUGHT: Why should anyone hear the gospel twice before everyone has heard it once?

January 23 -- Revelation 22:1-5
Heaven Is a Place of Eternity

Billy Sunday used to tell a story to illustrate the length of eternity. We would like to repeat his story here.

Suppose that a bird takes one grain of sand from this earth and flies for one million years to a distant planet where he deposits the grain of sand. He then flies back to this earth over the next million years and repeats the process until he has moved this earth to that distant planet. Suppose that he then flies at the same rate of speed and moves the earth back to its original position. By the time that he finishes doing all this it still would not be breakfast time in eternity. This is one way of saying that time has ceased to be and that we no longer measure the length of time in eternity.

In relating to eternity, the Bible uses the terms "for ever and ever." This means "ages on end." Everlasting means that it never comes to an end. It just goes on and on and on without end. The Bible says that this is the kind of life Christians have. We shall live forever with our Savior. The way that we get that life is by receiving Jesus Christ as our personal Savior. The Bible also makes it clear that those who do not receive Jesus as Savior are destined for the torments of hell for eternity.

Where do you plan to be in eternity? If you have not planned to be in the presence of the Lord by accepting Jesus Christ as your Savior, then you have planned to face everlasting punishment that was intended for the devil and his angels. You still can change your plans. Why don't you accept Him now?

THOUGHT: Eternity is the same length whether you are in heaven or hell.

January 24 -- Luke 19:11-27
Occupy Till I Come

Suppose that you have a tire on your car that is just about flat. You take it to the mechanic and you ask him to fix the tire. You tell him that you will stop by and get it later in the day. You come back in the afternoon and find your car filled with gas; it has new seat covers; it even has a new paint job, but the tire is still flat.

When you ask why the tire is not fixed and why all the other things which you did not ask for have been done, the mechanic has an answer. He tells you that he wanted to make the car look as nice as he could and that he wanted you to have plenty of gas. He cannot understand why you are so upset that he has done so many things to beautify your car.

Do you think that sounds silly?

Jesus Christ left here almost two thousands years ago and just before He left He gave us the command to "preach the gospel to every creature" (Mark 16:15). We have built beautiful church buildings and we have erected tall steeples. We have put together great choirs and we have put together perfect organizations. We have been involved in much other activity but the world is still lost. We are doing so little to reach the world for Christ.

The nobleman in the parable told his servants, "Occupy till I come." How faithful are we being in using what the Lord has given us to "occupy" until He comes back again?

THOUGHT: The duty of the many should not be the task of the few.

January 25 -- Revelation 22:1-5
Heaven Is a Place of Comfort

Some time ago I was called to a home where the husband had just told the wife that he no longer loved her and that he was leaving. With that, he took the family car and drove off into the dark, leaving a broken-hearted young wife and two small children behind to face an uncertain future.

Stories like this one are being told over and over again across our land. More people than we can imagine are living in misery and with heartache. These people wonder where the comfort of this life is to be found. If we were in their situation we would wonder the same thing.

In Luke 16:25 the word that was given to the rich man who cried out from the torment of hell was, "Son, remember that thou in thy lifetime receivedst thy good things, and likewise Lazarus evil things: but now he is comforted, and thou art tormented."

Lazarus lay at the gate of the rich man and wanted only the crumbs from the table. His body was filled with sores. He was not able to walk to the rich man's house himself but was laid there by his loved ones. He had little of this world's goods while he was on earth, but now we see that he is comforted in the presence of God and the rich man is tormented in hell.

Whatever the condition of the people of God in this life, we can rest assured that heaven is a place of comfort.

THOUGHT: Keep looking up toward heaven. Jesus may come today.

January 26 -- II Corinthians 5:6-9
Heaven Is a Place of Joy

Quite often people discuss what heaven is going to be like and what joy will be theirs after reaching that place. Quite often it is also fairly evident that they do not even know what they are saying.

Some people say, "I will be glad when I get out of all the trouble and trials of this old world." All of us will be glad to do that, but this is probably not the best and most justifiable reason for wanting to go to heaven.

Other people say, "I am looking forward to heaven so that I can lie down by the river and rest for a thousand years." Anyone who reads the scriptures as they relate to life after death will know that our stay in heaven is going to be active. We will neither have nor want many occasions to lie down and rest. The greatest joy one can have is the joy of serving others. Revelation 7:15 speaks of those in heaven as living before God and serving Him every day.

One of the greatest thrills that we can have in this life is that of helping someone else in their Christian life. When people tell me that my message was a great help and encouragement to them or that my counseling answered many questions and has helped them to live for the Lord, I have to bow my head in thanksgiving to God that He has allowed me to have this joy.

THOUGHT: The greatest joy that a Christian will ever know is that of serving God for eternity.

January 27 -- Ephesians 6:10-18
Normal Christian Life

Many of us think it strange that a person depends upon his own works and experiences for assurance of salvation. Yet, we so often depend upon these same things for assurance that we are following the Lord faithfully.

Verse 10 of today's scripture tells us to "be strong in the Lord, and in the power of his might." There is no strength in an abundance of work. There is no strength in a lot of experience. Rather than giving us strength, these prove to be our weaknesses because they never really satisfy. We usually find that our works are not enough or our experiences are not as sensational as those someone else has had.

God expects His children to live the Spirit filled life. This is the normal Christian life. We will live this kind of life only as we are surrendered to our Lord. We will be surrendered to Him only as we understand who He is. We will understand who He is only as we have a knowledge of the Word of God.

We will be strong in the Lord and in the power of His might only as we are strong in the Word of God and understand what it says.

Many people know about God but they do not know God. They know about the Bible but they do not know the Bible. They know about the Savior but they do not know the Savior. We will know Him as we know the Word.

THOUGHT: Most of us live such a sub-normal Christian life that if we see one living the normal Christian life we think that he is abnormal.

January 28 -- Revelation 21:14-18
Heaven Is a Big Place

Dr. T. T. Martin said that when he was a boy, he heard preachers talk people out of going to heaven by saying that smokers, chewers, stealers, and others of questionable character were not going there. Dr. Martin said that he grew up thinking heaven was such a small place that only a few people could ever go there.

Revelation 21:16 gives the dimensions of the capital city, the new Jerusalem. It is described as being a cube with 12,000 furlongs on each side. Broken down into feet, this would be about 6,984,000 feet, which is about 1,328 miles. One wall is said to be about 216 feet wide and it is made of solid jasper stone.

According to this description of heaven, it is a big place. If we were to allow fifty feet between floors, the city would be about 139,680 stories high. This is only the new Jerusalem. Think how big all of heaven must be, and how many people could be accommodated there.

Read Revelation 7:9, which says, "After this I beheld, and, lo, a great multitude, which no man could number, of all nations, and kindreds, and people, and tongues, stood before the throne, and before the Lamb, clothed with white robes, and palms in their hands."

Heaven is big enough to take care of all who will get there. The Bible says, "Whosoever will, let him take the water of life freely" (Rev. 22:17).

THOUGHT: Heaven is a place where all troubles, trials, and afflictions have come to an end.

January 29 -- Matthew 25:31-46
We Need Preaching about Judgment and Hell

Any preacher who preaches faithfully will preach on judgment and hell because the Bible has much to say about both of them. The Bible speaks of the "unprofitable servant" being cast into outer darkness where there will be weeping and gnashing of teeth. In today's scripture it says to those who do not accept the Lord, "Depart from me, ye cursed, into everlasting fire, prepared for the devil and his angels."

One of the most horrible descriptions of hell is given in Luke 16. Hell is described there as a place of fire and a place of torment. It is a place where there is no mercy at all and a place where there is no comfort. It is a place to which the occupants do not want others to come. These verses describe hell as a real place and a place where people go to suffer torment forever.

Parents have said, "I do not want my children frightened with stories about hell. I don't think it is right to preach on hell." We warn our children about the danger of getting too close to the fire or falling into the lake. When they are a little older, we warn them about the evils of drugs, alcohol, the dance, and other things that we do not consider to be wholesome.

The Bible says that it is appointed unto men once to die and after that comes the judgment. Whatever we may think of judgment, the Bible teaches that there is to be judgment and that those who do not know Jesus Christ will be sent to hell. In our day we hear little preaching about sin and we see more sin than at any other time in our life. We should encourage our preachers to preach on judgment and hell.

THOUGHT: Failing to preach about hell will not cause it to go away.

January 30 -- Acts 2:32-38
Repentance

Can you remember the last time that you heard your pastor preach on repentance? Many pastors no longer preach on repentance. Too many preach on just following Jesus as our example. Jesus is the example for the Christian but He is not the example for the lost person. Jesus must first become a person's Savior and then He becomes his example.

It is foolish to teach and to preach salvation without repentance. The word repentance comes from the Greek work "metanoeo," a word meaning "to have another mind." Repentance means to "change the mind in respect to sin, to God, and to self." A person will usually be sorry for his sin before he repents, but sorrow is not repentance.

Jesus illustrated repentance for us in Matthew 21:28-29. The father asked a son to go into the field and work. The son said that he would not go. The scripture says, "But afterward he repented, and went." He saw that he was wrong and he changed his mind. Then he did what he should have done at the first.

God is calling Israel to repentance in Ezekiel 33:11. He says, "I have no pleasure in the death of the wicked, but that the wicked turn from his way and live; turn ye, turn ye from your evil ways; for why will ye die, O house of Israel?"

John the Baptist came preaching, "Repent ye, for the kingdom of heaven is at hand" (Matt. 3:2). Peter said, "Repent, and be baptized every one of you in the name of Jesus Christ for the remission of sins" (Acts 2:38). Jesus told the people who had seen the deaths of many people, "Except ye repent, ye shall all likewise perish" (Luke 13:3).

THOUGHT: True repentance involves sorrow of heart and faith in Jesus Christ.

January 31 -- II Timothy 4:1-2
Preaching against Sin

We hear the expression today, "I don't like to go to that church; the preacher preaches about sin too much. I don't like to hear that."

A study of the Bible will reveal that the prophets of God preached against sin in general and that they also preached against particular sins.

Isaiah was on target in his first chapter when he said of Israel, "Ah sinful nation, a people laden with iniquity, a seed of evildoers, children that are corrupters: they have forsaken the Lord, they have provoked the Holy One of Israel unto anger, they are gone away backward" (Isa. 1:4). He said that the "whole head is sick, and the whole heart is faint" (Isa. 1:5).

Nathan was not mincing any words when he explained to David about the man with many lambs taking the only one his neighbor had. Then he boldly said to David, "Thou art the man" (II Sam. 12:7).

Malachi asked if a man would rob God. He told them that they had robbed God when they did not bring tithes and offerings to the storehouse. Read Malachi 1:7-15.

Our Lord Jesus Christ preached against particular sins. He said that if you had hatred in your heart for another, you are a murderer. He said that if a man had lust in his heart for a woman, he had committed adultery with her in his heart.

The Bible says that we should not lie or bear false witness or covet or have any other gods before the Lord. Yes, we need preaching against particular sins today.

THOUGHT: When we think we have no sin, the truth is not in us.

Chapter Two

••

February

••

Verse to Memorize

Psalm 56:3

"What time I am afraid, I will trust in thee."

February 1 -- Joshua 24:15
When Decisions Should Be Made

We take so many things for granted. The sun rose this morning; surely it will rise tomorrow. The mail came yesterday; surely it will come today. I lived through yesterday; surely I will live through today. I had the chance to be saved last Sunday; surely I will have that same chance next Sunday.

The Bible says, "Boast not thyself of tomorrow, for thou knowest not what a day may bring forth" (Prov. 27:1). And again we are told, "For what is your life? It is even a vapor, that appeareth for a little time, and then vanisheth away" (Jas. 4:14).

None of us know whether we will be here tomorrow or not. Death is certain in that it will come to us all; but death is uncertain in that none of us knows when it will strike us. Decisions we need to make in serving God need to be made now. They should not be put off to a later date.

Joshua was not one to play around with sin and good times in the world. He made his decision, and he proclaimed that he and his house would serve the Lord, no matter what Israel did.

Moses came down from the mountain to find Israel worshipping an idol that they had made from their gold earrings. Moses was very angry and said, "Who is on the Lord's side? Let him come unto me" (Exod. 32:26).

Yes, decisions to serve God should be made now. We have no promise that we will get another chance to make those decisions tomorrow.

THOUGHT: We must serve God one day at a time.

February 2 -- Matthew 9:35-38
Prayer for Missions

Some almost unbelievable stories are told by missionaries about pagan peoples around the world. These pagan people know that there is a need in their lives, but until they come to know Jesus Christ they can have no peace.

One missionary tells this story about traditions and superstitions in Africa. If a woman's child dies, the witch doctor may accuse the woman of killing the child. The woman must then climb a tree and jump out of it to the ground. If she dies in the fall, she is guilty of killing the child; if she lives, she is not guilty. This is the way of one false religion.

Another missionary from the Orient tells this story. In accordance with their religious and superstitious beliefs, parents will take a small child and saw her teeth off even with the gums. This is supposed to please the spirits so that the family will be able to have happiness.

A missionary from Algeria tells about some people with a custom of cutting gashes in their heads, packing the cuts with paper, and then setting the paper afire in order to appease the evil spirits.

In America it is hard for us to understand that there are people doing such things as that. We say that we have the good news of salvation in Jesus Christ, but what are we doing in order that others may have the good news also?

We should pray to the Lord of the harvest that He will send forth many laborers into the harvest field.

THOUGHT: Sympathy is no substitute for action.

February 3 -- Romans 1:16
The Gospel of Salvation

Paul says that the gospel of Christ is the power of God unto salvation. Many other people say many other things, but I am inclined to agree with the apostle Paul.

In I Corinthians, we read where Paul says that the gospel is described in these words: "How that Christ died for our sins according to the scriptures; and that he was buried, and that he rose again the third day according to the scriptures; and that he was seen" (I Cor. 15:3-5). These words are simple enough for any of us to understand.

John said that if any person comes and does not bring this doctrine of Christ, we are not to receive him into our house. If we do receive him, we are partakers of his evil deeds. (See II John 10-11.)

Paul tells us in Titus 3:5-6, "Not by works of righteousness which we have done, but according to his mercy he saved us, by the washing of regeneration, and renewing of the Holy Ghost; which he shed upon us abundantly through Jesus Christ our Savior." These words are simple and they are understandable.

We put our total reliance in the teaching of the Bible. We conclude that salvation was made possible by His shed blood on Calvary's cross. It becomes ours by simple faith in Jesus Christ. Any other way of salvation is man-made and is a fraud and it is not of God.

There is great peace in knowing Jesus Christ as personal Savior. Do you know Him? If not, trust Him today.

THOUGHT: If there is any other way of salvation, why did Christ die?

February 4 -- James 4:7-10
How to Grow as a Christian

Two men applied for a job driving a big cargo truck. They were both given the same examination which included a question like this: If you were driving this truck down a mountain road, and came to a curve of eighty degrees with a precipice of a thousand feet on the outside of the curve, how fast could you make the curve and how close could you come to the precipice without going over it?

One man wrote his answer as follows: "I have been driving this type of truck for many years on all sorts of roads. I could make the curve at 45 miles per hour, come within one foot of the precipice, and not go over the precipice."

The second man wrote his answer and said, "I have been driving trucks for many years on all sorts of roads. I would go around this curve as slowly as I needed to and I would stay as far away as I could from the precipice."

There is no need to ask who got the job, is there? No firm wants to hire a man who is going to carelessly endanger its equipment and his life.

It is sad that many Christian people play around with sin and still expect to have a growing Christian life. The Bible says, "Have no fellowship with the unfruitful works of darkness, but rather reprove them" (Eph. 5:11).

We should always make it a practice to avoid sin as much as possible, rather than to partake of all that we think we can get by with.

THOUGHT: Sin in the spiritual, as leprosy in the physical, makes man unclean.

February 5 -- Matthew 17:14-21
Reasons Why

One day a preacher friend said to me, "We are failing in this day to win people to Jesus Christ. Why do you suppose this is true?"

Well, I believe that I can list some reasons why we are not winning people to Christ. Most of us would find ourselves guilty for one or more of these reasons. Let's look at some of these reasons.

1. We live dirty lives. This was true with David. He cried out to God and said, "Wash me throughly from mine iniquity, and cleanse me from my sin" (Ps. 51:2).

2. We are lacking in faith. In our scripture for today, the disciples could not help this lad, and Jesus said, "O faithless and perverse generation." In verse 19 they asked, "Why could not we cast him out?" Jesus then answered them, "Because of your unbelief."

3. We are lacking in prayer. We read books on how to win friends and influence people and then we fail to pray for their salvation. The Lord Jesus Christ said, "Pray ye therefore the Lord of the harvest, that he will send forth laborers into his harvest" (Matt. 9:38).

4. We just don't care and we are not willing to go out after them. The Bible says that if you fail to warn the wicked of his wicked ways, and he dies in his sin, his blood will be required at your hands. (See Ezek. 33:8.)

THOUGHT: If you do not tell them, who will?

February 6 -- Hebrews 4:14-16
How to Grow as a Christian

There is a story about a family in which the mother and father were not speaking to each other. If the father wanted to tell the mother something, he would ask one of the children to pass the word to her. The mother would do the same. This caused total confusion among the children.

It is so sad to hear about a situation like that. Yet, there are many people who fail to talk to their heavenly Father and who must depend upon others talking with Him for them. This latter example is even more sad than the former example.

Our scripture today tells us that Jesus is now in the heavens. It tells us that He is touched with the feeling of our infirmities. It also tells us that we are to come boldly to the throne of grace at any time to receive that which we need.

What are some things about which we can come to the throne of grace and talk with God? We can talk to Him:
1. About sickness in our house;
2. About our work, whether at school or on the job;
3. About social activities, especially young people in selecting their dates;
4. About our church, pastor, teachers, and our own consistent walk with God;
5. And, about our Christian schools, missionaries, and evangelists.

You see, we can go to God in prayer at any time. We can pray about anything and on the behalf of anyone.

THOUGHT: Perhaps the greatest privilege God ever gave His children is the privilege of prayer.

February 7 -- Acts 1:1-9
How to Grow as a Christian

Physical exercise is a very necessary ingredient in the recipe for physical maturity, and spiritual exercise is likewise necessary for spiritual maturity.

A favorite passage of scripture for many people is found in Matthew 28:18-20. "And Jesus came and spake unto them, saying, All power is given unto me in heaven and in earth. Go ye therefore, and teach all nations, baptizing them in the name of the Father, and of the Son, and of the Holy Ghost: teaching them to observe all things whatsoever I have commanded you: and, lo, I am with you alway, even unto the end of the world." To read or to quote this passage is one thing but to observe its teaching in our daily living is quite another thing.

A person is being a good witness when Christ can be seen in his daily life. I ought to conduct myself at all times so as to allow people to see my good works and to glorify my Father who is in heaven.

However, witnessing is also telling others what Jesus has done for me and what He can do for them. The Bible teaches me to "go and tell."

It is a thrill to know that God has appointed you and me as His witnesses. We can take His Word and point lost people to a saving knowledge of Jesus Christ. The Bible says, "Let him know, that he which converteth the sinner from the error of his way shall save a soul from death" (Jas. 5:20).

THOUGHT: A witness tells only what he knows.

February 8 -- Proverbs 23:22-26
The Christian Life Is Positive

Paul said in Colossians 2:6, "As ye have therefore received Christ Jesus the Lord, so walk ye in him." Here in this verse the Christian life is pictured as a walk. A person who is walking is making progress. One person might walk faster than another person but both are moving forward.

Wouldn't it be strange if a person went about his life walking backwards? This would be a most awkward situation and would indicate that there was something dreadfully wrong with that person.

This same thing can be said about the Christian who does not seem to be moving forward in his Christian life; something is dreadfully wrong. We see people who pride themselves because they don't do a lot of things that a lot of other people do. However, being proud of things that you don't do is not the essence of the Christian life.

Two men had worked together at the post office for several years. One of them quit his job. It was several years later before they saw one another again. Upon meeting again one day the postal worker said to his friend, "I have not seen you for so long; what are you doing now?" The friend did not answer by saying, "I do not carry letters now; I do not deliver packages now; I do not work at the post office any more." His reply was, "I have my own business and I get great joy out of serving my customers."

Is your Christian life a progression of doing things that please God or do you spend your time talking about things that you "don't do?"

THOUGHT: Christians should be so busy "doing" commendable things that they have no time to "don't."

February 9 -- II Peter 3:10-18
How to Grow as a Christian

Just as one needs a balanced diet and proper exercise for consistent growth and good health physically, even so we need to follow a formula for spiritual growth.

The Bible is the Word of God. We need to read and study it regularly if we expect to be in good spiritual health. God has revealed Himself to us in the Bible. In it He tells us what we are without Him, what we are in Him, and what we can expect to receive from Him.

The Bible tells us about the devil, sin, the flesh, and the world; it also tells us of victory over all these things that is ours in the Lord Jesus Christ.

The Bible tells us about the sorrows and heartaches of the world. It tells us about the peace of God. It also tells us about the comfort of the Holy Spirit that is ours when we are yielded to Him and His direction.

The Bible gives us examples of some who served the devil and were destroyed. It also tells of some who served God and received His blessing, who rejoiced in His love, and who have gone to be eternally in His presence.

The Bible is filled with history that gives accurate reports of the past. It is filled with poetry that bestows praises upon our God. It gives us proverbs that tell us how to get along with our fellow man. It gives us prophecy that tells us of future events. It also gives us love letters that tell us of His great love with which He has loved us.

THOUGHT: Thy word is a lamp unto my feet and a light unto my path.

February 10 -- John 14:1-6
Heaven Is a Place

Some people do not believe that heaven is a place. They say that heaven is only the good influence that a person experiences in this life. If this be true, there are a lot of people who never know what heaven is like. Some of the dearest saints who ever lived had a life of suffering. Fanny Crosby is a classic example of this. Yet, she loved God and how she served Him faithfully all her life!

The Bible speaks of heaven as a place. In verse 2 of today's scripture reading Jesus said, "I go to prepare a place for you." He certainly would not tell us that He was going to do something that He did not do.

It is said by some people that heaven is just a condition. What kind of condition can you have without a place for it to be? If you have a cloudy condition, you must have the heavens in which to have it. If you have a riotous condition, you must have the streets or the ball park or some other place in which it can exist. Yes, there must always be a place in which the condition can exist.

If heaven is not a place, where are Abraham and Lazarus? Where are Jesus and the Father? Where are all the saints who have died down through the ages?

Verse 3 says, "That where I am, there ye may be also." The Bible very plainly teaches that heaven is a place and that the only way anyone can ever reach that place is by putting his faith in Jesus Christ.

THOUGHT: Heaven is the home of the redeemed.

February 11 -- Acts 1:10-11
Jesus Himself Is Coming

This same Jesus, Who walked in the garden with Adam and Eve;

This same Jesus, Who met Abraham under the oaks and talked of the son to be born in his family;

This same Jesus, Who wrestled with Jacob all night;

This same Jesus, Whom the prophets saw in visions and Whom men and women have known through the years as the true God;

This same Jesus, Who was born of a virgin, Who at the age of twelve baffled the theologians, and Who walked up and down Israel for three and a half years doing good, healing the sick, giving sight to the blind, and forgiving sin;

This same Jesus, Who sweated great drops of blood in the Garden of Gethsemane, Who was betrayed by His friend, Who was denied by His disciples, Who was given a mock trial, and Who was crucified for crimes that He did not do;

This same Jesus, at whose feet the leper fell and said, "If thou wilt, thou canst make me clean" (Mark 1:40);

This same Jesus, to Whom the Syrophenician woman came and said, "Lord, help me," as she begged Him to heal her daughter (See Matthew 15:22-28);

This same Jesus, Who in loving mercy cleansed me and made me whole, and established my goings;

This same Jesus is coming back again!

THOUGHT: In such an hour as you think not, the Son of Man will come.

February 12 -- I Corinthians 15:12-19
The Resurrection

Spring is a beautiful season of the year. Through the fall and winter months the leaves have died and fallen from the trees. When spring comes, new life breaks out everywhere. Flowers begin to bloom and trees begin to bud. The evidence of "resurrection," or new life, is seen everywhere.

Spring points to the resurrection of Christ because He no longer lies in death and because He has risen triumphantly from the grave.

Jesus' disciples were very disturbed. They had thought that He was the Messiah. They thought that He had come to deliver them from the authority of Rome. Then, He was crucified and He was placed in the tomb. They then seemed to have lost all hope. Some of them went fishing; others were busy about other things. All of them were cast down because their hope had been shattered.

Some of them went to the tomb on the first day of the week. Upon arriving there, they found that the stone had been rolled away from the door. They were astonished at what they saw, but the angel of the Lord said to the women, "He is not here: for he is risen" (Matt. 28:6).

The scripture says that with fear and great joy they left the tomb and went to tell His disciples that the Lord was risen.

Yes, the spring of the year with its new life everywhere reminds us of the resurrection of Jesus Christ.

THOUGHT: I know the Man Who actually came back from the dead.

February 13 -- John 1:1-2
The Living Word

The Greek term "Logos" is translated here "Word." Logos means a thought or concept and the expression or utterance of that thought or concept.

No one can express himself without the use of words. Even our thoughts must be through the use of the alphabet and in expressions using words.

Jesus said, "I am Alpha and Omega, the beginning and the ending" (Rev. 1:8). Alpha is the first letter of the Greek alphabet and Omega is the last letter. This would be the same as saying "I am the A and the Z."

The Son of God is said to be "the express image of his person" (Heb. 1:3). In Colossians 1:15 we read that He is "the image of the invisible God." Thus, as we look at Jesus Christ, we see God Himself.

Now, since Jesus is the express image of God, and since He is the physical manifestation of the invisible God, and He is the Alpha and Omega, He is the Word--the Living Word.

That which we want to know about God we can find in Jesus Christ. That which we want to know about the Living Word we can find in the Written Word. The Bible is the Written Word and Jesus Christ is the Living Word.

May God help us to apply ourselves in the study of the Bible so that we may know God through Jesus Christ.

THOUGHT: The only Christ some people know is the one they see in you.

February 14 -- John 3:16-18
Strange Sayings

Mr. A says that in order to get to heaven you must join the right church and you must be baptized the way his church baptizes. You must confess to a leader in the church and you must take mass periodically. You must believe the articles of faith of his church and you must believe that the head of his church does no wrong. You must live the best you can and then, when you die, you must live in purgatory until purified enough to go to heaven.

Mr. B says that you must believe on Jesus Christ as your Savior and be baptized for the remission of sins. After that, you must live the best you can and you will go to heaven.

Mr. C says that you must accept Jesus Christ as Savior from past sins and then you must live the best that you can, because heaven depends on how you live in this life.

Mr. D says that you must take Christ as your example and try to live by His teachings. He says that there might be a heaven and a hell or there might not be.

The Bible says that Jesus Christ is the only way of salvation and that whoever receives Him has complete salvation. We are saved by our faith and not by our works. In Jesus Christ there is full and complete redemption. He died for our sins on the cross, He was buried to take them away, and He rose again to give us eternal life. We have all that we need in Him and we do not need to look for anything else.

THOUGHT: Salvation is Jesus plus nothing.

February 15 -- Romans 6:19-23
Everybody Needs Salvation

We have heard people talk about their mother, grandmother, other loved one, or friend by saying that they have never known that person to curse or to raise her voice or to do anything wrong. They say that if there ever was a good person, that person was one. They say that if anyone was ever meant to go to heaven, that person was.

It might be true that those persons had a good name, but we should understand that no one goes to heaven because of being good. The only way people go to heaven is by faith in Jesus Christ as personal Savior.

One day a publican and a Pharisee went to the temple to pray. The Pharisee walked down to the front, lifted his face toward heaven and began to tell God what a good man he was and what a good life he was living. He told God that he was glad that he was not like other men. He also told God how he fasted and tithed and that he was not even like the publican who was standing nearby.

The publican would not even lift up his eyes, but he "smote upon his breast, saying, God be merciful to me a sinner" (Luke 18:13).

The Bible tells us that "this man went down to his house justified rather than the other" (Luke 18:14).

Yes, everyone needs salvation. No one is saved by being good and no one is saved by not doing bad things. Salvation is by faith in Jesus Christ and in Him alone.

THOUGHT: Jesus is the only Way, the only Truth, and the only Life.

February 16 -- Romans 10:8-13
Patched-up Religion

A certain biology professor was said to be able to identify any kind of bug one could find. A group of his students took several kinds of bugs and they cut each of them into several pieces. Then they took certain pieces and pasted them together to make them look like a bug.

They took their creation to the professor and asked if he could identify the rare bug that they had found. The professor observed the masterpiece very closely, looked at his students and said, "That, my friends, is a Humbug."

People often are not willing to take the Bible at what it says but they often want to add to it or to take away from it. Why should people be unwilling to believe God's Word? Why do people always want to please their feelings?

A three year old boy saw his dad working in the yard. "Let me come into the yard, Daddy," said the boy. "All right, jump off the porch," said the dad. The boy said, "No, I will fall." The dad said, "Don't be afraid; I will catch you." The boy then jumped into his dad's arms. The dad asked, "Were you not afraid?" The boy's reply was, "No, you told me you would catch me."

We should always trust our heavenly Father and we should take Him completely at His Word, just as this young boy did with his dad.

THOUGHT: Any kind of religion without Jesus Christ is a "humbug."

February 17 -- Acts 16:25-31
How to Get to Heaven

As two men discussed how to get to heaven, they disagreed in their thinking. After a while one of them finally said, "Well, we are all going to the same place but we are just traveling different roads."

This may have a good sound, but it just is not true.

One person said, "You know, it is like this: One person goes by way of St. Louis and another goes by way of Washington, but they both wind up in Chicago." This might be well for someone who is going to Chicago, but when someone wants to go to heaven there is only one way.

Jesus said, "I am the way, the truth, and the life: no man cometh unto the Father, but by me" (John 14:6).

This could not have been spoken any plainer, could it?

Our scripture today says, "Believe on the Lord Jesus Christ, and thou shalt be saved." Don't you suppose that Paul would have told the Philippian jailer if there had been more than one way? I believe that he would have.

The Bible says, "For God so loved the world, that he gave his only begotten Son, that whosoever believeth in him should not perish, but have everlasting life" (John 3:16).

The Bible says that God gave His only begotten Son, not that He gave several sons. We must believe in His only begotten Son. We do not choose between His only begotten Son and several other things. Salvation is by simple faith in Jesus Christ. Have you believed on Him?

THOUGHT: Strait is the gate, and narrow is the way that leads into life.

February 18 -- I Corinthians 3:9-11
The Foundation

I love to watch a building in the making. Some years ago I watched as a crew worked seemingly endlessly laying a proper foundation for a large building. They spent weeks on putting down pilings for the building. They did this because unless the foundation is sure, the building upon the foundation will not be sure either.

The Bible says that we should always be ready to give a reason for the hope that is within us. It also says that we should be so grounded in the faith that we will not be tossed about with every wind of doctrine.

Abraham was a man who had laid a good foundation. When God was going to destroy Sodom for the wickedness in that city, He came by and talked with Abraham about it. The Lord said, "Shall I hide from Abraham that thing which I do...for I know him, that he will command his children and his household after him, and they shall keep the way of the Lord, to do justice and judgment" (Gen. 18:17,19).

Our reading today says that there is only one foundation that is substantial and that foundation is already laid. Jesus Christ is the foundation provided by our Lord Himself. No other foundation is sufficient for us to build upon.

In Ephesians, Paul speaks about our life as a building. We must be careful of the foundation. Are you building upon Jesus Christ or are you building upon a foundation of your own making? Any other foundation will surely crumble under the crushing force of the floods.

THOUGHT: Other foundation can no man lay.

February 19 -- Hebrews 9:19-22
Pardon by Blood

Today's verse tells us, "Almost all things are by the law purged with blood." Does this mean that certain sins could be forgiven without blood? No, this is not the meaning at all.

In Old Testament times under the ceremonial laws, some clothes were cleansed by washing in water. Certain metals were cleansed by burning in fire. However, there has never been forgiveness of sin without the shedding of blood. It is still the same today. The blood of Jesus is all that avails to remove the stain, guilt, and penalty of sin.

When a person is pardoned of God, it is not something that will happen at some time in the future, but it is a present reality. It is not a thing that is received gradually, such as healing from a disease, but it is an instant work of God. When one receives Jesus Christ as Savior, that person has a present and positive pardon from sin.

John 5:24 says, "Verily, verily, I say unto you, He that heareth my word, and believeth on him that sent me, hath everlasting life, and shall not come into condemnation, but is passed from death unto life."

Pardon from sin is something about which we can know. We do not have to guess or hope or imagine. "He that believeth on him is not condemned: but he that believeth not is condemned already, because he hath not believed in the name of the only begotten Son of God" (John 3:18).

We ought to believe God for complete pardon in the blood of Christ. He says that we have pardon by our faith. Simple? Yes, it is simple but it is true.

THOUGHT: My sin cost God His only begotten Son, the Lord Jesus Christ.

February 20 -- Colossians 3:5-7
Your Members upon Earth

The "members which are upon the earth" which Paul speaks of here are not the members of our physical body so much as the members of the flesh, or our old nature. We are to mortify, or put to death, the old Adamic nature.

It is true that God has declared us to be justified by faith in Jesus Christ. We must understand that God has done this as Judge and it means that we are justified from sin. We will not be condemned to hell because we are risen with Christ. However, we must act to put to death our members on earth. Remember that Paul is talking about the members of our old nature, the Adamic nature. He is not talking about the members of our physical body.

The Gnostics, a group that claimed to have an advanced knowledge about God, also claimed that all matter was evil. Thus, they said, the human body was evil and it must be put to death. They tried to achieve holiness by punishing their bodies.

Paul is saying to the Colossians that the Gnostics were wrong. These bodies of ours are not evil except as we who live in them are evil. It is the old Adamic nature that needs to be put to death and we are not to follow its leading.

We are already saved from the penalty of sin. Through the grace and the strength that He makes available to us, let us also diligently try to be saved from the power of sin in our daily living. This would greatly please Him.

THOUGHT: The old nature is to be put completely out of operation.

February 21 -- Colossians 3:5-7
Put to Death

Someone has said that when you find the word "therefore" in the Bible, you should find out what it is there for. Paul uses the word in verse 3 and we should go back to the beginning of this chapter to get the significance of the usage of the word here.

In verse 1 of this chapter Paul uses the Greek particle followed by the indicative mode to make a definite statement. He does not use it to merely suggest a possibility, as may seem to be the case here in the King James Version. Paul is really saying, "Since you are, indeed, risen with Christ." This is a statement of fact. Thank God for the fact that every saved person is risen with Jesus Christ.

Now, in verse 5 Paul says, "Therefore, since you are risen with Christ, you should mortify your members." This is the natural thing to expect a person to do after being saved.

Did you notice that this is something for you to do? God has already declared it to be so. Now He wants you to make it so in your daily life. God's act is judicial, but your act is to be practical. God has declared you to be just and now He wants you to live like a justified man.

Mortify! This means to put to death or to make a corpse out of a body. You are to put forth a definite effort yourself to see to it that the deeds of the flesh are put to an end. When something or someone is dead, it or he is no longer able to produce. We are to put to death the members of the flesh so that they can no longer produce their evil fruit.

THOUGHT: Our earthly life should coincide with our heavenly citizenship.

February 22 -- Colossians 3:5-7
Our Responsibility

These are important verses. They give to us admonition that we should follow strictly. Paul was a very wise man. His instruction by the inspiration of the Holy Spirit is given that we might have rules to follow in our daily life.

He gives certain instruction in verse 5 and then he says in verses 6 and 7 that the wrath of God dwells upon those that do such things. He also says that all of us lived in these things at one time. Praise God for salvation.

Paul tells us five things that we are to mortify, or put to death. I remind you that it is our responsibility to work at putting these out of our life. Few Christians realize their great responsibility is in turning from evil to God.

Put to death fornication. This covers the whole field of immorality, including the look, the thought, and the act. Sin is conceived in the mind and desired in the emotions before it is realized in the will.

Put to death uncleanness of mind and action. Not only do we need clean hearts but we need clean minds to ward off sinful thoughts.

Put to death sinful affections. Evil passions are what we dwell on in our minds. If we do not deal with these, they will deal with us.

Put to death evil concupiscence. This is that inward yearning and craving for those evil things that are forbidden to Christians.

Put to death covetousness. God says that this is a form of idolatry and we must get rid of it.

THOUGHT: God really wants us to put these terrible things to death.

February 23 -- I Corinthians 3:11-15
Foundation

A building is as substantial as the foundation under it. Jesus told of two men who built houses. One man built his house upon the sand. When the winds and rains came, the house fell. The other man built his house upon the rock. When the winds and rains came, the house stood firm.

Paul speaks of the Christian as preparing a building of his Christian life. We are to be careful of the material we use. We must use good and acceptable material and we must refuse bad and unacceptable material. We are also to build upon the proper foundation, Jesus Christ. Any spiritual house built upon any other foundation will not stand the test of the storm.

Recently I watched with great interest in our city as a group of men prepared a good foundation for a multistory building. It took several months to complete the job. There were great pilings driven into the ground and finally the foundation was finished and the building was erected. It stands as a testimony to the foundation under it.

What is the testimony of your Christian life today? Does it speak of a good foundation or does it prove that you have built upon a soft, sandy, undesirable foundation?

In today's scripture Paul said, "Other foundation can no man lay than that is laid, which is Jesus Christ." With the good foundation of Jesus Christ, are you now preparing a good building on it?

THOUGHT: Building upon the wrong foundation can be said to be a lot like pouring water in a sieve.

February 24 -- John 10:1-11
Our Shepherd

Our Lord Jesus Christ is pictured in the Bible as a shepherd. There are at least three areas of His shepherding ministry that we want to consider.

In Psalm 22 He is pictured as the Good Shepherd. In our scripture today we are told that the Good Shepherd gives His life for the sheep. Psalm 22 describes His death on the cross. He is described as one upon whom ridicule and scorn is heaped. He is rejected by His own people, He is beaten by His enemies, and He is forsaken by God. There, as the Good Shepherd, He suffered for our sins.

In Psalm 23 He is pictured as the Great Shepherd living for, caring for, protecting, feeding, and leading His sheep during the age in which we now live. The writer of Hebrews wrote, "Now the God of peace, that brought again from the dead our Lord Jesus, that great shepherd of the sheep, through the blood of the everlasting covenant, make you perfect in every good work to do his will, working in you that which is wellpleasing in his sight" (Heb. 13:20-21). Jesus is at the right hand of the Father making intercession for us today.

In Psalm 24 He is pictured as the Chief Shepherd who is coming again. "Lift up your heads, O ye gates; even lift them up, ye everlasting doors; and the King of Glory shall come in" (Ps. 24:9). In his first epistle, Peter says, "And when the chief Shepherd shall appear, ye shall receive a crown of glory" (I Pet. 5:4). The way to be ready to receive Him at His second coming is to receive Him now as your Savior.

THOUGHT: What man thinks about Christ's second coming has nothing to do with what God says about it.

February 25 -- John 5:24
Assurance

Someone has asked, "How can I have assurance about anything?" Our assurance as Christians comes by simple faith in the truth of God's Word. Either the Bible is the Word of God, or it is not. As for me, I believe that it is. Thus, I have assurance based upon the teaching of the Word.

There is assurance over doubt about salvation. Jesus said that His sheep hear His voice, He knows them and gives them eternal life, and that no man can take them away from Him. This is plain enough; it is the teaching of the Word of God and it ought to be good enough to assure us.

Do you have doubts about salvation? You should go back to the time you received Jesus Christ as Savior and ask yourself the question, "Did I really trust Him? Did I ask Him to come into my heart and save me?" If you did, trust Him to do what He said He would do. If you are not sure, you should right now ask Him to save you.

There is assurance of His acceptance. God does not accept us based upon how good we are but He accepts us based upon our faith in Jesus Christ. Paul said, "He hath made us accepted in the beloved" (Eph. 1:6). We could never be acceptable, but we are made accepted in Jesus Christ.

There is assurance of no condemnation. "There is therefore now no condemnation to them which are in Christ Jesus" (Rom. 8:1). When we receive Christ, He comes into our hearts. We are accepted in the beloved. There is perfect salvation in Him and now there is no chance of any future condemnation.

THOUGHT: To believe is to have your personal assurance satisfied.

February 26 -- I Thessalonians 4:13-18
The Expectancy

"Mommy, is it today that we go see daddy come home on the plane?" Little Susie had expected daddy to return home every day since he left on a week-long business trip. She asked the same question every day. Little Susie had great expectancy and this was evident when the time drew near for her daddy to return home.

There should be the same eager expectancy manifested in the lives of the children of God as we look for the second coming of our Lord Jesus Christ. Our scripture today tells us that He is coming. In verse 16 Paul says, "For the Lord himself shall descend from heaven." He is not going to send someone else, but He is coming Himself.

In Acts 1:11 the disciples were asked by the angels, "Ye men of Galilee, why stand ye gazing up into heaven? This same Jesus, which is taken up from you into heaven, shall so come in like manner as ye have seen him go into heaven."

Yes, without any doubt, Jesus is coming again. A good question for each of us to ask ourselves is this: Am I ready to meet Him if He should come today? There is no question as to whether He is coming and there is no question as to whether I will stand before Him. The question is whether or not I am prepared to meet Him.

There is only one way that a person can be ready for the coming of Christ and that is to have received Him as personal Savior. If you have not received Him, you should do it today.

THOUGHT: Keep looking up, for the Lord Jesus may come today.

February 27 -- John 14:1-3
What It Will Be Like When Jesus Comes

The Bible says, "The Lord himself shall descend from heaven with a shout, with the voice of the archangel, and with the trump of God" (I Thess. 4:16). Do you ever think about what it will be like when He returns? Let's give a little thought to it today.

There will be a shout of victory. There will be a shout from heaven itself as the Son of God takes His own unto Himself. There will be a shout as the dead in Christ are raised from the dead and the living saints are caught up to meet the Lord in the air. There will be a shout of victory from the saint of God when he realizes complete victory over sin, the devil, and hell. Yes, friend, it will be some shout of victory!

There will be a shout of joy as the Bridegroom comes for the bride. It was a time of joy and excitement for me as I went one day to pick up that young lady who was to become my wife that afternoon. It will be a time of unprecedented joy when He comes for us.

The Lord Jesus is not interested in how big our cities are or how great our business might be. He is not interested in how wonderful our chambers of commerce might be or how beautiful our church buildings might be or how educated our people might be. His interest is in whether we are ready to meet Him when He comes again.

The only mention of joy in heaven is at the repentance of a lost soul. Have you caused joy in heaven? Have you received Jesus Christ as personal Savior?

The Bible says, "Believe on the Lord Jesus Christ, and thou shalt be saved" (Acts 16:31). If you have never done that, right now is the best time to do it.

THOUGHT: Unto them that look for Him, shall He appear the second time without sin unto salvation.

February 28 -- Psalm 138:1-7
When Is Revival Needed?

When there is a lack of brotherly love and Christian confidence among the people, revival is needed.

Sister Sally is mad with Brother Bob and Talking Tilly is gossiping about everything and not sure about anything. Somebody painted the hall the wrong color and everybody is upset because anybody should have known that we needed the heat on rather than the air conditioning. When there is dissension, jealousy, and evil speaking among the church members, there is a need for revival.

When people of the church are falling into gross sin, we need revival. The church cannot prosper and grow while Christians are involved in such things as drinking alcoholic beverages, using profane language, committing sex sins, and are guilty of the many other sins of the world. Even when God's people are trying their hardest to walk clean and pure before a lost world, there is still a lot of hurting influence.

When sinners are careless and unconcerned, when they have no respect for God and the church, and when they are needlessly falling into hell, there is need for revival.

Today the church and church people often have little effect upon a world loaded down with sin. Sinners go on unconcerned that they are breaking the heart of God and that they are sending themselves to hell. We need a heaven-sent revival that will call Christians back to God and that will renew faith in the church member and will bring glory to God.

THOUGHT: The gospel not only needs to be preached, but practiced.

February 29 -- Titus 3:4-7
Satan Told Me I Was Good Enough

One of the first things that I can remember Satan saying to me was that I did not need to trust Jesus Christ as my personal Savior. He told me that I was good enough to go to heaven and that I did not need salvation.

At the time I thought that I was a respectable young fellow. I did not do a lot of things that a lot of other boys did. However, I still knew that something was wrong and that God was not pleased with my life. All the time that Satan was telling me that I was good enough, the Word of God was telling me that "the soul that sinneth, it shall die" (Ezek. 18:4).

In Luke 18:10-14 we read the account of the Pharisee and the publican going to the temple to pray. The Pharisee stood and prayed thus with himself, "God, I thank thee, that I am not as other men are, extortioners, unjust, adulterers, or even as this publican." The publican prayed, "God be merciful to me a sinner." The Lord said that the publican went down to his house justified rather than the Pharisee.

Also, Romans 3:10 tells us that there is none righteous, no, not even one. Yet, Satan wanted to convince me that I was good enough to go to heaven.

Have you ever received Jesus Christ as your personal Savior? If you have not, Satan might be telling you the same thing that he told me. The Bible tells us that we are not saved by being good, but we are saved by faith in Jesus Christ. Jesus said, "I am the way, the truth, and the life" (John 14:6).

THOUGHT: All have sinned and come short of the glory of God.

Chapter Three

•••

March

•••

Verse to Memorize

Galatians 6:10

"As we have therefore opportunity, let us do good unto all men, especially unto them who are of the household of faith."

March 1 -- Nehemiah 1:5-11
When Will We Have Revival?

When the wickedness of a wicked generation grieves, humbles, and distresses the children of God, we can expect revival in the church.

Too often we talk about sin as though it is not exceeding sinful and as though it does not ruin the lives of God's people. We talk of it as though it does not break the heart of God and as though it does not send people helplessly and hopelessly to hell.

Prevalence of wickedness around us today does not mean that we cannot have revival. The hard heart and the unconcerned and indifferent spirit of man are the things that stand in the way. The Bible says, "When the enemy shall come in like a flood, the Spirit of the Lord shall lift up a standard against him" (Isa. 59:19).

The pressing need is for compassionate and brokenhearted people to humble themselves and to call upon God in prayer. We need mothers, fathers, teachers, deacons, and young people to be in sincere prayer for revival. When hearts are broken and spirits are troubled, and we are driven to prayer, then we will see revival.

We will have revival when Christians begin to confess their sins of lying, cheating, gossiping, drinking, envying, filthy talking, and to confess the many other sins that keep them from a closeness to God.

We will have revival when the preachers begin to give attention to the need and begin to preach the Word in the power of God's Spirit.

THOUGHT: Wickedness will drive people away from God--or to God.

March 2 -- Psalm 85:5-9
What Revival Will Do

Revival is much like the weather; people talk a lot about it but they seldom do anything about it.

Revival will bring conviction of sin upon the hearts of the church people. As people begin to listen to the Word of God being preached and as they call out to God with hungry hearts, they will find the convicting power of the Holy Spirit.

Revival will break the power of sin in the lives of God's people. As we experience conviction, we should confess our sin and surrender to God. As we experience conviction, we should cry out for His grace and yield to His Spirit. As we do this, we will find ourselves walking in the power of the Holy Spirit rather than in the power of sin. Only the power of God can break the power of sin and only as we yield to Him can He work through us in the power of the Holy Spirit.

Revival will bring renewed faith to the Christian. As God's people see their own sinfulness and experience the desire to serve Him, they will have renewed faith. As they confess their sin and receive God's forgiveness, they will have renewed faith. Just as a shower of rain brings renewed vitality to the life of a drought besieged flower, so the Holy Spirit brings new faith to a wayward Christian.

Revival will bring salvation to the lost as God's revived children become the good witnesses that God has intended for them to be.

Let us ask God for and let us look to God for a real revival in our own souls today so that we may be all that He wants us to be.

THOUGHT: Sin-laden Christians need revival.

March 3 -- Psalm 51:1-10
People in Despair

Moses made some wonderful choices during his life. Hebrews 11:25 tells us about one of them, where Moses chose rather to "suffer affliction with the people of God, than to enjoy the pleasures of sin for a season." Yes, there is pleasure in sin but it is just for a season.

There are people in despair all over the world today because of sin. Sin never brings happiness, but it always smites the conscience, breaks the heart, blights the mind, ruins the body, and damns the soul.

History reveals that nation after nation has gone down in defeat and ruin because of sin. To review the history of Greece, Rome, and Germany would substantiate this. America is on dangerous ground today because our people are sinful people. Our people appear to be determined to persecute and to antagonize the true believers. They seem to delight in mocking God and seem to be more and more intent on bringing the fire of God's judgment down on our nation.

So many people have warped, twisted, and broken bodies today because of sin. Many people are in mental hospitals because sin has ruined their minds. Many homes have no peace and are at the brink of disaster because of the sin of the parents. Many people live in despair because sin has ruined their public life. Many people cannot get jobs because no one wants to hire a thief, a liar, a drunk, a cheat, or a lazy person.

Let us pray daily that God will keep us clear of sin and close by His side.

THOUGHT: All of the devil's apples have worms.

March 4 -- Psalm 51:5-13
Sin Is a Disease

There was a time when my wife had a lot of time to work in the yard. She had many kinds of beautiful flowers. As one kind would finish its season, she would remove it and plant another in its place.

One day after working in the yard she noticed that she had a skin rash and that she was swelling. We immediately thought that it was an allergy because of a certain kind of foliage she had handled that day.

On the next day the rash, swelling and itching was no better. She decided that she needed to go to the doctor. She told the doctor about her work and that this must be an allergy. The doctor said, "No, this is not coming from without; it is coming from within you." He immediately wanted to know what she had been eating, what kind of medicine she had been taking, and if she was upset about anything.

Sin also comes from within a person. The Bible says, "The life of all flesh is the blood" (Lev. 17:14). We each have inherited our nature from Adam's sinful blood. This sinful nature is constantly expressing itself outwardly. However, the problem is coming from within and confession must be made to Jesus Christ in order that the needed inner cleansing may be received from Him.

THOUGHT: A man is not a sinner because he sins; but he sins because he is a sinner.

March 5 -- Jeremiah 17:7-10
The Cricket in the Spider Web

Did you ever see a cricket become caught in a spider web? That is a strange sight to behold. Many times I have seen that very thing happen.

The cricket might be able to pounce upon a spider with the intention of having a nice meal, but usually he will find himself in a trap. As he tries to place himself in the best position, he finds that he is caught in the web. As he frantically tries to release himself, he just becomes tangled up more and more in the web.

To the utter amazement of the cricket and to the delight of the spider, the cricket becomes the meal for the spider rather than the spider becoming the meal for the cricket. He is caught in a trap that he not in the least suspected.

Sin is a great web that catches many unsuspecting people. No one ever enters sin with the intention of remaining there, but in the end many people find themselves caught up in that trap.

In simple language, our scripture verse for today tells us that it is easier for us to do that which is wrong than it is for us to do that which is right. Have you ever stopped and given this any thought?

You might know some people today who are having what they think is a great time in sin. However, the day will come when they will want to turn from it but they will find themselves caught in its web. The best policy is to never become caught in the web of sin and this is done by staying clear of sin.

THOUGHT: It is much easier to stay out of sin than it is to get out of sin.

March 6 -- I John 1:5-10
What a Christian Can Do about Sin in His Life

It was the closing night of the revival meeting and the evangelist had preached faithfully each service. He had condemned sin and he had exalted Christ. He had noticed a certain woman who had been in every service. She had responded to every invitation that had been given. Each night she would walk down the aisle and would talk with the pastor and then she would return to her seat.

Finally the last invitation of the meeting was given by the evangelist. Along with several others, the same woman came down the aisle again. Since the pastor was busy at the time, the evangelist stepped out and went to meet the woman. The evangelist said, "I believe you have responded to the invitation each service. Is there something troubling you?"

She replied, "Yes, there is."

The evangelist said, "Tell me about it."

The woman then related to him something that she had done many years ago. He asked her if she had ever confessed it to God and she replied, "Yes, a thousand times."

The evangelist responded, "Well, you have confessed it nine hundred and ninety-nine times too many."

Now, what could he have meant by that? He meant that we should believe that God will do what He has said He would do. He has clearly said that if we confess our sins, He will forgive us. Our joy of forgiveness comes only when we trust Him to do what He says He will do.

THOUGHT: Faith should be thought of as simply taking God at His word.

March 7 -- James 1:12-16
Who Knows about Sin?

Everybody in the whole world knows something about the existence of sin. The psalmist said, "My sin is ever before me" (Ps. 51:3). Judas said, "I have sinned in that I have betrayed the innocent blood" (Matt. 27:4). Nehemiah said, "Both I and my father's house have sinned" (Neh. 1:6).

In the darkest jungles of the world those to whom we usually refer as heathens have a knowledge of wrong-doing. Missionaries come back from those lands and tell of the "gods made with hands." Those heathen people often try to appease the evil spirits by sacrificing their children, by cutting their own bodies, by making for themselves gods, and by performing all sorts of religious rituals.

People in America are also conscious of sin. There are some religious groups that will lay heavy burdens upon their people in payment for sin. Some people have to go to confession where they tell someone of their sin and then pay a sum of money supposedly in order to obtain remission of their sin. Some people will deny themselves certain foods or certain activities in order to hopefully make restitution for sins that they have committed.

For those of us who know the truth, we know that we all are sinful creatures and have been from the beginning of our life. However, we also know that there is a peace in knowing that Jesus Christ is the Savior and that in Him there is complete forgiveness of all sins.

THOUGHT: It is not what we know that saves us, but **Whom** we know.

March 8 -- I John 1:6-8
What Kind of Example Are You?

Many people rise in the morning and go about their work as though their life had to do only with themselves. They seem to have no thought of the other person and how others might be influenced by the lives that they live.

Do you wonder what kind of example you are to those people around you who may be watching you even more closely than you suspect?

It would seem that Lot never stopped to think how his life would affect others, even those of his own family. The Bible says that Lot "pitched his tent toward Sodom" (Gen. 13:12). Lot just kept moving in that direction until he wound up in Sodom. While he was there, he not only ruined his own life but he ruined the lives of his entire family.

Christians need to be very careful about what they do and where they go. They need to watch what they say and what company they keep. These things not only affect them but they affect others as well.

For example, I would not want my neighbor to see me go into a liquor store to get change for a parking meter. Would you? If we are seen going into a place like that, people may see us and may think we going there for the same reason that others go there.

It is much better for us to have the attitude that Joshua had. He said, "As for me and my house, we will serve the Lord" (Josh. 24:15). Having such an attitude as this would help us to keep from being caught doing anything that would damage our testimony or make people think the wrong thing about us.

THOUGHT: Be careful; your example is showing.

March 9 -- I John 2:1-6
What Sin Does in the Life
of a Christian

All of us understand that Christians do sin. That is not to say that Christians *must* sin but that it is a matter of fact that Christians *do* sin. A good question to ask is this: what does sin do in the life of a Christian?

Sin kills joy in the life of a Christian. David was involved in a very wicked sin. As you will remember from reading God's Word, David was very disturbed when he realized what he had done. His cry was not "restore unto me my salvation" but it was "restore unto me the joy of thy salvation" (Ps. 51:12). David had lost the joy of salvation and so will you and I if we have sin in our life.

Sin will also destroy peace in the life of a Christian. Isaiah said, "There is no peace, saith the Lord, unto the wicked" (Isa. 48:22).

Most of us know of people who have allowed sin to enter their life and who have lost their peace. These people are not now walking with God. They are troubled souls and a troubled soul cannot serve God effectively.

Sin will also destroy love in the heart of a Christian. When we allow sin in any form to come into our lives we begin to lose our love for God. His Word is no longer as precious to us as it should be. We lose the desire to pray. We do not have the hunger for His house or for the fellowship with His people. Sin takes love away.

THOUGHT: Sin will keep you from reading His Book, or reading His Book will keep you from sin.

March 10 -- Ephesians 2:4-10
Faith

Saving faith is faith in the personal work of Jesus Christ on the cross. Often the following illustration is used to help explain faith. You may have faith in a chair that it will hold you up, and so you sit in it. You do not examine it, or shake it around, or ask someone else to check it out for you. You just come in and sit down in it. That is exercising faith that the chair will not let you fall.

The chair is a good illustration of faith. That is a genuine faith, but that faith will not save us. It is not a faith placed in the right object. However, the right kind of faith placed in the right object will save us. The right object of our faith is Jesus Christ. It takes a simple child-like faith in Him. We must trust Him and Him alone and when we do that we are exercising a saving faith, which is the only faith that can ever save a person.

There is also a faith that works. The story is told about the great Blondin, the tightrope walker who walked across the Niagara on a tightrope. He once asked a lad, "Do you believe that I can walk across on this rope?" "Yes," the lad answered.

He again asked the lad, "Do you believe that I can walk across with you on my back?" The lad again answered, "Yes."

Once more he asked the lad, "Do you want to try it?" This time the lad very quickly answered, "No."

All too often we have faith that a thing can be done and that we can do it, but we do not exercise our faith by trying to do it. Saving faith is proved by a faith that works.

THOUGHT: Faith gives life; works prove that life really does exist.

March 11 -- John 1:40-42
There Is No Substitute for Personal Contact

All door to door salesmen know that there is no substitute for the personal contact and successful salesmen know that you should never give up on a prospect. The Avon lady keeps calling and the insurance man keeps calling. That is, those who are doing the selling keep calling.

Look at these figures that have been compiled about salesmen. Forty-eight percent of the salesmen call one time and do not call again. Twenty-five percent of them call twice and then call no more. Fifteen percent call three times and stop at that. However, twelve percent of the salesmen keep on calling and they do eighty percent of the selling. This means that eighty-eight percent of the salesmen quit after making no more than the third call.

How does our persistence in personal witnessing compare with the persistence of salesmen? Are we guilty of giving up because we do not see the results that we think we should see after the first try? Do we make a second attempt and quit? Do we make a third attempt and stop at that? Instead of stopping, are we faithful to keep on witnessing and trusting the results to God?

Someone has said, "I never get tired of the work, but I get tired in the work." Whether or not that applies in the lives of preachers or other "full-time" workers, most of us would have to admit that it applies to our personal witnessing. We need to be more faithful in this phase of our work. Remember the twelve percent of the salesmen who keep on calling and who do eighty-eight percent of the selling.

THOUGHT: If at first you do not succeed, try, try, and try again.

March 12 -- Luke 18:1-8
A Renewed Prayer Life

What would you say is the sin that is the greatest temptation to most people? Hebrews 12:1 tells us to "lay aside every weight, and the sin which doth so easily beset us." I have come to the conclusion that the sin that so easily besets most people is the sin of not praying. We need a renewed prayer life.

We need to pray for revival. We have reached the point where there is no revival in most places today. There are a few areas where some people are motivated from fleshly excitement to "go out after people." However, I see very little evidence of real revival when I take a look around me in America today.

When God's people are brokenhearted because God is being sinned against and when we are burdened for the souls of people who are destined for hell, then we will begin to pray for revival. When revival comes Christians will turn from sin, they will support the church, and they will be the kind of witnesses that God can reward with souls coming to Christ.

The psalmist cried out to God from his heart. He saw the wickedness of the nation. His heart was broken because of the sin of the people, and he cried, "Wilt thou not revive us again, that thy people may rejoice in thee" (Ps. 85:6)?

God said that if His people would humble themselves and pray, then He would do something. Read II Chronicles 7:14. Unless Christians humble themselves, they will not pray. Unless they do pray, revival is not going to come. May God teach us to humble ourselves and pray!

THOUGHT: Prayer gets to the heart of God.

March 13 -- Isaiah 35:1-10
Christian Joy

There are many reasons for Christians to express real joy in life. We will look at three of these reasons today.

Christians ought to express joy because we have deliverance. Paul said that the Father "hath delivered us from the power of darkness, and hath translated us into the kingdom of his dear Son" (Col. 1:13). Each of us is very much aware of the power of the devil. He is cunning and subtle. He walks around seeking whom he may devour, but he also changes himself into an angel of light. He is active on every hand and he is much stronger than you and I are. We need deliverance and we can have that deliverance from the devil's power only through Jesus Christ.

Christians ought to express joy because of our liberty. Lost people are bound by the devil. They are living in sin and they can do nothing about it within themselves. God's people have liberty and we do not have to live a life of sin. Paul said, "Where the Spirit of the Lord is, there is liberty" (II Cor. 3:17). He also said, "Ye have been called unto liberty" (Gal. 5:13). Yes, we have the liberty not to sin.

Christians ought to express joy because of our comfort. If we look at the condition of the world today and how it seems that the devil is running away with everything, we are apt to be very discouraged. When we look to Jesus, the author and finisher of our faith, and we realize that He is our Savior and Keeper, we have that deep comfort that He gives. A little fellow once quoted the twenty-third psalm this way, "The Lord is my Shepherd, I don't want nothing." He seemed to have had perfect comfort.

THOUGHT: We have liberty, not to please self, but liberty to please God.

March 14 -- Psalm 100
A Renewed Service

Churches need a good foundation. This they have in the Lord Jesus Christ. Churches also need a good structure built on the foundation. This they have in the teachings of the Word of God. Churches also need good workers, or good servants. We are good workers when we feed upon the Word of God, when we dedicate ourselves to God, and when we commit ourselves to the church for service.

The church needs people who will be faithful in attendance in the services. We should plan our church attendance and we should give it top priority on our schedule.

The church needs people to teach and to take care of the people who do come to the services. The pastor should not be expected to do all of the teaching and instructing. There is enough work to do around the church for all interested Christian workers to have a part in it. The church today is suffering because so many people will not serve and because many who do accept responsibilities do not take them seriously enough to serve faithfully.

Dr. Robert G. Lee tells about going into a candle shop. He said that he saw all kinds of candles and that he was immediately reminded of Christians. He said that some of the candles had never been lit, just as some Christians have never been on fire for God. Some of the candles had burned a while but then they had gone out. Other candles had burned themselves out completely. Which of these candles is an illustration of you and your life?

THOUGHT: Let your light shine so that others around you may see.

March 15 -- Isaiah 59:1-4
Another Lesson on Prayer

A preacher friend of mine told me of a young man in his congregation who did not believe in tithing and who would not tithe. He said that he just could not do so and that he did not believe that God taught tithing in the scriptures.

As time went by and the Word of God was preached, the young man was finally convinced that he should at least try tithing because God's Word did indeed teach Christians to tithe. He began tithing, but at the end of the first month as grocery time approached there was no money left to buy groceries. What would he do?

The pastor said that he determined to pray definitely that God would supply the need and that this dear young Christian would be convinced that he could trust God to meet his needs if he tithed his income. Sure enough, about the middle of the week, before their grocery shopping day came, this young fellow was given a substantial sum of money from a source that he had least expected.

Of course, I am aware that some people would say that this money would have come in whether there had been any prayer or not. However, we don't have any proof of that, do we? I am sure that one would have a hard time convincing this young fellow and his dear companion that God did not meet the need and that their financial requirements were not met by a direct answer to prayer.

THOUGHT: Receiving is in proportion to asking.

March 16 -- II Peter 1:1-2
Peter Was Committed

Peter said that he was a servant, or a slave, of Jesus Christ. This was his work. He was not to carry out his own desires, but he was to carry out the desires of his Master, the Lord Jesus Christ.

The word "servant" comes from the Greek word "deo" and is the word used for the most servile form of work. Peter is designating himself as a bondslave to the Savior.

The term designates one who is born as a slave. You and I were born as slaves to sin. Peter had been a slave to sin once but now he is a slave, or servant, of God.

Again, this term refers to one whose will is swallowed up in another person's will. The Christian is born into a willing and loving servitude to Jesus Christ. The lost person has his will swallowed up in the will of Satan but the Christian has his will swallowed up in the will of God.

The Christian and his Savior are bound together with bonds that even death will not break. We will serve Him in this life until He has finished with us here, and then we will go to be with Him where we will serve Him forever.

Do we look at our lives and wonder if we are as committed as we should be? Perhaps you have no questions in your mind as to your commitment. On the other hand, you may already know that you are not properly committed to the Lord Jesus Christ.

We should take constant inventory of our lives in order to make sure that we, as servants of God, are truly being faithful to Him.

THOUGHT: You serve him to whom you yield your members as servants.

March 17 -- II Peter 1:1-8
Before and After

In the first verse of this epistle Peter introduces himself and tells us something about himself. We have read about Simon Peter in the gospels and we know how impetuous he was. We also know what God did for him, but now we will let him tell us about it.

The name "Simon" means the old man or the unconverted man. Before Peter became a Christian he was called Simon. Jesus changed Simon's name to Peter when he was converted. The name "Peter" means a piece of rock. The Greek word is "Petros" and the Aramaic word is "Cephas." The English word is "Peter." The person called Peter is the new man.

The word "petra" in Greek means a massive rock and it is used to designate the Lord Jesus Christ. The rock, mentioned in the wilderness journey, from which Israel received water points to the Lord Jesus Christ. Paul said, "For they drank of that spiritual Rock that followed them: and that Rock was Christ" (I Cor. 10:4).

The word "Petros" means a rock in the sense of a piece of rock. Peter is telling us that he had become a new man in Christ and that he had actually partaken of the divine nature. This he tells us in II Peter 1:4.

Simon is the unconverted man and Peter is the new man in Christ Jesus. How is it with you? Would you have to be called by your old name of Simon or could you be called by your new name of Peter? Remember, there is salvation and a new name available for all who will call upon the Lord.

THOUGHT: The gospel is the power that makes the change in your life.

March 18 -- Psalm 103:1-22
Blessing God

God is not being praised today as He should be. Most people are too busy asking for things for themselves to spend much time praising God. There is a song that says something like this: "I didn't come to ask for anything, I just came to talk with you, Lord."

Every Christian should spend time just talking to God, loving Him, and praising Him for all His goodness. All that we have comes from God. All good and perfect gifts are from God. He provides our needs and He heals our sickness. He gives us protection and every benefit that we receive comes from our dear Savior.

Do you spend your time in discouragement and despair or do you spend your time in blessing the name of Jesus Christ? Paul tells us that God has given Jesus "a name which is above every name: that at the name of Jesus every knee should bow...and that every tongue should confess that Jesus Christ is Lord, to the glory of God the Father" (Phil. 2:9-11). Either we will do that in this life and receive life eternal, or we will do it at the great white throne of judgment and will be in eternity with the devil and his angels.

There is no doubt, I suppose, that some of the sweetest times that many of us have ever had have been while we were alone with plenty of time to think of Him and His love to us. At such times we worshipped God with all of our being. God becomes very real to us then. At such times we can tell Him of our love for Him and how we want to honor Him not only with our mouth but with our life as well. "Bless the Lord, O my soul" (Ps. 103:1).

THOUGHT: It is good to worship God alone when we can bless His name.

March 19 -- Psalm 103:1-5
Satisfaction

Many people seek the happiness and pleasure that the world offers, yet they never find what they seek after. Others have very little of this world's goods but they have a deep settled peace because they are depending upon the Lord.

Temporal things do not satisfy. Alexander the Great conquered the world of his day, then he sat down and cried because there was not more to conquer. He was a very unhappy man who lived a very unhappy life. He died while still just a young man, having never reached the happiness for which he sought.

We will be satisfied when Jesus comes again. Then we will be taken from this evil world to be in His presence, where we will honor Him and serve Him forever. We should be satisfied with Him until He comes. The Holy Spirit lives within us to give to us assurances and to bring encouragement. The Holy Spirit will show us God's love and He will make known to us God's will.

We are satisfied with all the good things that are ours. We have pardon from sin and we have cleansing through His blood. We have justifying righteousness and we also have sanctification by the Spirit. We are adopted as full grown sons and we are heirs of God and joint heirs with Christ.

Many people talk about the good old days of the past and the bliss of the future. However, ours is a God who satisfies our mouth with good things for the present.

THOUGHT: I am satisfied with Him, but is He really satisfied with me?

March 20 -- Romans 2:17-29
Man Will Be Judged According to Reality and Not Profession

These verses speak about the religious sinner. Here is the one who has made his claim about spiritual things and who has condemned those who are evidently unsaved. He has boasted about how good he is, about how he loves the Lord, and about how he loves to serve Him. However, he does little or nothing to let others see Christ in his life.

We find many people like that today. I know people who introduce me as their pastor and who talk about "our" church and what "we" are doing. Unfortunately these people are never there to support the church financially or in any other way. What these people say means little to the program of the church or to God.

Paul says that their religious profession will mean nothing in the time of judgment. They make their claims of good, yet they are guilty of doing the very same things that they accuse others of doing.

It does not take long to find out if people are real or fake. Usually their talk will give them away. If that does not immediately give them away, you will soon see in their lives whether they are real or fake.

No one likes an impostor. We like for people to "live up to the claims they make." God expects the same from His children and He will judge us all by the reality of our life rather than by what we profess.

THOUGHT: Precious stones will endure the fire.

March 21 -- Romans 2:12-16
Man Will Be Judged by the Secrets of the Heart

There is a man that I know who was accused of a certain violation. He consistently denied any wrongdoing. Others were exposed and some even admitted guilt, but this man did not. Eventually his own guilt was uncovered. Although he was not the "ring-leader," still he repeatedly denied involvement. When the secrets of his heart were disclosed, he was judged accordingly.

The Bible says, "Be sure your sin will find you out" (Num. 32:23). We can deceive our family and friends and our fellow man, but we can never deceive God. The Bible tells us, "Be not deceived; God is not mocked: for whatsoever a man soweth, that shall he also reap" (Gal. 6:7). The Bible goes on to say, "For he that soweth to his flesh shall of the flesh reap corruption; but he that soweth to the Spirit shall of the Spirit reap life everlasting" (Gal. 6:8).

One day all the secret things of the heart will come to light. What an outlook for the lost person! What do you think it will it be like for you as you have all the hidden things revealed before God?

This will be a great time for God's faithful, humble and obedient servants. They will be rewarded according to their works, whether they be good or bad. Since this is true, should we not be busy doing the things that are pleasing to Him?

THOUGHT: One day the secret things of the heart shall be made known.

March 22 -- Romans 2:1-11
There Is No Respect of Persons with God

Man is often guilty of showing respect of persons. One person means more to you and is a closer friend than another is. It is a hard thing for a person not to show partiality because we each have our own favorite friends.

In our human environment, we find that the educated, the cultured, the prominent, the strong, and the smart are sought after very much. They are often shown political, social, and religious preferences. On the other hand, we find that the poor, the sick, the weak, and the ignorant are often unfairly despised and rejected.

God sees man through the eyes of holiness and He will judge with perfect justice. This verse says that there is no respect of persons with Him. The phrase "respect of persons" means "to receive face." When the lost stand before the Judge at the great white throne judgment and when the saved stand before the Judge at the judgment seat of Christ, He will not look at their faces to determine His judgment.

Whether a person is a thief or a murderer or a drunk or whatever his character or his status in life, each one will be judged according to truth. Whether you are a great person in the eyes of the world or whether you are someone seldom heard of, the judgment will still be according to truth.

Rewards will be given to the Christian according to his works during his life and not according to his job status in this life. There is no respect of persons with a holy God and there will be no respect of persons in His judgment.

THOUGHT: Be careful how you live; it will surely come back again to haunt you.

March 23 -- Romans 2:12-15
Man Will Be Judged According to Performance and Not According to Knowledge

Salvation is not by good works of man. Salvation is by simple faith in Jesus Christ as personal Savior. Yet, the person who is saved will perform good works in obedience to the teaching of the Bible.

The person who rejects Jesus Christ as personal Savior, and who repeatedly spurns the love of God, will have to face God on the issue of knowing what to do and not doing it.

These verses tell us that the one who has the law will be judged by the law. They also tell us that the one who does not have the law will also be judged but not with the full penalty of the law.

This being true, would it not be to the benefit of everyone to study, to understand, and to walk according to the teaching of the law of God?

No one is excusable. God has done a work in every heart that teaches us that which is right and wrong. Even those people in the darkest countries know some right from wrong because they often sacrifice to their gods in order to try to escape punishment.

Our lives should manifest what our tongues claim. We should live the life that we claim to live. Others should be able to see in us what they hear from us. We will not be judged by our knowing, but we will be judged by our doing.

THOUGHT: It is not what you know, but what you do that means the most.

March 24 -- I Kings 8:54-61
Promises

When a person applies for a job, he wants to know certain things about the job. He wants to know what kind of work it is and just what will be expected of him on the job. He wants to know something about the working conditions, the atmosphere on the job, who the boss will be, the hours of work, and what days he is expected to work. He also wants to know the pay scale.

When a person looks for a church home he will ask several questions about the church that he is considering. For example, what is the doctrinal position of the pastor and of the church? Is there a liberal or ecumenical trend in the church? Does the church have a good music program and a good missions program? Will the church be able to minister to the needs of him and his family?

When a man makes plans to marry, he will also ask some questions. For example, can he expect the unfailing loyalty from the young lady he is considering for his wife? Will her love be a lasting one? Are there any reasons to doubt her love for him? Will she make a good mother for his children? Will she properly care for the children?

In every area of life we all want promises that will be fulfilled. This is as true in our spiritual life as it is in our physical life. Although people often make promises that they fail to keep, today's reading tells us of the absolute faithfulness of the Lord. When He makes a promise, you can be sure that He will keep it.

THOUGHT: Promises are worthless unless they are really trustworthy.

March 25 -- Proverbs 3:1-2
Long Life for Loyalty

These verses challenge us to faithfulness in our walk with God and they promise us fullness of life in return. We so often forget the teaching of God's Word. We forget His instruction that is given to us in the Bible. That is one of the reasons why we must have two preaching services on Sunday, a mid-week prayer meeting and Bible study, and frequent revival meetings.

Many times in the book of Proverbs we are told to deal with our own heart. Here we are told to let our heart keep the commandments. It is not enough that we have just a head knowledge of the Word of God. We need to hide it in our heart so that we might not sin against God.

God's promise in verse 2 is not so much a life of eighty years in length as it is an abundant and fruitful life, regardless of its length.

The fact that scientific and medical research has lengthened the life expectancy to above seventy years does not necessarily mean that it is a true sign of progress. Many people have a very fruitful life materially and they live to be old, but they must spend years in a nursing home or a hospital before death. After death there are many bills to be paid and there is often a lot of heartache in settling the estate.

We have known of people who only lived a short life here but who still had a very fruitful life.

THOUGHT: A life lived in obedience to God is lengthy and fruitful regardless of its length in years.

March 26 -- Proverbs 3:3-4
Favor with God and Man

There is an old man with a white mustache whom I remember well. He was in his seventies or eighties and he was a very dear old fellow. He always spoke kindly to you, he was glad to have visitors come to see him, and he always made you feel important.

These verses in today's scripture tell us to grow old gracefully and then God will give us good favor both with God and with man.

You have seen people who were irritable and just not pleasant to be around. They were forever not pleased with anything. Sometimes you would wonder if they drank vinegar to make them so sour. We would all agree that these definitely are not our favorite kind of people.

Let us all work hard to be kind and considerate of others. The writer of today's scripture reading says that we should not let mercy and truth forsake us. Let us live a life of integrity and a life of truthfulness. At the same time, let us be kind hearted and respect the rights of other people.

When Joseph was made ruler over all of the land of Egypt, Pharaoh put a gold chain about his neck (see Gen. 41:42). When the bridegroom in Song of Solomon described his bride, he spoke of the chains around her neck (see Song of Sol. 1:10). This speaks of beauty and of being acceptable.

We should work hard to let others see mercy and truth in us as they would see a chain of gold around our neck.

THOUGHT: Friendly people make friends.

March 27 -- John 3:1-5
Nicodemus

Nicodemus was a Pharisee. The Pharisees were a religious sect that was very strict in law-keeping. A key problem was that they overlaid the law with traditional interpretation and that they looked at laws as having come from Moses. The term Pharisee itself derives from a word meaning "separated." They were highly religious people but they were destitute of the sense of sin and need.

Nicodemus was of this sect. Along with all the others, he was self-righteous and could see nothing wrong with his life. He was a "ruler of the Jews," which undoubtedly speaks of him as being a member of the Sanhedrin, the supreme council of the Jews. He was well educated and he was a master, or teacher, of the Jews.

Why would a man such as this come to Jesus? He came because there was a definite need in his life. The fact that he came to Jesus at night is not nearly so important as the fact that he came. The time of his coming and the reasons for coming have been discussed by many. Nicodemus did come to Jesus and this is the important thing.

Here is a man who has experienced just about all that the world could offer. He is a clean and moral man. He studies the teaching of the Rabbi and he is a "keeper of the law." Indeed, he is a "godly" man. Why did he come to Jesus? He came to Him because even with all his religiosity Nicodemus realized that there was something lacking. He came to the One who he thought could give him some help. Had he never come to Jesus and made his inquiry, he probably would never have been saved.

Have you come to Jesus for something missing?

THOUGHT: **It is not our own goodness but it is Jesus who saves us.**

March 28 -- John 3:5-16
The New Birth

Jesus told Nicodemus of his need of the new birth. Just like so many people today Nicodemus did not understand. Most of us take the simple and make it profound rather than taking the profound and making it simple. Our Lord told Nicodemus several things about the new birth.

Jesus told him of its importance. Without the new birth a person cannot see the kingdom of heaven. This also means that he will be unable to understand spiritual things. The natural man just cannot understand the things of God because they are spiritually discerned.

Jesus told him of the instrument and the producer of the new birth. Man is to be born of the water and of the Spirit. The Word of God is referred to as the water of life. We are said to be washed by the water of the Word. The Holy Spirit applies the Word of God to our heart and we are born again.

Jesus told Nicodemus about the necessity of the new birth. One cannot enter the kingdom of God without it.

Jesus discussed the character of the new birth. The new birth is spiritual. The flesh always remains the flesh and it is not remade. The new birth brings a new man into life and we become new creations in Christ.

Jesus mentions the process of the new birth. Just as the wind blows and no one knows exactly when or where or how it blows, even so the Holy Spirit of God moves in ways that we do not understand. We are born again by the Spirit of God.

THOUGHT: The new birth makes a new man who is able to live a new life.

March 29 -- Nehemiah 8:1-10
Some Astounding Things

It is reported that nine percent of all money spent to reach people for Christ is spent on ninety-four percent of the people. Ninety-one percent of the money is spent on six percent of the people of the world.

Here are some other figures that should disturb us. These figures are several years old and they would be much higher today. However, these figures can still be used to illustrate our point.

The United States spends $300,000,000 per year on chewing gum; $146,000,000 on shampoo; $76,000,000 on lipstick; $325,000,000 on dog and cat food; $341,000,000 on greeting cards; $2,000,000,000 on travel; $5,000,000,000 on tobacco products; and $16,000,000,000 on amusements. These figures are astounding but they are made more astounding when we stop to realize that we spend less than $150,000,000 a year on all foreign missions projects.

We have some 38,600 missionaries on about 130 mission fields. There are about 300,000 villages that have no Christian witness. There are more than 2,000,000,000 people in the world today who have never heard the name of Jesus Christ. There are about a thousand languages that have never been reduced to writing and there are about two thousand languages that have no portion of the scriptures in them. As this is being written, the ratio of our missionary personnel to the unreached is shrinking twenty-five percent every eight to ten years. It is not that we have fewer missionaries than we once had but it is because our missionaries are not going out as fast as the population is growing.

THOUGHT: Go ye into all the world and preach.

March 30 -- Psalm 142:1-7
Love the Lost

I doubt that any one of us loves lost souls as we should. Are we convinced that every person without Jesus Christ as personal Savior is lost and on his way to an eternal, burning hell? Do we believe that it is not God's will that any should perish but that all should come to repentance? If this is true, we should be trying to persuade people to come to salvation in Jesus Christ.

We ought to love the lost because where there is no vision the people perish. When men forget souls they forget God. When we forget souls we forget morals and spiritual life. This was true in the day of Eli the priest. Even the priest turned from God and there was no word from the Lord. There was no vision and the people perished.

We ought to love the lost because where there is no burden and concern, people die without hope. Our scripture verse for today tells of a sad occasion when no one cared for a lost soul.

I do not want to stand in the way of a soul reaching God. Instead, I want to be used to reach the lost for the Lord. The greatest need among God's people today is a consuming passion for lost souls. Too many Christians are satisfied to play at being a Christian and they never witness to the lost.

Our reading for today says, "No man cared for my soul." How sad that this should be true! May God give to us a vision and a compassion for the lost people who are all around us. May we be someone who cares for that soul.

THOUGHT: We cannot save people, but we can tell them about Jesus.

March 31 -- I John 4:16-21
Love the Brethern

All of us need to have and show more love for the brethren. There is much said today about love. Most of the love talked about is the love of the flesh and the love of the world, rather than the love of God.

Do you really love your fellow church member? How long has it been since you have told someone that you love them in the Lord or since you have sincerely shown them that you loved them? In a service recently our visiting preacher asked our people to go to someone and to tell that person that they loved them. This is a good thing to do, but love should be more than just words from the mouth.

It is easy for us to make claims. It is easy to tell people on Sunday that we love them and then not be available on Tuesday to share their burden. We can talk about love and put up a false front. We can face people with piety and then cut one another to pieces behind their back. What we need is a life-changing love for our fellow man.

The Bible says, "We know that we have passed from death unto life, because we love the brethren" (I John 3:14). This is the kind of love that will overcome hatred and that will overlook unkindness and harsh words. It is a love that will refuse to believe gossip and that will refrain from backbiting. It is a love that will definitely keep us from being just a make-believe Christian.

Paul said that if we speak with the tongues of men and angels and do not have love, we are nothing and can accomplish nothing for the Lord. (See I Corinthians 13.) Let us love one another sincerely.

THOUGHT: Love is a sure sign of salvation.

Chapter Four

•••

April

•••

Verse to Memorize

Luke 24:6

"He is not here, but is risen: remember how he spake unto you when he was yet in Galilee."

April 1 -- I Peter 2:1-5
Simon Peter

First Peter was written to encourage believers who were being tested. Second Peter was written to warn of dangers that the church was confronting.

In Peter's day there were certain dangers that hindered the church. Peter points out some of these dangers. He introduces himself in chapter 1 and mentions certain great truths of the faith.

We see in Peter a very good example of a converted man. Simon was the old man and Peter is the new man. (Peter is the English word and Cephas is the Aramaic word, while Petros is the Greek word.)

In Matthew 16:15-17, Christ asked, "Whom say ye that I am?" Peter answered, "Thou art the Christ, the Son of the living God." Jesus said, "Flesh and blood hath not revealed it unto thee, but my Father which is heaven."

Jesus then told Simon that he would be called Petros; he was a new man. From that time on, he was called Simon Peter. The miracle of conversion had transformed him into a new creature. Second Corinthians 5:17 says, "Therefore, if any man be in Christ, he is a new creature."

Have you become a new person in Christ? Have you committed your life to Him? There is only one way of salvation and that is the way of simple faith in Jesus Christ. One day Simon received Him as personal Savior and he was transformed from that very moment. You can be transformed also, because the scripture says, "For whosoever shall call upon the name of the Lord shall be saved" (Rom. 10:13).

THOUGHT: Except you be born again you cannot see the kingdom of God.

April 2 -- I Peter 1:1-3
Calling

A young man came by my study one time and told me that God had called him as a missionary. He was trying to raise the money to go to a foreign field where he said God had called him to serve.

This happened to us often. Our church was interested in missions and we helped many missionaries around the world. When young men learned that we were people who were concerned about missions, they wanted to come by to talk about their work and about the possibility of getting financial support from us.

Peter tells us in the first verse that we read today that he is a missionary. Now, he did not spell it the same way we spell it today, but that is what he is saying.

In the strictest sense of the word "apostle," it means "sent by the Lord Himself." In order for a person to be an apostle in that sense, he would have to see the Lord and be sent personally by Him. In another sense of the word, any person who is called and sent out by the Lord can be said to be an apostle of the Lord Jesus Christ.

In this sense every missionary is an apostle and every Christian worker is an apostle. We are all witnesses for Him. What a joy it is to be a special messenger for the Lord and to be called and commissioned by Him to take the gospel to the lost people of the world.

Peter goes on in these and the following verses to show to his readers what Jesus Christ has done for them. We need more "apostles" today; that is, we need more people who are sent by the Lord Himself.

THOUGHT: How shall the people hear without a preacher?

April 3 -- II Peter 1:1-4
Grace and Peace

When we think of the grace of God, we usually think in terms of how it relates to salvation. It certainly takes the grace of God to reach down into the depths of sin to find the lost sinner and to give him life in the Son of God. However, that is only one aspect of His grace.

Grace does not end there. Yes, we are saved by the grace of God, but we are also kept by the grace of God. After one becomes a Christian he really needs the grace of God. Satan will do all in his power to cause God's children to slip and fall. Only by His grace can we avoid the many pitfalls of the devil.

The entire sanctifying experience of the Christian is dependent upon the grace of God. How often we come to God and confess sin and promise that we will never be guilty of that again. Then we find ourselves going out and committing the same offense again. God in His grace understands our weakness and He is willing to supply our need. He is always willing to forgive us when we confess our sins to Him.

Grace comes first and then peace comes afterwards. We can have peace in all areas of our life and under all circumstances, if only we will rely upon Him for it.

This grace and this peace come through a knowledge of the Lord Jesus Christ. This knowledge is the evidence of our calling in Christ and it is the symbol of our election. It is the channel of our communion and it is the root of our grace. It is the substance of our hope and it is the passport to glory.

Do you know Him?

THOUGHT: The weakest believer shares the blessing with the strongest apostle.

April 4 -- II Peter 1:1-3
Commitment

Peter says that he is a servant. This word comes from the Greek word "deo," which is the most servile term used for a servant. The word is used to designate a person who is born as a slave.

Whether a lost person realizes it or not, he is born a slave to sin. Regardless of how morally clean he might be, he remains a slave to sin until he is born again. Peter is saying here that he has been born again and that now he is a slave of Jesus Christ.

The Christian is born into loving and willing servitude to God. This refers to one whose will is completely swallowed up in another. The will of the lost person is swallowed up in Satan. The will of the saved person is swallowed up in the dear Savior.

The Christian and Christ are bound with bonds that only death can break. Since Christ will never die again the bonds can never be broken. The death of Christ at Calvary broke the bonds of the devil, but Christ died once unto sin and now He lives unto God.

This bondage refers to one serving another and completely disregarding his own interest. The Christian is committed to Christ and, forgetting his own likes and dislikes, he now lives this life to please God.

To be a slave of Jesus Christ means to be possessed by Him. It means to be at His disposal and to be motivated by His love. This is the kind of person the grace of God made of Peter. This is the kind of person the grace of God will make of us if we will surrender to Him.

THOUGHT: He is the potter; we are the clay.

April 5 -- II Peter 1:1-3
Precious Faith

Faith without an object is not really faith at all. Faith in Jesus Christ must be faith in some point about Him. Here Peter refers to faith in the person of Jesus Christ and to faith in His work on Calvary. He also refers to faith in His shed blood. It is the blood of Jesus Christ that cleanses us from all sin.

The blood of Christ also cleanses us from all the stain and guilt of sin. We become new creatures in Him. The guilt that has made some of us run and hide for years is now gone. We no longer have that guilt complex because the blood of Christ has removed it.

The Lord no longer sees our heart and life as stained with sin because the blood of Christ has washed all that stain away. Rather than the blotches and blackness of sin there is now the spotless whiteness that only the blood of Christ can give us.

The precious faith in Jesus Christ brings to us the power of God that cleanses from the greatest sins, delivers from the greatest danger, and supplies the greatest need.

It is a precious faith because it is in a precious Person, because it brings precious redemption, and because it gives precious promises.

How wonderful it is to know that God wants us so much that He works this precious faith in us. He does this so that we might be cleansed by the blood of His Son and some day live eternally with Him. It is not done because of who we are or because of what we have done. It is done because of who He is.

THOUGHT: This precious faith will produce a precious practice in a believer.

April 6 -- John 1:6-8
John the Baptist

The Bible says in today's reading that John the Baptist was sent from God. He was the son of a preacher. He was rugged and he denounced sin fearlessly. First and foremost, however, he was a man sent from God.

There have been many other people who have been sent from God. Martin Luther was sent to turn Christianity from formalism and ecclesiasticism back to God.

D. L. Moody was sent to break hearts and to call people to evangelism and compassion for the lost.

John Wesley was sent to go up and down the new world and to melt the icicles of religion and turn people from their troubles to the Savior.

Billy Sunday was sent to take the drama of his soul and to kindle revival fires in the hearts and souls of people all across this great America.

Not only was John sent from God, but he was also a man and not an angel. God has always used man to reach man with the gospel of Christ. God did not have to use man. Only in His infinite wisdom did He choose not to use angels or to create a special messenger. He gave man the privilege of preaching the gospel to the ends of the earth.

He still gives us the same privilege today. We have the opportunity of taking the simple gospel and pointing men and women to Jesus Christ. We cannot save the lost but we, like John, are sent from God to warn men and women to change their ways and to turn to the Son of God.

THOUGHT: We are His witnesses.

April 7 -- John 1:6-8, 29
More on John the Baptist

John the Baptist had a very special job. God had a special purpose in sending him into the world. He came to be a very special witness. These verses tell us that he was not that Light but he was the witness of that Light.

John's purpose in the world was to point people to the "Lamb of God, which taketh away the sin of the world." John was to tell what he knew and only what he knew.

The people to whom John was preaching were very religious people. They did not like for someone to try to change them. John and his message were rejected and he was eventually beheaded because of his preaching. All of this happened because he was doing the job for which he came into the world.

It is a tragedy that God would send the Light into the world and that man would not know about it. Only the blind person has to be told that the sun in shining. It is pathetic and sad indeed that man goes on sinning when Jesus came "to seek and to save that which was lost" (Luke 19:10).

John came to be a witness. You and I who are saved are also witnesses. John was not the Light and he could not save, but he could be the witness that he was sent to be. As witnesses, we are to point the lost to the "Lamb of God, which taketh away the sin of the world."

John was sent to point to Jesus, the Light, "that all men through him might believe." Even so must we consider this to be our work today.

THOUGHT: A witness tells what he knows.

April 8 -- II Timothy 2:15-19
Study

There are several words or phrases in this verse that would make good subjects for research. I want us to notice three of them.

1. Study. The first word in the verse is perhaps the key word. Do you want to grow in the Lord? Then you must study. Do you want to know the Word of God? Then you must study. There is no short cut and there are too many Christians who think that they can get by without study. Study is the act or process of applying the mind so as to acquire knowledge or understanding, such as by reading or investigation. All of you who have done this know that studying is a hard job. God tells us to apply ourselves in this way so that we might be able to know Him better.

2. Approved. To approve is to give one's consent to; to sanction; to confirm; to be favorable toward something. A person who studies the Word of God receives God's approval. This is the only way to have God's approval upon our knowledge. The article of clothing that you bought from the store had a little slip of paper with it that tells that it was inspected by someone. This means that it has been approved according to the standards of the manufacturer and that it is now ready for sale.

3. Needeth not to be ashamed. Every child of God ought to study the Word of God in order to have assurance and to be able to tell others of the hope that he has. Too many times we are ashamed before man and unable to answer his questions. We should be much more ashamed before God if we neglect to study as we should.

THOUGHT: When we study we can meet God's specifications.

April 9 -- Proverbs 9:9-12
Understanding

Have you made an inventory of your understanding of the Word of God recently? Most of us would be shocked if we knew just how little we understand the Word of God. People do not know God because they do not know the Word of God.

We can know God only as we know His Word. The Bible is God's written revelation of Himself. We can look at the creation and know that God exists. How could we have such a universe as we have without God having created it? Yet, the universe, the creation itself, tells us nothing about the character of God. Only the person who knows Jesus Christ as Savior can understand God and that person can understand God only as he has a knowledge that comes from the Bible. You can measure your knowledge of God by your knowledge of the Bible.

The knowledge we are referring to here is not an intellectual knowledge but it is an experiential knowledge. This is an inner knowledge that comes from the "fear of the Lord" or from an inner experience of Jesus Christ as revealed in God's Word, the Bible.

Have you committed yourself to Him? Don't try to be like God unless you have let Him transform you. You cannot know God intellectually, neither can you grasp His Word intellectually. You receive strength in the inner man as you receive the Word in the inner man.

THOUGHT: There is no knowledge of the character of God apart from the Word of God.

April 10 -- Jeremiah 15:15-21
Eating the Word

Jeremiah said, "Thy words were found." If we are not careful we will overlook the Word of God. We might read daily and completely miss the thing that God is trying to point out to us. All of us have read certain passages many times, only to have them suddenly take on a special meaning one day when we read them once more. As it happened with Jeremiah, we found the words of God.

Jeremiah said, "I did eat them." The Bible is our spiritual food. It is the food for our souls. The Bible is the written Word of God, while Jesus Christ is the living Word of God. Jesus said, "I am the bread of life" (John 6:35). We partake of Him, this bread, as we read the Bible.

We should meditate upon the Word. Only as we do this will we find out what God is saying to us. If the Word of God is not our spiritual food and our refresher, giving us spiritual vitality, we have failed in our attempt to "find" the words and to "eat" them.

The Bible ought to be more than read; it ought to be more than understood. It ought to be more than remembered. It ought to be "eaten." This means that it ought to be digested and then applied to our daily lives.

Once it is applied, the Bible will bring joy and rejoicing to our heart. Nehemiah tells us, "The joy of the Lord is your strength" (Neh. 8:10). The joy of the Lord will fill us as we know Him better through the study of the Word. Thus, we are brought back to the Bible, the Word of God. We are to find it and to eat it. Through our rejoicing we are to share it with others so that they may have the same joy.

THOUGHT: As food is to our body, so is the Bible to our souls.

April 11 -- Joshua 1:6-8
Study Daily

Meditate day and night. Should we never sleep? Is there no time for work and rest? Are we to spend all day and all night in meditation? Of course we are not.

What is meditation? It is the act of meditating; it is deep, continued thought; and it is deep reflection on sacred matters as a devotional act. The verse that we have read today says that we are to "meditate therein day and night."

We should give ourselves to reading the Word of God every day. Too often we find ourselves reading the Bible only as we go to Sunday School or to preaching service. This is not the way it was meant to be. Unless we have the Word in our heart it is hard for us to meditate upon it during the day while we are at work or during the night while we are asleep.

I recommend to young Christians that they read the Bible every day. I do not tell anyone how many verses or chapters they should read each day. Some have time to read more than others. The important thing is that we daily read His Word.

As we read the Word the Holy Spirit will point out things that we would not otherwise see. We should spend time thinking about these things. As we go to our job, we can meditate upon the Word that we have hidden in our heart. As we sleep at night our subconscious continues to meditate upon the Word of God. The Word can then be applied to our heart and it will become an active part of our daily living as we grow in the "fear of the Lord."

THOUGHT: Spiritual food is more important than physical food.

April 12 -- II Kings 6:13-17
We Should Recognize His Presence

The king of Syria had warred against Israel. Elisha told the king of Israel about Syria's plans and the plans were thwarted. The king of Syria asked his wise men how this could be. They told him that Elisha, the man of God, had told the king of Israel about Syria's plans.

This made the king of Syria mad with Elisha and the king asked where Elisha was so that he might capture him. Upon learning that Elisha was at Dothan, the king of Syria sent to take him captive.

In the morning when the servant of Elisha rose early and went outside, he saw that they were surrounded by horses and chariots of the king of Syria. He was afraid and reported the matter to Elisha, asking, "What shall we do?" Elisha was not afraid. He knew that God would take care of His own. He simply asked the Lord to open the servant's eyes so that he might see. His eyes were opened and he saw the hosts of God, horses and chariots of fire, round about Elisha.

The Lord has said to His own, "I will never leave thee, nor forsake thee" (Heb. 13:5). We are assured of God's presence and we should always conduct ourselves as in His presence. The Lord said to Moses, "My presence shall go with thee, and I will give thee rest" (Exod. 33:14).

The way to keep from despair, discouragement, and despondency is to practice the presence of Jesus Christ.

THOUGHT: Why should I be afraid when I'm in the presence of my God?

April 13 -- Proverbs 3:5-6
Daily Guidance

Notice the Lord's instructions in today's reading: "Trust in the Lord with all thine heart, and lean not unto thine own understanding. In all thy ways acknowledge him, and he shall direct thy paths."

Simple, is it not? Yet, this is a hard thing to do. Most of us want to think we know a little about a lot of things. We like to do things our way without asking anyone else. This is evidence of a proud heart. Nothing could be more futile and more wicked than to lean to our own understanding.

We should trust in the Lord and acknowledge Him in all our ways. We should let Him direct us in everything that we do. Someone has suggested that we let Him direct us in our dining room, bedroom, classroom, and work room. This is just another way of saying, "In all thy ways acknowledge him."

Did you notice the promise? "He shall direct thy paths." This I want! Unless we commit ourselves and all our activities to Him all the time, we cannot expect His constant direction. However, when we lean upon Him and not upon ourselves, we can expect to receive the daily guidance that we all need.

Do you have His leadership in your life? Do you take everything in your life to Him for His guidance? Perhaps most of us need to make some new commitments to Him in accordance with today's scripture verses.

THOUGHT: We can have His guidance when we expect it from Him.

April 14 -- Proverbs 3:7-8
Good Health for a Holy Life

Man has lost the fear of God. Having done this, he has lost sin consciousness. Elsewhere in Proverbs we read, "A wise man feareth, and departeth from evil: but the fool rageth, and is confident" (Prov. 14:16). The very fact that man has lost the fear of God results in failing to depart from evil.

We are being taught today that the word "fear" in connection with God means reverential fear and respect. In a sense this is true, but there is also at the same time an element of alarm in the heart.

God is a God of love, but He is also a God of wrath. God hates sin and He will punish the sinner. There should be an awe and a profound reverence for such a wonderful and loving God. There should also be a fear and dread of a God of wrath who has a hatred of sin.

God promises health, both physical and spiritual, in return for a holy life. Caleb is a good example of this. Forty-five years after he spied out the land and was promised by Moses the area of mountains and giants that he had investigated, Caleb said that he was then eighty-five years old. "As yet I am as strong this day as I was in the day that Moses sent me...Now therefore give me this mountain...then I shall be able to drive them out, as the Lord said" (Josh. 14:11-12).

How is your life today? Do you suffer physically and spiritually because of a lack of fear and a lack of departing from that which is evil?

THOUGHT: A life lived for God is a life that is lived for good.

April 15 -- Proverbs 3:9-10
God Will if You Will

We often hear someone say, "I cannot afford to tithe." If any thinking person will read the Word of God and give due consideration to this matter, he will come to the opposite conclusion. He will conclude that he cannot afford *not* to tithe. If we are not willing to trust God with our finances, how can we trust Him with our family, our time, and our souls?

These verses tell us that God will abundantly bless us materially if we will be faithful to Him with our material possessions. He says that our barns will be filled and our presses will burst.

I can remember the time that my wife and I began tithing. We thought that we could not do it. At the time, we were living on a very limited income. I was in college and we also had a daughter in school. We knew that God asked for the tithe and we wanted to be obedient to Him. We began giving the tithe regularly. During those years we had some rather difficult times, but we have never stopped tithing. We are now giving more than the tithe, which is true to the Word of God. He has never failed to provide for us yet.

In the final analysis, we must answer the question, "Do we believe that God is going to remain true to His Word?" If the answer is yes, we cannot fail to tithe.

Don't forget that Jesus Christ said, "Seek ye first the kingdom of God, and his righteousness; and all these things shall be added unto you" (Matt. 6:33).

THOUGHT: God blesses the cheerful giver.

April 16 -- Romans 1:16
Are You Ashamed?

This verse in Romans is a wonderful verse of scripture and we plan to spend several days examining it. In the first fifteen verses Paul has given several reasons for this statement. Paul says, "I am not ashamed of the gospel of Christ."

There are some things we should be ashamed of.
- We should be ashamed of the oftentimes poor testimony of the church.
- We should be ashamed of poor church attendance.
- We should be ashamed of the poor financial support for the church.
- We should be ashamed of the poor witness by the members of the church.

Some things we should not be ashamed of.
- We should not be ashamed of suffering as a Christian. See I Peter 4:16.
- We should not be ashamed of the second coming of Christ. See I John 2:28.
- We should not be ashamed of talking about Jesus. See Mark 8:38.
- We should not be ashamed of the gospel of Christ. See Romans 1:16.

Paul refers to the gospel as the gospel of God (Rom. 1:1); the gospel of His Son (Rom. 1:9); and the gospel of Christ (Rom. 1:16). He tells us where the gospel came from, what the gospel is about, and what the gospel will do.

Gospel means "good news." We need this good news because there is so much bad news around us. This good news is salvation in Jesus Christ. Those of us who have it rejoice in it and those who do not have it need it. Let us spread it.

THOUGHT: The gospel is a matter of life or death!

April 17 -- Romans 1:16
The Person of the Gospel

The gospel is not just a group of facts. We sometimes hear people say, "Now that is the gospel truth." Usually what they have reference to has absolutely nothing at all to do with the gospel of Christ.

A concise definition of the gospel is given to us in I Corinthians 15:3-4, where Paul says, "For I delivered unto you first of all that which I also received, how that Christ died for our sins according to the scriptures; and that he was buried, and that he rose again the third day according to the scriptures."

The gospel is a Person and that Person is the Lord Jesus Christ. Any time Christ is taken out of the gospel message you are left with a blank frame of words. There is then no life and there is no hope. The Son of God is the Person of the gospel.

All that Christ is and all that He has done for us is included in the gospel. Had He not been all that the scriptures say about Him, He could not have been our Redeemer. We think of His pre-existence and of His virgin birth. We think of His sinless life and of His sacrificial death. We think of His bodily resurrection and of His physical ascension into heaven. Perhaps more than anything else we think of His imminent personal return. When we think of these things we are thinking about all that makes Him our wonderful Savior and the Person of the gospel.

What does Jesus Christ mean to you? Have you received Him as your Savior? If you haven't yet received Him, you should do so today while you still have the opportunity.

THOUGHT: The gospel without a living Person is like a building without walls.

April 18 -- Romans 1:16
The Purpose of the Gospel

Paul says that the gospel of Christ is the power of God unto salvation. It is plain for us to see that the purpose of the gospel is salvation. When the angel talked with Joseph about the coming birth of Jesus, he said, "And thou shalt call his name JESUS: for he shall save his people from their sins" (Matt. 1:21).

God created Adam and Eve and placed them in the Garden of Eden. He told them that they could partake of every tree in the garden except the tree of the knowledge of good and evil. He told them that the consequences of eating of that tree would be death.

Satan came to Eve disguised as the serpent. He told her that God was being selfish and that He was withholding from them something that they should have. He told her that they would not die and that they would become as gods and would know good and evil. He beguiled Eve and she ate of the fruit. She gave to Adam and he ate of the fruit as well.

At that moment Adam and Eve lost their contact with God. They became sinners and sinful. Being the man who would become the father of mankind, Adam plunged into sin all those human beings who would come after him. Because of their acts of disobedience they fell into sin and as the result all people need salvation.

Through Jesus Christ coming into the world and taking our sin to Calvary, God has provided salvation for all who will believe on Him. The purpose of the gospel is to provide salvation for all of the lost.

THOUGHT: By putting faith in Christ one passes from death unto life.

April 19 -- Romans 1:16
The Power of the Gospel

This world is mad over power. There are power tools to drive nails, to shell beans, to sweep floors, and to mix cake batter. There are power machines to mow lawns, to cool houses, and to propel you down the road at a hundred miles per hour. There are powerful processes that convert wood into paper and that convert iron ore into frying pans. There are powerful space ships that place men on the moon and then bring them home again.

All of this power is great in its place, but the greatest power this world has ever seen is the power of the gospel.

The word "power" is from the Greek word "dunamis," from which we get our word dynamite. Everyone knows what dynamite will do. We have all seen giant holes blown in rock for the building of roads. The gospel message has exploded in the heart of many a drunk and has blown the beer out of the refrigerator and has blown the desire for other strong drink out of his appetite.

The gospel has exploded in broken homes and it has blown the devil out of hearts. The gospel has restored loved ones to each other.

There is no problem too great for God. He will take care of the problem if people will allow Him to use the power of His gospel message in their lives.

Sin is also very powerful. We have all seen it's ugly work many times. We have also seen the work of the gospel. I would rather see problems solved by the power of the gospel than to see problems created by the power of sin.

THOUGHT: The gospel can pull the devil off the throne of your heart.

April 20 -- Romans 1:16
The Program of the Gospel

The gospel is for everyone. Paul says, "It is the power of God unto salvation to every one that believeth."

A college education is not for everyone. Even though we have a system of public education, there are many who are still unable to obtain a good education. There are also those who do not have the faculties to get a good education.

Everyone cannot have a big auto, a big house, a lot of money, or a long vacation. We could think of more things that a person cannot have than we could think of that he can have. However, every person in the world can have salvation.

Christ said that we are to go into all the world and preach the gospel to every creature. See Mark 16:15. We are told that God is not pleased that anyone should perish, but He desires that all should come to salvation. See II Peter 3:9.

"For God so loved the world, that he gave his only begotten Son, that whosoever believeth in him should not perish, but have everlasting life" (John 3:16). The Bible teaches that whoever believes on the Son has everlasting life. It also teaches that whoever does not believe on Him shall not see life, because he has not believed on the Son.

Jesus said, "Whosoever will, let him take the water of life freely" (Rev. 21:17).

Yes, the gospel is for everyone. Since this is true, you and I should be involved in taking it to the ends of the earth.

THOUGHT: God does not know a person for whom Christ did not die.

April 21 -- I Timothy 1:1-4
An Apostle

The writings of Paul abound in the New Testament. He wrote almost half of it. He is a dominant figure in the unfolding of the polity of the New Testament church. His name begins the church and pastoral epistles.

Paul grew up in Tarsus as a person named Saul. His name was changed when he was changed by salvation in Jesus. He led an illustrious life.

Paul tells us a little about himself in Acts 22:3, where he says, "I am verily a man which am a Jew, born in Tarsus, a city in Cilicia, yet brought up in this city at the feet of Gamaliel, and taught according to the perfect manner of the law of the fathers, and was zealous toward God, as ye all are this day." Paul then goes on in verse 4 to say, "And I persecuted this way unto the death, binding and delivering into prisons both men and women."

In I Timothy 1:13 Paul tells us that all his acts of persecuting the saints were done in the ignorance of unbelief. He did not understand what he was doing because sin had blinded him.

In our verse for today we are told that he is now an apostle of the Lord Jesus Christ. The One whom he had earlier persecuted he is now proclaiming as the Savior.

It is great to know that we who were once opposed to God have also been changed. We are now reconciled to God by the blood of the Lamb, the Lord Jesus Christ. Let us give praise to the Lord for his power to change us.

THOUGHT: Once I was lost, but now I am found.

April 22 -- I Timothy 1:3-4
Instructions to Timothy

Paul's purpose in writing this first letter to Timothy is given in these two verses. According to our first verse today, Paul had already given this charge to Timothy in person and by word of mouth. He writes to him so that he might remind him and impress him with the importance of the message. He also writes so that he might leave the same instructions for those of us who would come after Timothy.

Timothy is to charge some in Ephesus that they teach no other doctrine. Paul had taught in Ephesus for two years at one time. The people were well instructed in the doctrine of Jesus Christ. False teachers are now beginning to creep in among the people. Paul charges Timothy to warn these people of the false doctrine.

Paul loved the church at Ephesus. He loved all the churches but he seemed to have had a particular love for these people. They had ministered to his needs and he does not want to see them turned away from Christ.

Later in this important letter to the young preacher, Paul continues to advise him further, "If any man teach otherwise, and consent not to wholesome words, even the words of our Lord Jesus Christ, and to the doctrine which is according to godliness; He is proud, knowing nothing, but doting about questions and strifes of words, whereof cometh envy, strife, railings, evil surmisings" (I Tim. 6:3-4).

Let us follow the advice of Paul. Let us determine that we will listen to no doctrine other than that of the Lord Jesus Christ as taught in the Bible.

THOUGHT: Someone said to me once, "Stay with Jesus till you can do better."

April 23 -- I Timothy 1:3-4
More about Instructions

Verse 4 warns against listening to fables. A fable is an untrue story. In Timothy's day false teachers were coming into the churches with what they called a superior knowledge. They taught that they had a knowledge that Paul did not have. According to them, those who followed the teaching of Paul were not saved people.

They also taught that God gave off certain emanations over a long period of time. (An emanation is something that comes forth from a source.) They claimed that Jesus was the last of these. They said that He was the most god-like of them all but that He was not God. Timothy was told to rebuke these false teachers and to warn the church about them.

We have the same thing to contend with today. There are those of the so-called "scholarship" who deny the truth and authority of the Word of God. They claim a knowledge far beyond that of the Bible. They say that certain parts of the Bible cannot be true because God is not that kind of person.

The Bible claims to be the authentic Word of God. Jesus Christ spoke of the scriptures and the truth of them. The apostles claimed to be inspired. We would do well to listen to what the Bible teaches and not to listen to what some unbelieving intellectual may say. Paul's word to us today is the same as it was to Timothy long ago. Let us pay attention to this important instruction.

THOUGHT: God's Word plus nothing is truth!

April 24 -- Romans 2:1-3
God's Courtroom

Trial by jury is one of the great American rights. Any person can request and get a jury trial. Under the American system, an accused person is supposed to be considered innocent until he is proven guilty. In our courtrooms, witnesses are called to the witness stand to tell what they know about the case at hand. After their testimony is received the jury is asked to bring a verdict based upon the evidence given. It is similar to this in the courtroom of God, except that God is the Witness, the Jury, and the Judge.

Three classes of sinners are condemned in Romans:

1. The renegade, or down and out, sinners (Rom. 1:18-32). These are the people who have rejected Christ and are living in open sin.

2. The respectable, or up and out, sinners (Rom. 2:1-16). These are the people who are morally clean and are respected as citizens, but they are lost.

3. The religious, or in and out, sinners (Rom. 2:17-29). These are the people who are in the church, but they are out of Christ. They claim something but they do not produce anything spiritual.

Paul says that all of these sinners have committed the same sin. They have not necessarily committed murder or robbery or have lived immorally, but they all have rejected Jesus Christ as Savior.

Paul also says that they are all faced with the same judgment. In Romans 2:3 Paul asks whether you think that you can commit the same sin as others and still escape judgment. The answer is that you cannot escape judgment.

THOUGHT: Be sure, your sins will find you out.

April 25 -- Romans 2:1-3
Man Will Be Judged According to Truth

Man really does not understand his heart. The Bible says, "The heart is deceitful above all things, and desperately wicked: who can know it" (Jer. 17:9)? Unless the Holy Spirit convinces a person of his sinfulness, he will never understand just how sinful he really is.

God sees the facts. He knows the truth and He will reveal it and He will judge man accordingly in the judgment. Paul said that God "spared not his own Son, but delivered him up for us all" (Rom. 8:32). God knows all about each of us and He will judge each of us according to the truth.

It is very possible for man to escape human authorities. He may commit crimes that are never known and he might get by without getting caught all through his life. He might even escape from the authorities after they have discovered his crime. Through some smart move of his lawyer or through the ignorance of the prosecutor or through the lies of his witnesses, he might even escape being convicted in court.

However, this will not be true in the Court of God. God knows the truth about each one of us and this truth will be exhibited at the judgment. With God as the Prosecutor, the Jury, and the Judge, you can rest assured that there is absolutely no way for any person to escape from the truth.

THOUGHT: Trust and obey, for there is no other way to be happy in Jesus.

April 26 -- Romans 2:1-5
Man Will Be Judged by Accumulated Wrath

Imagine a man living a lifetime without Jesus Christ, thinking all the while that he is having a great time following the lust of the flesh and rejecting the call of God. He is actually piling up wrath upon his own head. It is a wrath that will be executed against him in that great day of judgment.

Some people say that they do not believe that God is a God of wrath. They say that He is only a God of love. God is indeed a God of love but He is also a God of wrath. Since He is holy and can only condone holiness, He must also be a God of wrath. As a God of wrath He expresses His hatred and indignation against that which is sinful.

Verse 4 tells us that the goodness of God leads us to repentance. Who was it that kept you from dying in your sleep last night? Who was it that supplied you with food to eat, clothes to wear, and air to breathe? Who was it that gave you a family to love, friends to fellowship with, and a church to love, support, and attend? It was the God who loves you.

As we consider His protection, provision, and promises, it should lead us to repentance for our sinful ways.

If you reject all that God is doing, you are laying up for your treasure the wrath of God. His wrath is sure to come upon all who reject Him. Won't you accept the escape that He has made available to you?

THOUGHT: To receive the life of Jesus Christ is the only way to escape the wrath of God.

April 27 -- Romans 2:6-10
Man Will Be Judged According to His Works

God does not desire to judge and send people to hell. He says that He is "not willing that any should perish, but that all should come to repentance" (II Pet. 3:9). If man will not receive Jesus Christ, he leaves God no alternative but to judge him. He must do that according to man's works.

The person who rejects Christ will stand before the white throne judgment. This is not to determine where he will be in eternity, but it is to have the sentence executed against him. That sentence is to be cast into the lake of fire.

The child of God will stand before the judgment seat of Christ. This is not to determine where he will be in eternity, but it is to receive the reward from God.

Each of these people determines where he will be in eternity by what he does with Jesus Christ in this life. Each one will be judged by his works; the sinner will be judged to determine the degree of punishment in hell and the Christian will be judged to determine the degree of reward in heaven.

The lost person will be punished according to his works. The saved person will be rewarded according to his works, whether they are good works or bad works. Which judgment do you want to come upon you?

Yes, judgment is surely coming to one and all. Thank God for His gracious offer of mercy.

THOUGHT: A person is saved by faith; lost by unbelief; judged by works.

April 28 -- John 4:1-4
How the Zeal of Jesus Affects Me

The Bible says some thought-provoking things about our Savior. "The Son of man is come to seek and to save that which was lost" (Luke 19:10). "While we were yet sinners, Christ died for us" (Rom. 5:8). "Who gave himself for our sins, that he might deliver us from this present evil world" (Gal. 1:4). "For he hath made him to be sin for us" (II Cor. 5:21). These and many other truths concerning our Lord and Savior provoke us to thought and they create in us certain desires concerning Him.

I want to know Him more clearly. It is one thing to know about Him; it is something entirely different to know Him. It is one thing to be saved and to know Him as Savior. However, it is something entirely different to be committed to Him and to know Him as Lord. Paul said that he counted all that was dear to him as loss so that he might know Jesus. He wanted to know Him in the power of His resurrection and in the fellowship of His suffering. He wanted to know Him in the passion of His death and in the pattern of His life.

I want to love Him more dearly every day. John said, "He must increase, but I must decrease" (John 3:30). I want to know the reality of that statement. The psalmist said, "O God, thou art my God; early will I seek thee: my soul thirsteth for thee, my flesh longeth for thee in a dry and thirsty land, where no water is" (Ps. 63:1).

I want to follow Him more nearly. I want to walk so close to Him that I can hear His heart beat. I want to be sensitive enough to His call so that I can hear the still small voice as it says, "This is the way; walk ye in it" (Isa. 30:21).

THOUGHT: A desire for God will cause a person to walk with God.

April 29 -- Isaiah 55:1-7
Pardon

To parole a person is to release him from prison upon good behavior before all his sentence is served. To pardon him is to erase the crime from his record; thus, it is as though he never committed the crime. It is even said that to pardon one is to declare that he never committed any crime. God gives His own a pardon.

Pardon from God is possible from all sin. If there is repentance, there is remission. Whatever the sin is, God forgives it when we confess it to Him. No sin is too big or too black for God's pardon to cover.

Pardon from God is complete. Paul said, "There is therefore now no condemnation to them which are in Christ Jesus" (Rom. 8:1). The sin has come before God and He has seen it. The sin is washed away in the blood of our Savior. When God forgives, He does it completely. The prodigal son came home to ask to be made a servant and he was restored as a son (see Luke 15:11-32). We take the place of a son who is fully forgiven when we come to God.

When God pardons a sinner, that sinner stands before God accepted in the beloved. It is as though he had never sinned. When the thief on the cross called upon the Savior, he was told, "To day shalt thou be with me in paradise" (Luke 23:43). That could mean only one thing; he had been granted full pardon from his sins. This is possible only in Jesus Christ.

THOUGHT: Pardoned from sin means to be accepted in the Beloved.

April 30 -- I Corinthians 1:18-31
The Church at Corinth

The church at Corinth had allowed the spirit of the world to invade the church. We have much the same today. When we allow the world to come into the church we lose the authority of the Bible. When we lose the authority of the Bible, we have no answers for the problems of the day.

Corinth was a great center of philosophy. Philosophy is not wrong as long as it keeps the eternal values in order. When philosophy forgets Jesus Christ and rests upon what man can do, it is a danger rather than a help.

The church at Corinth had allowed luxury to invade it. The people had lost their concern for one another. Some people would bring great meals to the Lord's Supper. They would eat and drink and would forget those who had nothing.

The church had allowed immorality to enter the fellowship and they were doing nothing about it. Paul seems to say that they were glorying in the freedom allowed in the church. They were morally depraved and they were religiously materialistic.

Paul had to tell them to forget man's wisdom. God has chosen the weak things of earth. He has chosen the foolish things to confound the wise. God chooses no man based upon that man's merits or philosophy. He chooses a person because of His love and mercy.

Let us be thankful that God chose to give us salvation in His Son.

THOUGHT: The wisdom of the world says that the Bible is not authoritative.

My Prayer List

1.

2.

3.

4.

5.

6.

7.

8.

9.

10.

Chapter Five

•••

May

•••

Verse to Memorize

John 5:24

"Verily, verily, I say unto you, He that heareth my word, and believeth on him that sent me, hath everlasting life, and shall not come into condemnation; but is passed from death unto life."

May 1 -- Job 1:1,8
Job Was a Man of Principle

Job was perfect, which means that he was a mature son of God. He had grown up in his knowledge of and walk with God. He was a well-rounded character. Nothing was lacking in his life of godliness. He was a consistent man of God. Job was not one who just had both good traits and bad traits. He was one who had knowledge, who loved God, and who had faith. He was not at the same time envious, jealous, and critical. No, Job was a mature believer.

Job was an upright man. He had holy reverence before God and he served God. He was a person who fulfilled the writings of the psalmist even before they had been written. The psalmist said, "Stand in awe, and sin not" (Ps. 4:4).

Job was a man who feared God and who turned away from evil. He followed the principle of Paul in Romans 13:14, "Put ye on the Lord Jesus Christ, and make no provision for the flesh, to fulfill the lusts thereof." He turned from evil because it was not of his makeup to sin against God. His actions with his children proved that.

This is not Job's testimony of himself but it is God's testimony of Job. This is what God saw when he looked at Job. God called this to the attention of the devil.

What does God say about us today? Does he see us as people who are perfect and upright and who shun evil? Is God's testimony of us entirely different from what it was of Job? If we saw ourselves as God sees us we just might make some changes.

THOUGHT: What God knows about me is more important than what a person thinks about me.

May 2 -- Job 1:2-3
Job Was a Man of Property

Someone said, "Money is not everything, but it helps." Riches can be a great asset in serving the Lord, but so often riches take people away from God rather than calling them closer to Him.

Not all Christians have great material fortunes. God cannot trust all of His people with wealth. Too many riches prove a stumbling block rather than a means of serving God. The psalmist advised us, "If riches increase, set not your heart upon them" (Ps. 62:10).

Paul said, "The love of money is the root of all evil" (I Tim. 6:10). It is such an easy matter to set your heart upon worldly goods and not upon Christ. One preacher was heard to announce from the pulpit that the church needed to pray for a member who was becoming rich. Job was a rich man, but he knew how to handle his riches.

Although we are not all rich materially, all Christians are rich spiritually. God has given to us all spiritual blessings in heavenly places in Christ Jesus. We are blessed with eternal life and the blessed hope of the soon coming of Christ. We are blessed with the privilege and power of prayer and the joy of searching the scriptures. We have the presence of the Holy Spirit. These are only a few of His blessings upon us.

Job lost his material possessions but he never lost his spiritual possessions. Material things will pass away but spiritual things will abide. Solomon said, "Better is little with the fear of the Lord than great treasure and trouble therewith" (Prov. 15:16). Job had twice as much in the end as he did before Satan put him through the fire.

THOUGHT: With all your getting, get wisdom.

May 3 -- Job 1:4-5
Job Was a Man of Prudence

We have all seen people who had great personalities, great material possessions, many friends, and maybe good looks, but they seemed to have no wisdom about things present or things to come. Job was not deceived by the selfish pride that seems to afflict many of God's people.

Job had a deep concern about his children. He knew where his children were and what they were doing. He was not like so many parents today who let their children run to and fro with little guidance and discipline. Verse 5 says, "Thus did Job continually."

Job knew the need of regular worship. Being a godly man, he provided this for his family. There was no time when he was not aware of the need in his own family. He was continually concerned about their spiritual welfare.

Too many families have fried preacher, boiled teacher, or stewed deacon at almost every meal. This is not conducive to training up a child in the way that he should go and then expecting him not to stray from it.

Job prayed daily for his children. Lest they get into something that they should not get into, Job made special offerings for them. Job honored God with his example as well as with his teaching.

Does our home life show that we make wise decisions? Are we examples of wisdom? When God shows us to others, what do they see in us? Job was seen as a wise man.

THOUGHT: Wisdom is characteristic of a genuine person of God.

May 4 -- Job 1:9-10
Job Was Protected

Satan is arrogant! His desire is to take every child of God away from the Savior, but the truth of the matter is that he cannot do it. These verses prove that Satan has no power except that which God allows him to have. He is limited in what he can do.

We see that God put a hedge around Job's person. "As the mountains are round about Jerusalem, so the Lord is round about his people from henceforth even for ever" (Ps. 125:2). Paul said that the people of God are hidden with Christ in God. There is no way the devil can get to our life. He can do much to hinder our testimony and because of this we need to be very careful, but Satan cannot touch our life.

God put a hedge around Job's family. It is true that the children were killed by the great wind, but this is not the end of the story. We must read the last chapter of Job to see that God restored Job's children to him.

God put a hedge around Job's belongings. God did not promise Job anything. Destruction came and his belongings were taken. His family was destroyed and his body was tortured with boils. We must go to the last chapter of Job in order to find what the final outcome for Job was. We read, "So the Lord blessed the latter end of Job more than his beginning" (Job 42:12).

Let us never forget that "the angel of the Lord encampeth round about them that fear him, and delivereth them" (Ps. 34:7). Let's do just as David did, who said, "I have set the Lord always before me: because he is at my right hand, I shall not be moved" (Ps. 16:8).

THOUGHT: Whatever the circumstances and need, we have an unfailing God.

May 5 -- Proverbs 3:5-6
How to Get Rid of Fear

Be assured that God wants you to be free from fear. He can take your fears from you. Jesus rebuked the disciples for being fearful and for having so little faith. The storm was rough and the sea tossed the little ship around, but Christ Himself was there. This should have been enough to reassure the disciples.

To be free from fear you must first be sure that you want to be free. Many people enjoy being sick or having other hindrances that bring them attention from others. They love the attention and they love the fears that allow them to escape responsibilities. Jesus asked the impotent man by the pool, "Wilt thou be made whole" (John 5:6)?

To be free from fear you must admit that you have fears. It is easy to hide them and to refuse to recognize and admit that you are fearful, but as long as you do this there is no freedom. It is good to write down the things that you fear most. Look at them. Tell someone about them. Rahab told the spies how she had heard of their God and she feared Him. This was a good thing for it brought salvation to her house.

Ask God to remove all your fears. David said, "I sought the Lord, and he heard me, and delivered me from all my fears" (Ps. 34:4).

Practice the presence of Jesus Christ. The Lord is my shepherd right now. He is by my side and He lives within me right now. He supplies all my needs right now. He has said, "I will never leave thee, nor forsake thee" (Heb. 13:5).

Dwell in the Word of God. "He that dwelleth in the secret place of the most High shall abide under the shadow of the Almighty" (Ps. 91:1).

THOUGHT: Forget about all of your many fears and praise the Lord.

May 6 -- Acts 2:42-47
The Gospel Attracts

At Pentecost three thousand people were saved. Immediately after Pentecost people were added to the church daily. The leaders of that day did not like this at all. They threatened the disciples. They beat them and they commanded them not to preach in the name of Jesus again. The disciples went out from them and with boldness they began to proclaim the message of salvation in Jesus Christ. People responded and they saw the church grow.

People found in Jesus Christ a peace that they had not found before. There was a fellowship with God's people that they had never known before. The leaders of that day said that there was nothing to it. They said to just leave it alone and it would soon go away, but it did not work that way. These people were not superficial, neither was the Christ that they followed. Rather than just playing church, they were genuine and sincere.

The attracting power of the gospel as seen in the first church was manifest in several ways. It gave them power to overcome the opposition of the enemy. They were called in before the magistrates and were told to stop preaching their doctrine. They were threatened and beaten, yet they went out to speak the Word.

The gospel had made witnesses of them. They went from house to house preaching the Word of salvation. When we are busy we will win some to our Lord.

It made good stewards of them. They sold what they had and they put the money in the treasury of the church so that the less fortunate could be fed. They constantly exalted Christ in their daily life. Let us follow their example.

THOUGHT: A consistent witness will always attract others to Christ.

May 7 -- Acts 5:12-18
The Gospel Repels

The early church presented a real problem for the people. They either had to be in the church or out of it. When a man came to know Jesus Christ as Savior and joined the church, he was a marked man. He was immediately hated by the Jews because he had embraced Jesus Christ.

Once they became members of the church, the people lived holy lives. Miracles were performed and signs and wonders were seen. The people were known to be followers of Christ and for this they were persecuted. It cost the early church members something to follow the Savior.

Our scripture today says that when they saw God's judgment upon certain disobedient church members none of the people wanted to join the church. The gospel message repelled those who were not willing to walk with God.

Churches where the gospel is preached with power and where the people turn from the evil practices that dishonor God usually do not have a great influx of people. The gospel message has a repelling force.

Many people want to be members of churches where they are not advised against dancing, drinking, going to movies, and many such questionable things. We have a mixed multitude that sometimes wants to compromise their Christian testimony in order to have a good time in the world.

May God help us to know the truth, to be made free by the truth, to live according to the truth, and to reach others with the truth.

THOUGHT: Demands of Christianity divided the saved from the unsaved.

May 8 -- Genesis 5:21-24
Walking with God

To the best of my knowledge there are only two men of whom it is specifically said that they walked with God. The Bible said of Enoch that he walked with God and he was not, for God took him. It also said of Noah that he was a just man and perfect in his generation and that he walked with God.

When I have finished the work that God has given me to do and I am off the scene, I want to be remembered as one who walked with God.

In order to walk with God there must always be a beginning point. This comes when a person receives Jesus Christ as his personal Savior. You cannot walk with one with whom you are not in agreement. You are not in agreement with Christ until you receive Him as your Savior. Enoch agreed with God and he embraced Him. From that time on the two walked together.

Enoch began walking with God when his son was born. The son's name was Methuselah, which means "when he dies, destruction will come." God was warning Enoch of His coming judgment upon this earth. Enoch heeded the warning and began walking with God.

Many people come to know Christ and begin walking with God during a time of crisis. Usually at such a time a person's heart is tender and he is ready to seek help and peace from God. Many children promise their dad or mother that they will come to Christ. After having a wreck or facing some other kind of crisis, a person is usually more willing to talk about accepting Jesus Christ. We should always be alert to such occasions.

THOUGHT: The best walking partner a person can have is God Himself.

May 9 -- Isaiah 24:1-6
Wrong to Be Gone

A mother left her infant son in bed in their mobile home while she ran next door to see a neighbor. While she was away, a short circuit in the electrical wiring set the home on fire. Before she could get back to the mobile home it was destroyed and the baby died in the fire.

A defense plant hired a man to patrol the place at night. His job was to walk around the plant. He stopped at a sandwich shop one night for a snack, but while he was stopped someone entered the plant and set a device that caused an explosion the next day.

Peter was absent from the Lord's side as he was ill treated by the soldiers. Peter had walked afar off; now he curses and swears that he has never heard of Jesus Christ.

Thomas was absent from the upper room when Jesus appeared to the disciples after His resurrection. Because of this Thomas missed seeing the Lord and missed the fellowship with the other disciples. Thomas doubted that Jesus had arisen and came to be called "doubting Thomas."

Demas loved the pleasures and excitement of the world. When the going got rough on the missionary journeys of Paul, Demas left him.

David was absent from battle when in reality he should have been in the front lines. While out of place he became a very sinful man and had to pay dearly for his sin.

It pays to be in the right place at the right time.

THOUGHT: There is a French proverb that says that the absent one is always wrong.

May 10 -- John 4:1-4
Christ Must Go through Samaria

No faithful Jew would dare go through Samaria on his way to Galilee. He would have gone from Jerusalem through Jericho, crossed the Jordan River, and gone up the east bank of the Jordan. Wasn't this a longer route? Yes, it was a longer route but he did not want to "contaminate" himself with the mixed race in Samaria.

Our scripture says that Jesus must go through Samaria. If others would not go through it, why must He?

Jesus must go through Samaria because there was a woman there deep in sin who was ready for the Messiah. This was His business in the world. See Him as He goes into this despised place in the midst of these despised people. See Him as He sits upon the well curb and waits. See Him as He talks with this fallen woman and offers her the water of life that, if she drinks of it, would cause her never to thirst again. This was His work.

He went through Samaria because He was always about His Father's business. Jesus had said, "Other sheep I have, which are not of this fold" (John 10:16). The business of the Father was bringing people to Him; Jesus was doing this.

He went through Samaria because it is not His will that any should perish but that all should come to repentance. This woman needed salvation and Christ came to die for her just as He did for any person in Israel.

He must go through Samaria because "God so loved the world, that he gave his only begotten Son, that whosoever believeth in him should not perish, but have everlasting life" (John 3:16). He will save anyone who calls upon Him.

THOUGHT: The same principle that sent Him to Samaria sent Him to the cross.

May 11 -- John 3:17-21
Sad Condition

When Jesus came to this world He did not find peace and love among the people. He did not come because He expected to find them. He came because the world was lost and needed a Savior. He came to seek and to save that which was lost. What did He find when He came?

He found a priesthood in Israel that was blinded with the traditions of men and the elements of the world. The religious leaders of the day came out to meet Him and asked, "Who are you?" They should have known who He was. John the Baptist knew who He was.

He found a nation with no joy. How could they have joy when they had rejected the very source of joy? Where the blood is rejected there is no joy, no assurance, no conviction, and no fellowship. It is the same today. Many people sacrifice their principles on the altar of worldly pleasure.

Jesus found the temple desecrated. He had to chase the business operators out of the temple on two occasions while He was on earth. It is our belief that He would make some vast changes in the church if He should walk in on the scene today. Much goes on in the name of the church that must not be pleasing to Him.

He found Himself in a world that hated Him. He was not received by those who should have been the first to greet Him. The world hated Him because their deeds were evil and the same situation exists today. Yet, in the midst of sad conditions, Jesus Christ came to save the ungodly. It was while we were still sinners that Christ died for us.

THOUGHT: God's love penetrates sinful hearts.

May 12 -- Matthew 6:25-34
Seven Arguments against Anxiety

Anxiety that comes from a lack of confidence in our God causes ulcers. Headaches are caused by lack of relaxation in Jesus Christ. We are offered peace in our Savior. Why do we continue to bring problems upon ourselves?

Anxiety manifests ungratefulness. Verse 20 tells us that there is no need to be upset and anxious about food and clothes. God has given us our own bodies and even life itself. These are more important than food, drink, or clothing. Can't we trust Him for secondary things?

Anxiety is unreasonableness. The fowls do not reap and store up food. They are content to leave all these things to our heavenly Father. Should we not be content also? The Bible says that we are much better than the fowls are.

Anxiety is unavailing. Which of us can make ourselves any bigger by worry? The Lord asks the question about which of us can add a cubit to our stature. Since anxiety avails nothing, it is not good to be anxious and worried.

Anxiety shows unbelief. God says that the lilies are clothed and cared for, although they do not toil or spin. He says that we have little faith when we do not trust Him for those things that we need.

Anxiety is uncivilized. It is a mark of the heathen to fret and worry. We should know better than to fret and worry, for we should trust our Father.

Anxiety is unnecessary. Verse 34 says to let every day take care of itself. We have enough today to be concerned about without worrying about things of tomorrow.

THOUGHT: Worry indicates a lack of faith.

May 13 -- Luke 14:16-24
Visitation at Work

The way to reach other people for Jesus Christ is to go out there after them. If we consistently put ourselves in the presence of people, God will use our good witness to bring some of them to Himself.

Jesus was always with people. On a well curb He brought a sinful woman to Himself. By the roadside He opened the blind eyes of a beggar and gave to him eternal life. By the river He called Andrew to Himself and Andrew went out immediately to bring his brother to Jesus.

There once was a businessman who was challenged to soul winning upon seeing the list of unchurched people that resulted from a census his church took. He asked for a list of names and he went out and enlisted enough of these people who had not been reached to have the largest Sunday School class in his church.

Dr. Lee Roberson came to Highland Park Baptist Church when there were about six hundred in attendance. He emphasized visitation to his church people. The church rose to the challenge and Sunday School attendance rose to over six thousand, with hundreds being baptized each year.

Dr. Dallas Billington went to a little church in Dayton, Ohio, when it had thirteen members. The people there took seriously his challenge on visitation and began visiting and winning the lost to Jesus Christ. In time membership in the church rose to over six thousand.

This is God's plan for reaching the lost. It has never failed. It will not fail today if we will use it.

THOUGHT: The place to win people to Jesus is where they are.

May 14 -- Acts 20:17-21
Visitation Evangelism

Visitation evangelism can be defined as going to people for the purpose of talking to them about their relationship with God. Many times churches will mark off several blocks in a town and will go from house to house witnessing to the people. If some people would ask our authority for this we would point to Jesus Christ Himself. He came to seek and to save the lost. This is how Jesus called Peter, James, John, Andrew, and the rest of the disciples.

Jesus commanded that you and I be busy at it. He said at various times, "Go ye...behold, I send you...launch out into the deep...ye shall be witnesses...go after that which is lost...as my Father hath sent me, even so send I you." Visitation is emphasized in the parables of Christ. The shepherd went after the lost sheep until he found it. The good Samaritan ministered to the unfortunate man. At the great supper the servants were sent out into the highways and hedges to bring in people. Nowhere in the Bible are sinners told to "go to church," but we who are saved are constantly told to go out after the lost.

There are at least three reasons why God's people should be busy reaching out for others. First, it is because of the weakness of the flesh. Second, it is because of the temptations of the world. Third, it is because of the powerful forces of evil.

What are you doing about witnessing to others? Do you know some lost people? Perhaps God has appointed you to be a missionary to bring those people to Him.

THOUGHT: Visitation evangelism: Jesus did it; He commanded it; and He taught it to His disciples.

May 15 -- Psalm 1
Why Be Concerned?

Every Christian ought to be concerned for the lost and for the unconcerned church member. The blood of Jesus Christ was shed on Calvary for every person. There is no reason for any person to be lost and there is no reason for any Christian to be in a backslidden condition.

Go into any city or town on a given Sunday and you will find fewer than thirty percent of the people in anybody's church. You will also find fifty percent of the church people who are not faithful to their church. Perhaps part of the reason is that many pastors do not preach the truth of salvation. They do not preach that salvation is by faith in Jesus Christ, who shed His blood for sinners like us.

Every year there are billions of dollars spent by the government fighting crime. Billions of dollars are spent on booze. Murder and rape and other major crimes are occurring every few seconds around the country. Should we be concerned about this?

The Bible and prayer have all but been removed from our schools. Satanic forces and satanic practices have replaced them. False and soul-damning heresy is being preached on every hand. We are being told to identify with things and movements that do not honor God.

Why should we be concerned? We should be concerned because this world is rapidly turning its back upon Jesus Christ and is fast following money and pleasure.

Let us resolve to dedicate ourselves anew to reaching people with the life-changing message of the gospel of Christ.

THOUGHT: Saying no to Christ means no salvation and no hope.

May 16 -- Proverbs 11:24-30
Words about a Soulwinner

Our scripture today tells us that the one who wins souls is a wise person.

James says, "Let him know, that he which converteth the sinner from the error of his way shall save a soul from death, and shall hide a multitude of sins" (Jas. 5:20). A man is wise when he is about the business of God.

A soulwinner usually has a better knowledge of God's Word than most people. He must study the Bible in order to be able to help others. He helps himself long before he helps others. In studying the Bible and looking for ways to reach people for salvation he comes to know Jesus Christ better and he will grow in His favor.

Soulwinners will be regular in services in their church and faithful in their obligations. They will be dependable and will usually be leaders in their church.

Because of a deep love for God and a love for lost souls, soulwinners will live a life of dedication to God. They will follow the words of Paul when he said, "I beseech you therefore, brethren, by the mercies of God, that ye present your bodies a living sacrifice, holy, acceptable unto God, which is your reasonable service" (Rom. 12:1).

Worldliness will be much less attractive to soulwinners and they will be respected in their community. They will have a great influence upon others and the devil will not be able to toss them about with every wind of doctrine.

A soulwinner is a person who is busy about the primary business of God. Let us be faithful in this work.

THOUGHT: Remember that bringing the lost to Jesus is our primary work.

May 17 -- Job 4:14-21
What Fear Does to Us

Fear is a strange thing. It will make us do things that we would not otherwise do. Fear makes us unhappy and brings us into its bondage. It brings great destruction in our everyday lives.

Fear undermines our health. Just as Job was in our scripture today, we too will become tense and our emotions will become upset. Many people are sick today simply because of fear that they have not been able to control.

Fear breaks down the nervous system and affects the entire bodily function. Fear will take one's appetite away and will completely upset the digestive track. I know of a young man who has had such a problem because of fear that crept in upon him. In addition to this all his hair fell out, including his eyelashes and eyebrows.

Fear causes rheumatism and other diseases of the joints. It causes pimples on the face and blotches in the complexion. Paralysis is often the result of fear. The writer of Proverbs said, "The wicked flee when no man pursueth: but the righteous are bold as a lion" (Prov. 28:1).

Fear robs many people of their sleep at night. The mind becomes clouded. Moses said, "In the morning thou shalt say, Would God it were even! And at even thou shalt say, Would God it were morning! For the fear of thine heart wherewith thou shalt fear, and for the sight of thine eyes which thou shalt see" (Deut. 28:67).

Fear robs many people of joy, peace, power, poise, testimony, and the freedom to serve God. May God help us to be delivered from this kind of fear.

THOUGHT: Fear is an enemy of man's well-being.

May 18 -- Psalm 27:1-14
The Kind of Fears That Beset People

Usually general fears set in, but sooner or later particular fears present themselves in the lives of individuals. What kinds of fears bother you? Let's look at some of those besetting fears.

Fear of failure plagues many people. No one wants to be a failure and each of us must learn to live with this real concern. Paul said that it was difficult for him to keep from projecting himself. He feared that such self projection might cause him to be put on the shelf as far as carrying on the Lord's work was concerned.

There is fear of responsibility. Many people are ambitious but at the same time they are cautious. Here again Paul had his fear. He said that he not only had those things that were without and those things that came upon him daily, but he had the care of all the churches. There was the fear that he would not be able to properly care for them. Every pastor has some of this fear.

There is fear of danger or harm. I suppose that this was more real to me the first time I ever rode in an airplane. I could imagine the plane falling and plunging me to my death. All of us have a fear of danger or harm.

Many people have great fear of the future. Every unsaved person has this fear, and even some of us who are saved have it. We fear the thought of old age coming upon us or of being disabled or being a burden to others. Yes, there is a fear of the future.

We will have no worry if we will completely commit ourselves and all that we have to our dear Lord and Savior. We are His and He will take care of us.

THOUGHT: What could be better than resting in the Lord Jesus Christ?

May 19 -- Genesis 1:27-28; 2:18-25
The Home

The nearest thing to heaven on earth is a godly home. This is a home where dad and mother love each other and where the children love one another. The parents love the children and the children respect and love the parents.

Home can also be a hell on earth. If dad and mother fuss and fight all the time, home is not what God intended it to be. If there is drinking, cursing, and nagging, then home is not what it should be. If the parents do not love one another and the children do not love and respect their parents, home can become a place where God is not known. If this is true it does not resemble heaven at all.

God instituted the home with godly parents. Adam and Eve once knew no evil but they did know God. The time came when they turned away from God and they got away from the real intent of the home. No home can be godly without God at the head of it.

The home is the basic unit of our society. We need to see a revival in the home in order to see our complete society changed for the better. Any laws that are passed or any social changes or community programs that do not improve the family and the individuals in the family can only offer temporary relief for society. The nation will rise no higher morally, educationally, or spiritually than the level of the home.

Let us work diligently to help our home and family to become God-honoring as it should be.

THOUGHT: As the home goes, so goes the nation.

May 20 -- Ephesians 5:22-33
How to Prevent Unhappiness in the Home

Much can be done before the wedding to prevent unhappiness in the home. This might seem a strange thing to say but it is true. If certain precautions are taken before marriage, many heartaches and problems will be avoided. The couple should ask several questions about one another. Let's look at a few of these questions.

Is the person whom you plan to marry a Christian? If he or she is not, you should proceed no further. God's Word is explicit in its teaching that we are not to be unequally yoked together. The Bible never permits saved people to marry unsaved people. When you do this you are always out of the will of God.

You should consider whether the person would make a good husband or a good wife. There might be little or no reason why the person should not make a good husband or a good wife for someone else, but this person might not be God's selection for you.

Will this person make a good father or a good mother for your children? This is a good question to ponder and about which to pray. The other person's ideas about a family might be completely different from yours. It is better that you discuss this before the marriage.

Is the beauty we see in each other more than skin deep? Often we are infatuated with what we see, but the real beauty of the soul is not there. It is much better to have a person with a beautiful personality and disposition, who perhaps does not have such beautiful physical features, than to have a person with beautiful physical features and a bad personality and disposition. Let's look first for the beauty of the inner person.

THOUGHT: Marriage is for a long time. Make it a serious business.

May 21 -- Psalm 1
Rules for a Happy Home

Begin the home with God. My advice to the bride and groom is to begin a family the first night of your married life. If this matter is put off till later, it can be easily overlooked. Homes that are established upon God and homes that look to God through the family altar have a greater chance of holding together than those that do not.

Be considerate of one another. It is my thinking that much unhappiness comes about from a lack of consideration for one another.

Each member of the family should take the appropriate place. The woman should be a woman and the man should be a man. Too often the woman does not want to be a woman and the man does not want to be a man. The woman should remain feminine and the man should remain masculine. When this is not done, trouble most likely will arise.

The family should live within its means. The Bible says to be content with what you have. Many young couples get themselves into trouble by living above their income. Someone has said that if our outgo is above our income, then our upkeep will be our downfall.

Plan a family early. God speaks of children as being a blessing to a home. The home that does not have children is missing much from God. If we will let God direct in this matter, He will bring honor to Himself.

Avoid all appearance of evil. Do not say things or conduct yourself in a way that would be improperly suggestive.

THOUGHT: Love, consideration, and humility in the home spell a happy home.

May 22 -- II Corinthians 6:14-18
Be Not Unequally Yoked
Together in Marriage

The passage of scripture we have read today touches every area of our life. We are not to be yoked unequally in any phase of our activities. Lost people and saved people have nothing in common and they are not to be yoked together in business life, social life, or married life. God says in verse 17, "Come out from among them, and be ye separate."

The person with whom we are united in marriage will help mold our entire life, whether it be social, business, community, or church life. We are never to take a companion for ourselves without praying about it and without having assurance that this is God's choice for us.

The home is a type of the church. The groom and the bride represent Christ and the church. If a saved person marries a lost person, that type is broken and that particular home can never show forth the glory of God as long as one member is lost.

Consecration is all but impossible for a saved person who has a lost companion. Paul said that those who are married are mindful of the things of the world and how they might please one another. It is difficult for a saved wife to follow fully the instructions of Romans 12:1-2 if she has a lost husband. Regardless of how smoothly things might go in the home, he will always have demands that will take the wife away from serving God as she should. "The flesh lusteth against the Spirit, and the Spirit against the flesh" (Gal. 5:17). This will always be true in mixed marriages.

THOUGHT: God's Word never permits a saved person to marry a lost person.

May 23 -- Matthew 19:3-6
More on Unhappiness in the Home

In another devotional we considered preventing unhappiness in the home by taking certain precautionary measures before marriage. Today I want us to look at some things we can do, or perhaps I should say, some principles we should observe after we are married. These can be recognized before marriage as well as afterward, but married people should be aware of these and let them work in the home and lives of the individuals.

We should know the purpose of marriage and the home. There are two general purposes and whatever we could think of would probably fall under one of these.

The purpose of marriage is the companionship and fellowship of the married couple. After God made all the animals, fowls, and fishes of the sea He saw that Adam was still not completely happy. God made Eve to be Adam's wife. This pleased God and He saw that it was good. He intended that man and woman be together and enjoy the company of one another and work together in harmony to make the home a place of joy.

The purpose of the home is to raise a family. The psalmist said that children were a heritage of the Lord. God told Adam and Eve to multiply and replenish the earth. This is a very solemn purpose of the home; the husband and wife should give themselves to this purpose.

In Old Testament days a woman who had several children was looked upon as being blessed of God. You remember how Hannah prayed for a man child and how God heard her prayer. Happiness was usually linked to having several children.

THOUGHT: In all of its activities the home has a duty to honor God.

May 24 -- Philippians 4:5-7
The Peace of God

The peace spoken of in these verses is the peace that characterizes God Himself. God knows what He is doing, why He is doing it, how He is going to do it, and when it is done. Can you imagine God being nervous and upset about something and having to take tranquilizers? God is not anxious about the wonders we are witnessing. He is not anxious about the spread of communism or about Red China or about any other matter that causes you and me to run a fever of anxiety.

God offers us the same peace that He experiences. This is the peace that passes understanding. It is not only a peace of heart for eternity but it is also a peace of mind for the day in which we live.

Jesus Christ said, "Come unto me, all ye that labor and are heavy laden, and I will give you rest" (Matt. 11:28). This is the peace and rest that comes when a person is saved. Jesus also said, "Take my yoke upon you, and learn of me; for I am meek and lowly in heart: and ye shall find rest unto your souls" (Matt. 11:29). This is the peace of God that passes all understanding.

The Lord Jesus Christ is the peace that God gives to His people. When we receive Him, we receive peace. When we learn to know Him better, we find that lasting peace. God wants us to have both. One comes when we are saved. The other comes as we study to show ourselves approved unto God and as we follow close by His side.

God has provided all that we need in Jesus Christ. Let us relax in Him.

THOUGHT: Be steadfast in the storm; we know that the experienced pilot is at the wheel.

May 25 -- Romans 5:1-8
Peace with God

The dictionary looks at peace in several different ways depending upon the dictionary you use. These do not give different meanings of peace but in reality they are several illustrations of peace.

Peace is said to be made between warring nations. This means they cease from their military operations against each other. This is what happens when we receive peace from God. Let me illustrate.

Japan and the United States were engaged in war during World War II. The time came when the Japanese could no longer pursue their interests and they called for peace. The United States made peace terms and representatives of the two nations gathered on the USS Missouri and signed the treaty. Japan had no terms to offer but agreed to accept peace terms offered by the United States.

We have the same kind of proposition between God and man. Man is the aggressor in his war against God. When man determines that he wants peace, he comes to accept the peace offered by God. This peace is unconditional surrender on the part of man. He accepts the peace offered by God. That peace comes by faith in Jesus Christ.

The wonderful thing about the peace terms God offers is that they are always best for man. God never takes advantage of man but He gives man all spiritual blessings in heavenly places in Christ Jesus, in exchange for sin and rebellion against God.

Do you have peace with God today?

THOUGHT: God makes the terms of peace and man accepts them.

May 26 -- James 1:21-27
Obeying the Word

The new preacher came to the church. He was happy that God had sent him and the people were glad to have him in their church. He preached Sunday morning and the people were receptive. He did the same for the next two Sundays.

The deacons asked to speak to the pastor and said, "Pastor, our people know how well you can preach the message you have preached six times now, but they want to hear something else."

The young pastor replied, "You have not done what I told you in that sermon yet. When you do something about that one, I will preach another."

Well, I am not sure that this was the best philosophy for the pastor to have, but we hear so much that we do nothing about. We must receive and know the Word before we can obey it, but we most assuredly should obey it upon hearing it. Paul says, "Faith cometh by hearing, and hearing by the word of God" (Rom. 10:17).

To constantly hear the Word of God and to do nothing about it is of no benefit at all. There would be no profit in going to the store several times without buying the supplies that we are needing while we are there. There is no profit in hearing the Word without obeying what we hear.

James says that to hear and to not do is like looking into a mirror and going away and forgetting what we look like (see James 1:23). We are to obey the Word and to continue to walk with the Lord.

THOUGHT: Hear the Word; receive the Word; and obey the Word.

May 27 -- John 1:40-51
Work of the Pastor

Many years ago pastors served two or more churches. Notice that I said served, because there is a great question in my mind as to whether a person can pastor more than one church at a time. Most of us do not do the best job of pastoring just one church, much less several of them. The Bible refers to the pastor in several capacities. Let us look at a few of these ways and perhaps we can then pray for our pastor more effectively.

The pastor is referred to as a husbandman. The husbandman is one who cares for the vineyard. He is a farmer. He is to care for, feed, water, and cultivate the vineyard so that there will be an abundance of fruit. Likewise, the pastor is to feed the flock of God so that they also will bring forth an abundance of fruit.

The pastor is referred to as a shepherd. The shepherd protects the flock and leads it to food, water, and shelter. The pastor has a duty to provide for the people in the same way through the Word.

The pastor is referred to as a watchman. He is to watch for the enemy and he is to warn the people when the enemy approaches. He is not to fight alone, but he prepares the people to fight their battles in the Lord.

The pastor is referred to as a captain. The captain is the one who guides the ship or who leads the troops. The people should look to the pastor for leadership.

The pastor is referred to as an overseer. He is to have the oversight of the church of God. His job is great and he needs the prayers and support of all the people.

THOUGHT: And to some He gave pastors.

May 28 -- Mark 10:46-52
From Darkness to Light

One of the saddest things that I know of is a blind person. It seems to me that nothing could be worse physically than being blind. The account in our scripture today is a picture of one who is spiritually blind. Consider this man.

He was blind. He was not even as another man had been, who was able to see men as trees walking. This physical blindness pictures spiritual blindness. Aaron was blinded by material possessions, Samson was blinded by pleasures, and Demas was blinded by the world.

He was a very poor man. He was a beggar and had nothing with which to help himself. This is how it is with every unsaved person.

He knew his condition. He was very much aware of his needs. It is sad indeed when one is blind spiritually and does not know his situation.

He called upon Jesus. The people around him tried to get him to stop calling, but he knew his need and he felt that Jesus could meet that need for him.

He got the attention of Jesus as He passed by. Every time a lost person calls upon Jesus, He hears. Paul said, "Whosoever shall call upon the Lord shall be saved" (Rom. 10:13). This is good to know.

He came to Jesus. He was not willing to be denied. He arose from his place and he turned to the "Lamb of God, which taketh away the sin of the world" (John 1:29).

He asked for sight. This is getting right down to business. Have you asked Him for your sight? He followed the Lord. We too must follow and serve Him.

THOUGHT: He who receives Christ receives the Light of the world.

May 29 -- Luke 19:1-10
Jesus at Work

Jesus grew in stature and wisdom and in favor with God and man. His public ministry was announced and He was a busy man meeting the needs of people.

Nicodemus was a well-known man. He was a leader in government and a teacher in Israel. In spite of all this he knew that something was lacking in his life. He came to Jesus by night and Jesus knew just how to handle a man like him. It was hard for Nicodemus to make spiritual application of what Jesus said to him, but the Bible indicates that he did receive God's salvation.

Jesus stopped by a well one day and sat on the curb while his disciples went into town for food. While He was there a woman, who was down and out spiritually, came by. Jesus knew that she was coming and that is why He was there. He told this sinful woman the complete story of her sordid life, but He also told her that He would give her the water of life if she would ask. She did ask and He gave her life everlasting. She went back into the city witnessing for Him.

Jesus walked by a pool one day and saw there a man who was crippled. This man was unable to help himself at all. Jesus had compassion upon him and asked him if he would like to be healed. Then Jesus told him to rise and to take up his bed and walk.

All these are accounts to illustrate salvation. I was lost and helpless, wanting to be saved, but I could do nothing about it. Then Jesus came along and by faith in Him I received the water of life and was born into His family.

THOUGHT: Only the Lord Jesus could take a sinner and make a saint.

May 30 -- Mark 16:15-20
Evangelism

Evangelism is not so much a program to be taught as it is an atmosphere to be caught. It is not that we should have evangelism on a certain night of the week. We should have evangelism in the home, in the Sunday School, in the Vacation Bible School, and in every area of our life.

The key word to the mission of a believer is witness. Acts 1:8 says, "Ye shall be witnesses unto me." The Bible does not say that we should be witnesses, or that under certain circumstances we will be witnesses. Every child of God *is* a witness. We might not be the kind of witnesses that we should be, but we are His witnesses.

We are told to go into all the world and to witness. The Lord is really saying, "Upon your going into all the world," preach the gospel. Since we are Christians, it is taken for granted that we will go, and unless we do go the message of salvation will not be heard.

We are to preach the Word, to evangelize. As we go our message is to be the death, burial, and resurrection of the Lord Jesus Christ.

He says that we are to go to every creature. This is a personal thing with the children of God. Not only are we to go to the foreign fields with the Word, but wherever we go we are to be busy sharing the gospel of Christ with those around us.

We are not to do this alone. In Matthew 28 Jesus tells us that He is with us unto the end of the world. Our job is to be busy; His part is to empower His Word. Thus, people around the world will be saved.

THOUGHT: Fishermen must go to where the fish are found.

May 31 -- Revelation 12:7-17
The Devil Works Evil

Satan is pictured in the Word of God as a seven-headed, ten-horned, seven-crowned incarnation of evil. He is a liar from the beginning and he is the father of liars. He shows his fury, anger, and malice on almost every page of God's Word. Never a tear falls, or a heart is broken, or a vision is crushed, or a life is ruined but that it is the work of Satan.

Job was a mature man, a son of God who eschewed evil. Satan set his sights upon Job and asked permission of God to try him. Satan said that he could make Job curse God to His face.

God turned Satan loose on Job and He told him that he could do anything but take Job's life. He took his material possessions, his children, his friends, and even caused his wife to doubt Job and to tell him to curse God and die.

Satan was not successful in causing Job to curse God, nor will he ever be successful with any other saint of God. Job clung to God and in the end he had twice as much as he had in the beginning. God had the glory and Satan was defeated.

Satan walks around as a roaring lion seeking whom he may devour, but he can never devour a child of God. Yes, there are times when he causes us to fall by the wayside, but when we confess our sins God is still faithful and just to forgive us.

The day is at hand when the Lord is coming again to take His own out of this evil world and away from the mockery of Satan. Hallelujah, what a Savior!

THOUGHT: Satan is a defeated foe foundering for a short time.

Chapter Six

•••

June

•••

Verse to Memorize

Matthew 6:20

"But lay up for yourselves treasures in heaven, where neither moth nor rust doth corrupt, and where thieves do not break through nor steal."

June 1 -- Revelation 12:7-12
There Is Power in the Blood

We are redeemed by the power of the blood. Revelation 1:5 says, "Unto him that loved us, and washed us from our sins in his own blood." The blood of bulls and goats as they were sacrificed in Old Testament days could never wash away sin, but the blood of Jesus Christ, God's Son, cleanses from all sin. Paul said, "For I am not ashamed of the gospel of Christ: for it is the power of God unto salvation" (Rom. 1:16). Again Paul said, "In whom we have redemption through his blood" (Eph. 1:7).

We are cleansed by the power of the blood. The Bible says that the blood of the Lord Jesus Christ cleanses "your conscience from dead works to serve the living God" (Heb. 9:14). Peter said that it was not by silver and gold but by His blood. In Hebrews we read that "without shedding of blood there is no remission" (Heb. 9:22).

We are justified by the blood. In Romans 5:9 Paul said, "Much more then, being now justified by his blood, we shall be saved from wrath through him." Justification is the judicial act of God whereby He declares a sinner just. He does this by the power of the blood.

We are kept by the power of the blood. Paul explains in Romans 8:31-39 that we have all that God has for us in Christ Jesus. God has already delivered Him to death for us. Now He will supply all things through Him.

We are overcomers by the blood. "And they overcame him by the blood of the Lamb" (Rev. 12:11). Let us thank God today for the blood of the Lord Jesus Christ through which there is victory.

THOUGHT: We are overcomers in Him.

June 2 -- John 19:16-30
Jesus at Calvary

Jesus did not go to Calvary for Himself. He went there for you and me. He had no sin but He took upon Himself our sin and paid our sin debt. God made Him to be sin for us. Calvary is a place of victory.

We bring our sin to Calvary and there we receive His righteousness. We bring to Him our ruin and in return we receive His perfection. We bring to Him all our despair and we receive His assurance. We bring to Him our darkness and we receive His light. We bring to Him all our suffering and sorrow and we receive His joy. We bring our hell and we receive His heaven.

The brutality Jesus suffered is beyond human description. He was condemned and crucified. On the cross He committed His mother to the care of John. He was forsaken of God and darkness covered the earth for a period of three hours.

Many scriptures were fulfilled by events surrounding the death of Christ. As the prophets had foretold, He was betrayed by His friend. He was forsaken by His disciples. He was falsely accused. He was silent before the judges but He was proven guiltless. He was numbered with the transgressors. People gambled for His garments. He prayed for His enemies. He was mocked and He was crucified. And, He was forsaken by God.

Just as God in His love had planned, His Son tasted death for every man. Helpless man could do nothing for himself, but Jesus paved the way to God in His own blood. Have you received Him?

THOUGHT: Jesus took our sin with Him to the old rugged cross.

June 3 -- Colossians 3:1-4
Risen with Christ

To my friend I said, "If you are going by this place of business, I would like to ride with you." In reality I was asking my friend if he was going in that direction.

If we look at this verse as it is written and do not understand the mood in which it is written, it will be suggesting that we might be risen with Christ. In our King James Version of the Bible this phrase is written in the subjunctive mood, which suggests that a thing is a possibility. It says that this could be the case, or that it may not be the case. In the Greek it is not this way at all. There we have a Greek particle followed by the indicative mood, which is emphatic. What this statement really says is, "Since we are indeed risen with Christ." There is absolutely no question at all. It is a direct statement of fact.

What a wonderful thought it is that we are risen with Christ. This means that our old man (our old life) was crucified with Him. We were buried with Him and we have been raised from the dead with Him. Because of this we now have everlasting life.

It is a great joy to know that we are in the family of God. We are born into His family. It is not something for which we have to work but it is something that is given to us when we put our faith in Jesus Christ.

Have you received Him as your Savior? If you have not, you should do so now. If you have received Him, tell someone else about Him today.

THOUGHT: To be risen with Him is to have victory over death.

June 4 -- Colossians 3:1-4
Seeking

Luke tells us in chapter 15 of his gospel that a shepherd came to the fold at night with his sheep. He counted the sheep as they came into the fold. There were ninety-nine of them, but when he had gone out that morning there had been one hundred sheep. One of them was now missing.

This shepherd went out and searched for the lost sheep. The ninety-nine were safe but there was one that was lost. As that shepherd looked for the lost sheep until he found it, he pictured our Savior seeking for you and me until He found us.

In the scripture reading for today we have a different kind of seeking. Now that we have been found and have been brought into the fold by our Shepherd, we are to seek to follow Him in all our ways. We are to seek those things that are above. Jesus did not instruct us to lay up for ourselves treasures on earth where rust corrupts and thieves steal. He instructed us to lay up treasures in heaven where rust does not corrupt and thieves do not steal.

Later in this chapter Paul gives a long list of things that we are to seek. All of these things point us toward Jesus Christ. We are to try to be like Him.

The Bible tells us that the fruit of the Spirit is "love, joy, peace, longsuffering, gentleness, goodness, faith, meekness, temperance: against such there is no law" (Gal. 5:22). These things should be the fruits seen in our lives.

As we surrender ourselves to Him and let the Holy Spirit work in us, we will be busy seeking those things that are pleasing to Him.

THOUGHT: Seek the Lord's pleasure only.

June 5 -- Colossians 3:1-4
Gravity

We are told that Sir Isaac Newton was sitting under his fruit tree. A piece of fruit fell from the tree and hit him on his head. This was the beginning of man's theory of gravity.

We know that everything is drawn to a center. The force of gravity is such that it causes everything to cling to the earth. When rocket ships are sent to the moon, a great force must be used to break them free from the gravitational pull of the earth. On the return to earth they must re-submit to this pull in such a way as to have a safe landing.

Our lives have a gravity center also. We have our citizenship in heaven and we have a desire to seek those things that are above. We need to set our affections upon those things that please God. If our lives are lived in accordance with the evil system of this world then that is a pretty good indication that we are not in the family of God.

I used to have as my closest companions people who did not know the Lord and who did not serve the Lord. I used to go to places that I should not go. I did things that I should not do and I said things that I should not say. When I came to know Jesus as my Savior, that all changed.

Now I have a different gravity point in my life. I want to read my Bible and to pray for myself and for others. I want to do good things for people and to be in church and serving God. The difference is that I now know and love Christ and want to serve Him. My point of attraction is not on the earth any more, but it is now in heaven.

THOUGHT: Jesus Christ is our guiding star; let's set our sights upon Him.

June 6 -- Hebrews 10:11-14
Redemption Completed

In Old Testament days the high priest went into the Holy of Holies once each year with the blood of atonement. He would sprinkle the blood upon the mercy seat for the sins of the people. There was no throne there and he came back out into the presence of the people. Each year he went in with the blood of atonement. Each year he found no place to be seated and he came out again. His work was not completed.

Jesus Christ came to earth and He lived here a little over thirty years. He went to the cross as our sacrifice. He was buried and He arose the third day and ascended to the Father. He entered that heavenly tabernacle and He sprinkled His own blood. He sat down at the right hand of the Father. His redemption work was completed.

Paul said that Christ died once unto sin and now He is alive unto God. He also says, "Likewise reckon ye also yourselves to be dead indeed unto sin, but alive unto God through Jesus Christ our Lord" (Rom. 6:11).

We can add nothing to our salvation. By exercising simple faith in Jesus Christ we become the children of God. It is not by church membership or by baptism or by any other works that we can do that we are saved. Christ completed the work of redemption; we are to receive it from Him as a gift.

It is a joy to know that the Lord has taken all our sins and has destroyed them completely. We are made complete in Him and now He lives to make intercession for us in the presence of God.

THOUGHT: The blood of Jesus Christ washes away all sin--past, present, and future.

June 7 -- Ephesians 5:18-20
Thanks

A group of employees decided to play a trick on the boss one morning. When he came in, one of the men asked, "Sir, do you feel well this morning?" "Yes," he answered, "I feel fine."

Soon another man asked, "Boss, did you sleep well last night? You don't look well." He answered, "Oh, yes, I slept well, and I feel fine."

A little while later still another asked him, "Are you sick? You look pale and you look like you don't feel too good." This time the boss agreed that he was not feeling as good as he would like. Very shortly after that, he told the secretary that he was going to see the doctor.

We should make it a habit to thank God constantly for all that He is doing for us. We are apt to take good health for granted. We forget that God gives it and that He deserves our thanks. One man said to his friend, "You ought to thank God for everything." His friend said, "You mean, even when my wife wants to argue?" "Yes," the man answered, "thank God that she is able to argue."

A young preacher had cancer. He had entered the hospital for what appeared to be the last time. The next day he asked his wife to bring him a card that had the word "Romans" on it. She brought it and asked him why he wanted that. He told her to put it alongside the room number on the door. The room number was 828.

We should always be submissive to God's will. We should take all that comes our way as something that God wants to use in our life for our good and for His glory.

THOUGHT: Find something every day for which you can be thankful.

June 8 -- I Timothy 3:14-16
The God-Man

The Lord Jesus Christ was in the beginning with God and He was God. John 1:14 tells us that He became man. In this act God Himself took upon Him a body and He became man. He lived upon this earth as you and I live. Paul says that this is a great mystery but that it is a fact.

There are many things about Jesus that point to the fact that He was both man and God. The Bible teaches that He was born as a baby. He grew as any normal child grows. He learned by asking questions. He became weary in body and He hungered. He became thirsty and He slept. The Bible also says that Jesus wept and He prayed. He rejoiced and He also groaned in spirit. All of these things point to the fact that our dear Savior was man.

To point to the fact that Jesus was God, the Bible says that He spoke with wisdom. He acted in divine holiness and He displayed divine law. He read men's minds and He knew what was in men's hearts. He moved hearts of men and He compelled wills. Nature was subject to Him and disease fled from His presence. He stilled the storm. He fed the hungry and He raised the dead. He claimed to be God.

Is this a great mystery? Yes it is, but nevertheless it is true. We do not try to understand how this can be true. We just take God's Word at what it says because we believe that it is true.

THOUGHT: Jesus Christ is God of very God, but man of very man.

June 9 -- Colossians 1:1-8
Christ Seen in Personalities

People are different in many ways. Some are large and some are small. Some are educated and some are not. Some are great singers and some can't sing at all. There is one common characteristic of every Christian, however; every Christian has Christ living within.

In these verses we have examples of four distinct personalities. Christ is seen in each of these examples.

Paul, who was a highly educated man, was one who was respected as a "law keeper" before he came to know Christ. He once was a Pharisee of the Pharisees and a Hebrew of the Hebrews. Since his conversion, he had become very concerned about missions. He gave himself completely to the Lord and he spent himself in His service.

Timothy was a younger man than Paul. He had grown up in a Christian home. His mother and grandmother taught him the scriptures from his youth. He became a preacher under the instruction of Paul. Paul even called Timothy a brother.

The saints at Colosse were brethren in Christ and they were faithful to Him. However, as you will find in any congregation, there were people among them from many different walks of life.

Epaphras was perhaps the pastor of the church. He was a very sweet-spirited man and he was someone who loved the people.

All of these, although different in their own personalities, manifested Jesus Christ in their lives. Let us also show forth Christ in our daily lives.

THOUGHT: Let Christ be seen in you.

June 10 -- Colossians 1:3-6
Christ Seen in Praise

Paul was in prison in Rome, which was several hundred miles from Colosse. Yet he received word of the welfare of the church there at Colosse. It was a good report. Paul mentions four areas of their testimony for which he praises the Lord.

He praises God for their faith in Jesus Christ. It is always good to recognize good qualities in people. Paul probably did not know the people, but he did know of their faith and he gives praise to God for them.

He praises God for the love that they had for all saints. This is a sweet way to manifest Christ in one's life. The world needs love and who are better qualified to love them than God's people. The Christians at Colosse were loving people. They didn't leave anyone out but they let Christ love everyone through them.

He praises God for the hope laid up for them in heaven. This was not a hope that comes from wishful thinking. This was a hope that comes from an absolute knowledge. They knew what the future held for them and it was a sure hope.

He praises them for the fruit that was continually seen in their life. He praises them for the fruit that sprang from their faith, hope, and love.

What do people say about us? Do they see in us faith, hope, and love? Do they see the fruit which springs from these things? Whoever we are, we can let Christ be seen in us so that our life might bring praises to His name.

THOUGHT: Witness with words and work.

June 11 -- Colossians 1:13-29
Christ Presented to the Colossians

Paul was writing to the Colossians to warn them of certain errors beginning to creep into the church. To combat the errors, he presents Jesus Christ. He is the right answer to every attack of Satan. In these verses Paul presents Christ in five relationships. The Colossians need not be concerned about any lack in these areas. They are complete in Christ. Let us look at these relationships.

1. Christ's relationship to redemption (verses 13-14). We have redemption in Him; it is complete redemption and we need not look elsewhere.

2. Christ's relationship to God (verse 15). He is the physical manifestation of the invisible God. God is Spirit, but He has revealed Himself to us in Christ. He is also the Head of all creation.

3. Christ's relationship to the universe (verses 16-17). All things were created by Him and for Him and He holds all things together.

4. Christ's relationship to the church (verses 18-19). He is the Head of the church and all the needs of the church are supplied by Him.

5. Christ's relationship to the believer (verses 20-29). He is the believer's reconciliation. He is the believer's continuation and his inspiration. He is the believer's mystery and his perfection.

All that we need is to be found in Jesus Christ. Do we need assurance or wisdom or encouragement? Do we need companionship or strength or daily guidance? Whatever we need, it can be found in Him.

THOUGHT: In Jesus Christ all fullness dwells.

June 12 -- Colossians 2:8-15
The Peril of Rationalism

There is nothing wrong with philosophy. Philosophy is the love of wisdom. All of us should desire to have a certain amount of wisdom. However, we should be afraid of the philosophy that leaves out Christ.

Paul warns that there is a philosophy that is according to the traditions of men and not according to Christ. This worldly philosophy is what we are to shun.

In these verses Paul tells us why we are to follow Christ rather than the philosophy according the world. First, in Christ we have the fullness of God and we are complete in Him. He is our Head and we need no outside help. Second, in Him we have the circumcision that is without hands and which is of Jesus Christ Himself. Third, in Him we were buried in death, we were raised to new life, and we were made alive for new service for God. Fourth, in Him all ordinances and laws are fulfilled and we have complete victory over the enemy.

There is a growing group of people today who say that the Bible "contains" the Word of God. They say that if the Bible is talking about history or archeology or science or some related subject, it might be the Word of God or it might not be. They say that if it is speaking about how to be saved, it is God's Word. They say that we must always remember that the Bible was written by man and that man makes mistakes.

Paul is saying that we do not need what education or the tradition of man or the wisdom of the world can give. We have God's revelation of Himself in Christ. Let's follow Him. He is the living Word and the Bible is the written Word.

THOUGHT: The Bible does not merely contain the Word; it is the Word.

June 13 -- Colossians 2:16-17
The Peril of Ceremonialism

In Old Testament days the Israelites ate certain meats and refrained from eating others. They observed certain feast days and other holy days. They observed their regular and special Sabbath days. Paul says that all of these were shadows being cast by the Lord Jesus Christ and now that He has come we no longer need these things.

If we are going to observe certain days as part of our religious ceremony, why do we not go all the way? Why do we not have the sacrifices and observe the feasts and make the offerings? Why do we not follow all of the rituals of the Old Testament law?

Of course, our answer comes from the Word of God. It says, "For Christ is the end of the law for righteousness to every one that believeth" (Rom. 10:4). Our salvation is in Him and we need no other help. Observance of days and eating and drinking or abstaining from eating and drinking can be of no help to us in obtaining eternal salvation.

Someone once asked me what we were going to do on Ash Wednesday and what kind of special services we were going to have during Lent. My answer was that I do not even know when and what Ash Wednesday is and that we would have our usual schedule of services. We do not observe special days of this nature.

Our salvation is complete in Jesus Christ. Nothing I can do or refrain from doing in the way of observing days or in eating or not eating, can add anything to what He has done on Calvary. It is not our task to observe certain ceremonials so that our salvation may be more complete. It is our task to rest in Him and to serve Him daily.

THOUGHT: It is not days or eats, but it is Jesus Christ who is our redemption.

June 14 -- Colossians 2:18-19
The Peril of Mysticism

It is strange to hear of so many radio preachers who have had visits from Jesus Christ, or have seen angels, or have in other ways received special "revelations" from God. According to the book of Revelation, if we add to or take from the words of the Bible, we will suffer the plagues of the Book. See Revelation 22:18-19.

Recently I heard a radio preacher tell how Christ appeared to him in his bed. He claimed that Christ told him of things that were to happen. He also claimed that Christ told him to cut up his bed sheet and to send pieces of it out to people who would write to him. The people who did so would be healed after wearing the piece of sheet next to their body.

As far as I can find, there is no Bible verse to support this kind of thing. However, I do find Bible verses that speak against this sort of thing. Our scripture for today condemns this kind of activity. I wondered how large a bed sheet this radio preacher must have had in order to be able to send a piece to the radio audience.

God's revelation of Himself to man is closed. We have the Bible and there is nothing to be added to that. When Jesus Christ arose from among the dead, He ascended back to the Father and sprinkled His own blood upon the mercy seat in the heavenly tabernacle. He then sat down at the right hand of the Father. His wonderful work of redemption was complete. Let us take the Bible as God has given to us rather than seeking further revelation by "intruding into those things" that we have not seen.

THOUGHT: It is not through angels, but through the Bible that God communicates to us today.

June 15 -- Colossians 2:20-23
The Peril of Asceticism

Once I had the occasion to visit a group of people who had shut themselves off from the rest of the world. They lived within a walled city. They had their own system of religion, although they called it Christianity. They had the Bible and they had the cross, although it was not the cross as I know it. They also had their own rituals.

The only contact they had with the outside world was in buying their supplies. They considered that it would be contamination for them to have the usual association with the world. They felt that they must be separate from the world in order to be holy before God.

There was something that was hard for me to understand about the people. The day that I was there they were having a wedding celebration. There was dancing and drinking of which I could not be a part. These people seemed to go from one extreme to another.

Paul says that this is will worship. We are to separate ourselves from the ways of the world, but even Christ said that we are still in the world. He did not ask that we be taken out of the world but He asked that we be kept from the world.

It is foolish for us to try to separate ourselves from the world physically. We are in the world and we must remain here for our allotted time. We should be separated from the evil ways of the world, but Paul says that to close ourselves away from the world is of no benefit to us.

THOUGHT: One is not made holy because of what he does but by putting his faith in Jesus Christ.

June 16 -- I Peter 1:15-19
Blessings of the Blood

Someone has said that at his death Bishop Hamilton said, "I only want more confidence in the blood." To make us appreciate the blood of Christ more let us look at some things about the blood of Jesus Christ.

Blood averts judgment against sin. In Exodus 12:13 God told the children of Israel, "When I see the blood, I will pass over you." Judgment has been averted only if the blood of Christ has been applied to the sinner.

Blood converts the one who believes in the Substitute. The blood of cleansing changed the position and condition of the leper. In Revelation 1:5 we are told that Christ loved us and washed us from our sins in His own blood.

Blood inverts the position we once had in the world. Once we were a part of the world system. Now we are just in the world. God has put a division between His people and the world. See Exodus 8:23.

Blood inserts us into a new place. Moses was made nigh unto God by the sprinkling of the blood. The people said concerning God's commands, "All that the Lord hath spoken we will do" (Exod. 19:8). Ephesians 2:13 says that we are made nigh by the blood of Christ.

Blood asserts the wonderful blessing of pardon, peace, power, and purity.

Blood exerts a powerful influence in at least three ways. It kills sin; it slays self; and it overcomes pride.

Blood subverts the powers of hell. They are conquered by Christ's death.

THOUGHT: We are new creatures in Christ Jesus.

June 17 -- Hebrews 11:1-4
Faith of Abel

Hebrews 11 is a treatise on faith. No better one is to be found. This chapter is known as the faith chapter of the Bible. Here we get a glimpse of the presence of faith and the principle of faith. We also see the power of faith and the possibilities of faith when it is operative in the lives of people.

Abel's sacrifice was more noble than Cain's because he brought that which God had given him. He did not bring something that he had produced with his own hands.

Abel is the first man of faith mentioned in the Bible. Many others are mentioned after him. There is no doubt that God had instructed Adam and Eve in the sacrifices. They had taught their children. Abel believed and obeyed but Cain did not believe and he brought the fruit of his own hands. Abel's sacrifice was accepted by God but Cain's sacrifice was not. Abel worshipped God and God respected him.

Enoch is said to have walked with God and God took him. Noah is said to have walked with God and God saved him from the destruction of the flood. Before one can walk with God or work for God, he must worship Him. In order to worship God, a person must exercise faith in Him.

Abel exercised faith in God, which made him acceptable to God. It enabled him to worship God and it assured him of salvation.

It is through our simple child-like faith that we are accepted by the Lord. Let us not try to make it a hard task.

THOUGHT: Faith is the indispensable quality for which God looks.

June 18 -- Genesis 4:4 and Hebrews 11:1-4
Abel's Faith Acknowledged Sin

There is an account in the New Testament about a Pharisee and a publican who came to the temple at the same time. The Pharisee told God how good he was and how he tithed and fasted. He told Him how he did not do a lot of things that some others did. The publican would not so much as look up toward God, but he said, "Be merciful to me a sinner" (Luke 18:13). The Bible says that the publican went away justified rather than the Pharisee.

There is no conversation recorded between God and Abel, but that which happened points to certain things about Abel. By bringing the offering that God required, Abel admitted at least five things.

1. He admitted that God was totally righteous in the requirements that He had made.

2. He admitted that he was a guilty sinner who could do nothing for himself and that he deserved death.

3. He admitted that God is holy and that because of this He must punish sin.

4. He admitted that God is merciful and that He would accept this substitute.

5. He admitted that he expected acceptance with God in the coming Savior.

Have you acknowledged sin in your life and have you come to the point that Abel did? It is only as you look to God's substitute that you have assurance of salvation.

Jesus said, "As Moses lifted up the serpent in the wilderness, even so must the Son of man be lifted up: that whosoever believeth in him should not perish, but have eternal life" (John 3:14-15).

THOUGHT: Faith laughs at impossibilities.

June 19 -- Genesis 4:1-8 and Hebrews 11:4
Abel's Faith Obeyed God

If one is to obey, he must know what to obey. He must be taught. Adam and Eve were clothed when God slew the animals and made them coats of the skins. He must have taught Adam and Eve at the time and Adam must also have taught his children. They knew that they were to bring an offering to God.

Cain brought the product of his own hand and it was not accepted. Abel brought that which God had provided and that which they both knew that God required.

Neither you nor I can do anything to bring salvation. We have access to it only by faith in God.

There are two kinds of hearing. One is merely outward hearing. It only informs and instructs and does nothing to mold the life. The other is an inward hearing. It influences and molds the heart and moves the will. Cain had the first kind of hearing; Abel had the second kind. Abel's offering anticipated the coming Savior.

There is only one way for a sinner to approach a holy God and that is God's way. His way is through the shed blood of an innocent substitute.

John said, "Behold the Lamb of God, which taketh away the sin of the world" (John 1:29). He has made a way for us. He has pointed us to the Savior through the Word and He has called us by His Holy Spirit. What more can we expect Him to do?

What kind of faith do you have? Do you have Cain's kind, which points to what you can do; or do you have Abel's kind, which does what God says to do?

THOUGHT: Faith discounts human schemes and believes God.

June 20 -- Genesis 4:1-8 and Hebrews 11:4
Abel's Faith Admitted His Unworthiness

Some would say, "Poor Cain, he had no offering to bring. He just didn't know what to do. Abel should have helped him."

No, each of us is accountable to God. Genesis 4:7 tells us that Cain did know what to do and that he could have brought the acceptable sacrifice. He brought the work of his own hands, knowing that it was in direct disobedience to God.

By bringing a lamb Abel is saying, "God, I know that I am unworthy and that I have sinned. Thou art holy, and I am unholy. I am bringing the firstling of my flock which Thou has given to me. Please accept this innocent substitute for me." Abel's offering was one of faith, while Cain's was one of pride and rebellion.

Matthew 22 gives us the account of a wedding. Many people were invited; some came and some did not come. For all those who came there was provided a wedding garment. When the king came in, he saw the man without the wedding garment and he had him put out from the wedding. No one could remain at the wedding except those who were properly dressed for the occasion.

It will be the same in heaven. No one will be there who thinks that he is good enough to be there. The only way we can be there is to have on the wedding garment that comes by faith in Jesus Christ.

THOUGHT: The person who thinks himself worthy is most unworthy.

June 21 -- I Corinthians 1:1-3 and 3:1-3
Babes in Christ

There is no question but that these people are saved. Paul says that they are "sanctified in Christ." They are Christians but they are not living as they should. The rest of the book teaches us that this is the case. Like many church members today, they are saved and satisfied, but they are not growing in the Lord.

They are unspiritual. In chapter 3 they are said to be carnal. They are filled with envy and other sins. By having salvation they possess all they need from God but they are achieving nothing for Him. Their belief is one thing and their behavior is another.

They were immoral. Chapter 5 describes the terrible immorality that they allowed to prevail in their church. This does not speak of a church that knows the Word or a church that tries to follow the teaching of the Word.

They were impatient and selfish. In chapter 6 they go to law with brothers rather than trying to settle issues between themselves. In chapters 7 and 8 we note that they do not show the understanding that mature Christians should show. Babies always want things their way. We are not showing maturity when we conduct ourselves selfishly.

They were unthoughtful. They were critical of one another. When people allow selfishness to invade their ranks or begin a war of gossip or choose one over the other, trouble is in the making.

May God help us to grow up and not to remain babes in Christ. Study to show yourself approved and to walk so that you show yourself to be mature.

THOUGHT: There is nothing wrong with being a baby, unless you continue to remain a baby.

June 22 -- I Corinthians 10:23-31
Should I, or Should I Not?

Christians face many problems and learn many lessons daily. The Christian life is not an easy life and those who think it is must not have really tried it or they are not facing the facts as they are. Granted, one who is totally surrendered to God finds little problem living for Him. The problem he finds is that of keeping himself surrendered.

The way of the Christian is a narrow way. It is dangerous and we are likely to slip and fall at any time. We are watched by man and Satan alike. We are criticized on every hand. We are often misunderstood. Sometime I think that people intentionally try to misunderstand us.

Always there are questions that arise. What do I do about this? How do I react to that? What choice should I make about another matter? What company should I keep? We could continue to ask questions. Answers are not easy to find. Yet if we break certain rules it brings disgrace to self and to the church. It also brings reproach upon the Lord.

Christians must leave many things alone for testimony's sake. What will this do to my Christian testimony? Are others watching that might be hurt if they see me do this or that thing?

Paul said, "And whatsoever ye do in word or deed, do all in the name of the Lord Jesus, giving thanks to God and the Father by him" (Col. 3:17). As long as we follow this rule, we will be safe.

THOUGHT: God might let others do some things that He will not let you do.

June 23 -- Judges 18:1-10
The Danger of Careless Living

The Bible warns against careless living. Isaiah 32:9 warns careless daughters about their living. Much of the book of Proverbs warns against careless living. Paul writes to churches and warns them about the errors of the day and against careless living in their midst. John warns about being careless to follow false prophets. Throughout the Bible we are told to avoid evil.

Verse 7 of our reading today says that these people "dwelt careless...quiet and secure; and there was no magistrate in the land." Let us mention three symptoms of careless living.

First, there is a lack of concern for spiritual things. The latter part of verse 7 says that they "had no business with any man." We find this to be true today among some Christians. This is not good, for we need to fellowship with other Christians and we need to be concerned for the lost.

Second, people do not listen to and obey God. Through Isaiah the Lord said, "Hear my voice, ye careless daughters: give ear unto my speech" (Isa. 32:9). The Lord is saying that He cannot get people to listen to His Word. We ought to be willing to listen and willing to obey.

Third, people want to live to themselves and for themselves. The Bible says that no man lives to himself and no man dies to himself. We need one another and it is just a careless thing to try to live for God in isolation.

THOUGHT: Careless living is not a part of God's plan for His children.

June 24 -- I John 1:5-10
Christians Do Sin

It puzzles many Christians to realize that they do sin. If you are puzzled, it is because of one of two things. Either you have not been properly taught or you do not remember what you have been taught. The point that I am making is that Christians do sin and not that Christians have to sin.

Every Christian has the potential of committing any sin in the book. We are still in the flesh and as long as we are in the flesh we have the fleshly desires and inclinations. Paul tells us about our waiting for the redemption of the body. We "groan within ourselves," Paul says in Romans 8:23. We look toward that time of redemption of the body. Of course, we are already redeemed in spirit but we are not yet redeemed from this body.

Sin in the life of a Christian might be coldness of heart. It might be indifference about our Christian service or it might be deep sin. Whatever it is, it is sin in the sight of God and we must repent of sin.

God tells us that if we say we have no sin, we just do not know what we are saying. If we say that, we make Him a liar. He tells us to "love not the world, neither the things that are in the world" (I John 2:15). Paul tells us to put off the old man and to put on the new man. He also tells us to stop doing a lot of things that are not commendable for Christians to do. All of this is really telling us that it is possible for Christians to sin. Indeed, it tells us that Christians do sin.

When we sin, we should confess it to God and accept His forgiveness.

THOUGHT: Someone said, "I am not afraid to sin, but I am afraid of sin."

June 25 -- Matthew 16:21-28
Valuables

People place value upon things that appeal to them. Some time ago I saw a 1926 Model T Ford advertised for sale for $600.00. This is twice as much as it sold for when it was new. Also, there was a 1931 Model A Ford advertised for $1,950.00. This is five times the original selling price.

There are people who are antique lovers. Their homes are filled with antiques and the people seem to be fascinated by them. They will pay fantastic prices for certain items that some of us would not even want at all.

God says that your soul is worth more than all these things put together. He says that your soul is worth more than all the world. You cannot help yourself by gaining the whole world and then losing your soul.

Man has been away from God since Adam sinned in Eden. God placed such a value upon the soul of man that when Adam sinned God provided a way of redemption. In order to do this He had to pay the sin debt Himself. This is what He has done in the person of Jesus Christ.

I heard of a young scholar who could solve any problem presented to him. Any time local businessmen or school personnel or government officials had problems they would bring them to the scholar. One day the question was asked of him, "What is a man profited if he gain the whole world and lose his own soul?" He had no answer to that question. There is no answer to it.

THOUGHT: Don't take chances; take Christ.

June 26 -- Galatians 6:1-9
God Is Not Mocked

God knows where we are all of the time. He knows what we are doing and He knows why we are doing it. He also knows just how hard we are trying to cover up some of our acts or motives.

We can expect to reap exactly what we sow. At a time when the flesh is filled with lust and it seems that no one in the world will ever know, just remember that God knows already. We might be able to keep something from our family and friends but we can never keep anything from God.

The Bible says, "The Lord knoweth the thoughts of man, that they are vanity" (Ps. 94:11). Again, the Bible says, "For the word of God is quick, and powerful, and sharper than any twoedged sword, piercing even to the dividing asunder of soul and spirit, and of the joints and marrow, and is a discerner of the thoughts and intents of the heart" (Heb. 4:12).

We cannot fool God. He knows what we do and the Bible tells us that we will reap according to how we sow.

My father was farmer. During planting seasons he planted corn where he wanted to reap corn. He set out strawberry plants where he wanted to harvest strawberries. He never did plant one crop and expect to reap another. It will be the same in our life. Whatever we sow, we will reap. Be reminded that God keeps good records. The best thing we can do is to reprove evil and to have no fellowship with it at all.

THOUGHT: No one ever mocked God and won.

June 27 -- Ephesians 5:6-11
Companions

God speaks often in the Bible about His people being careful of their companions. He often warned Israel about associations with the nations around them. They were not to give their daughters to those nations nor to take the daughters of those nations for Israel's sons to marry. They were not to be identified with those nations at all. God is a holy God and He wants His people to be holy people.

The cautions in the Word of God do not mean that we should not work with lost people. It does not mean that we should not associate with or witness to the lost population. It means that we are not to embrace their ways. The problem is that we are usually like the people with whom we spend a lot of time. We also spend a lot of time with people who have the same interests as we have.

Take a sponge and lay it in a pan of vinegar. What will happen? The sponge will soak itself full of vinegar. Now, take it from the pan of vinegar and place it in a pan of water. What happens? It will soak up a little of the water but in so doing it will contaminate the whole pan of water.

It is strange that God's people who make friends with the world come to be like the world. God knew that this would be true and He tells us to "come out from among them, and be ye separate" (II Cor. 6:17).

We should love everyone. We should never consider ourselves better than others. God loves everyone. However, we should not be caught in Satan's trap by having as our good companions those who mingle with the evil of the world.

THOUGHT: Birds of a feather flock together.

June 28 -- Matthew 9:1-8
A Cheer of Salvation

In today's reading, four friends had shown their affection for this man and had shown their faith in the Lord Jesus Christ. They brought the man to Jesus and He forgave him of his sins and said to him, "Son, be of good cheer; thy sins be forgiven thee."

Salvation involves a lot of things, but let's look at just three things in particular. In salvation we have forgiveness of sin. No matter what has happened or what will happen in the life of an individual, the greatest thing that could ever happen is to receive God's forgiveness of sin. Paul said, "In whom we have redemption through His blood, the forgiveness of sins, according to the riches of his grace" (Eph. 1:7).

In salvation we are delivered from bondage. The man in our scripture for today had never walked. He was in bondage to this disease and not only was he helpless but he was also hopeless. When they brought him to Jesus he was delivered from bondage. Jesus said, "Ye shall know the truth, and the truth shall make you free" (John 8:32).

In salvation we have hope. The palsied man had been in bed all his life with no hope of ever walking. He could not even get himself to Jesus. His friends brought him to Jesus and the Savior not only gave him hope but He gave him new life.

The Bible says, "Now faith is the substance of things hoped for, the evidence of things not seen" (Heb. 11:1). By our exercise of simple faith in Jesus Christ, the cheer of salvation fills our heart.

THOUGHT: Christ saves from sin, not in sin.

June 29 -- Isaiah 30:15-19
God Wants to Bless His Own

The Bible is filled with occasions when God poured out His blessing upon rebellious people. Israel would sin against God. This in turn would bring God's judgment upon them. When they called upon Him and turned back to Him, He always forgave them and blessed them abundantly.

We are all inclined to be as the prodigal son was. We take journeys into a far country. The journey into the far country is usually made for more than riotous living. It is also made to get away from the Father. Man still thinks he can get away from God.

This was the problem that Jonah faced. He did not want to do the job that God called him to do. He thought that he could get away from the job and away from God. He was in for a rude awakening. Everyone who tries to run away and hide from God is also in for a rude awakening.

David found that he could not escape the presence of God. He could not escape even if he fled to hell or to heaven or to the mountains or to the sea. "Even there shall thy hand lead me, and thy right hand shall hold me" (Ps. 139:10).

God's Word tells us and His actions prove to us that He wants to bless His own. He offers peace in the time of trouble and comfort in the time of affliction. He offers companionship in the time of loneliness and strength in the time of weakness.

He tells us that we are blessed "with all spiritual blessings in heavenly places in Christ" (Eph. 1:3). Let us look to Him and receive blessings from Him.

THOUGHT: God's best is for those who trust Him.

June 30 -- Luke 16:19-31
Heaven Is a Place of Comfort

The rich man had all his physical and material needs met in this life. Lazarus suffered in about every way that one could suffer. Both men died, as all men will. The rich man went to hell and awoke to the torments of that place. Lazarus went to heaven and began to enjoy all the bliss of God.

The rich man began to plead for a little water to cool his parching tongue. He was reminded that he had received his good things in this life and that Lazarus had received his evil things. Now the rich man was greatly tormented while Lazarus was comforted.

We know many devout Christian people who are suffering physically in this life. The time will come when all of this will be past. Our bodies will be made like Christ's glorious body and we will be comforted there in His presence.

Just to be with those who are in heaven will make it a place of comfort. Hebrews 12 tells us that we will be in the city of the living God. There we will be with the innumerable company of angels. We will be with the general assembly and church of the first born. God the Judge of all will be there and Jesus the Mediator will be there. These will all combine to make heaven a place of comfort.

Let us praise God for the fact that we will not always be living and struggling in this land of evil. We will one glorious day begin to be comforted in His presence. Then we will realize fully the meaning of the song that goes, "Heaven will surely be worth it all."

THOUGHT: To be with the Lord Jesus Christ will be comfort indeed.

Answered Prayers

1.

2.

3.

4.

5.

6.

7.

8.

9.

10.

Chapter Seven

●●●

July

●●●

Verse to Memorize

Mark 16:15

"And he said unto them, Go ye into all the world, and preach the gospel to every creature."

July 1 -- Isaiah 35:1-10
Heaven Is a Place of Joy

It is a joyous occasion for God's people to meet together to study the Word. It is a joy to pray together and to sing the great songs of Zion. That is just one reason why we should always take advantage of every opportunity we have to be in our church services.

It is a joyous occasion when we think of the blessings of God in our own lives. It brings a time of joy just to think of forgiveness of sin and of the indwelling Holy Spirit. It is a joy to be kept by the power of God and to have the continuous deliverance from the power of Satan. It is great to be in the family of God.

One of the greatest joys that we have is when someone tells us our ministry has been a blessing to them. We know that we can do nothing on our own. Jesus said, "Without me ye can do nothing" (John 15:5). We know that this is true and when our life and our testimony are a blessing to others, it is only because He has blessed them through us. We rejoice that He chooses to do this.

When we get to heaven we will not spend our time lying along the banks of the river resting. We will spend our time serving God completely, where we will be unrestrained by the devil and sin. This will be the greatest joy that we could possibly have.

Yes, we will rejoice in victory. We will rejoice in being released from the temptation of Satan. We will rejoice in being in His presence. Most of all, we will rejoice in serving Him to the utmost.

THOUGHT: In heaven there is no devil, no sin, and no restraining power. We will just be serving God.

July 2 -- Exodus 2:11-15
Committed to a Task

Moses wanted to deliver his people from Egypt. He felt this to be his responsibility. The problem Moses faced in this chapter was that he was taking the responsibility upon himself rather than looking to God's leadership. He was working in the energy of the flesh.

Moses had a deep concern for his people. Upon growing up and seeing the terrible suffering that they were experiencing under their taskmasters, Moses decided that he would do something about it. Taking things in his own hands, he set out to relieve his people of their burdens.

Moses was committed to the task. We must be committed to our task if we are going to see God at work. However, we must not be committed to a task and to a method that does not have God's blessing upon it.

Moses had a deep conviction that something must be done for his people. He did not get God's approval upon his way of doing things. Again he overstepped his bounds by carrying out his desires rather than seeking God's direction.

The conclusion that Moses reached was a good one for him. It is too bad that he had to come to it this way. He saw that he could not do God's work in the energy of the flesh. He had attempted and he had failed. It was true with Moses and it will be true with us as well. Jesus said, "For without me ye can do nothing" (John 15:5).

THOUGHT: It is better to wait upon God than to work in the flesh and fail.

July 3 -- Exodus 3:1-12
Committed to God

Moses had just had a very bad experience. He had taken upon himself, in the energy of the flesh, to deliver Israel from the bondage of Egypt. In making his attempt he had killed an Egyptian and after doing so he had to flee the country to escape Pharaoh.

God sent him out to the back side of the desert where he began keeping sheep. Moses had much time there to reflect upon his former actions and to listen to God speak to him. Here in the desert, God visited Moses and ordained him to go back to Egypt and to deliver Israel from the wicked hands of the Egyptians.

Moses was amazed at God's approach. Here was a bush in flame, yet it was not consumed. The voice from the bush caused Moses to be in awe because he began to recognize the greatness of God.

In verse 5 we read, "Draw not nigh hither: put off thy shoes from off thy feet." This is the living God, the most Holy God! Moses began to understand something of the holiness of God as well as the great compassion that God has for His people. The very presence of the Almighty caused Moses to sense his own inadequacy.

We will later see that Moses even asked that he not be sent to deliver Israel. He requested that someone else be sent instead. However, Moses was now committed to God and to His way and not to man or to man's way.

THOUGHT: When we are committed to God, He does the work.

July 4 -- I Peter 1:17-20
I Sat at the Trial

It was my experience to sit through a trial recently of a man who had been convicted of a crime and had spent some time in prison. He was an "honor grade" prisoner, which meant that he was not being guarded when he was released during the day to work on a civil job.

One day he left his job and came into town. There he got drunk and committed a robbery. He had been apprehended and now he was being tried for leaving prison, breaking and entering, and receiving stolen goods.

The setting was interesting to me. The judge was on the bench. The prosecuting attorney presented the evidence to which the prisoner pleaded guilty. He had to plead guilty because he had committed the act and he had been caught. His defense attorney really had no defense to present and he could only ask for the mercy of the court.

How different it is with us. We are guilty and we have pleaded guilty. The crimes that we have committed have been presented to the court but our defense attorney, the Lord Jesus Christ, has already paid the debt for our crime. There is no sentence going to be passed upon us because Jesus has served the sentence already. We have been allowed to go free because of the fact that His blood washes away all our sin.

We were guilty but Jesus paid the penalty for us. How does that make you feel about Him?

THOUGHT: Jesus, our advocate, paid the full sin penalty for us.

July 5 -- I Samuel 7:1-4
Serving God

Many people make great ado about their life of serving God when really they are serving themselves and are not aware of what they are doing. If we are faithful to serve God, it will be evidenced in certain ways in our life.

We will be careful of the company that we keep. Proverbs 13:20 says, "He that walketh with wise men shall be wise; but a companion of fools shall be destroyed." Elisha walked with Elijah and after Elijah was gone he was given a double portion of his spirit. He performed twice as many miracles as Elijah did. Samson carelessly walked with the fools of the world and he was destroyed.

We will be careful of our habits. We cannot partake of the evil things of this world and still be pleasing to God. We cannot run with the devil's crowd and go to the devil's places and still serve God faithfully. John said for us not to love the world and the things of the world.

We will be careful of the thoughts that we entertain. The Bible says about man, "For as he thinketh in his heart, so is he" (Prov. 23:7).

We will be careful of the affections that we cultivate. Paul said, "Set your affections on things above, not on things on the earth" (Col 3:2).

We will be careful of the motives that we have. Whatsoever we do, whether we eat or drink, we are to do all to the glory of God. See I Corinthians 10:31.

THOUGHT: Let us always be careful to serve God, and not self.

July 6 -- Luke 16:19-31
Heaven Is a Place of Eternity

When a person leaves this world he goes to the place where he will be in eternity. The Word of God speaks of eternal life and eternal damnation.

In our verse for today the rich man was told that there was a great gulf fixed. No one would be able to leave hell for heaven, nor would anyone leave heaven for hell. It is just as true that no one could leave either place for earth. The Lord Jesus Christ was the only one who could leave either place and visit the other.

How long is eternity? How does one measure eternity? The word eternity is used only once in the Bible. The Bible says, "For thus saith the high and lofty One that inhabiteth eternity" (Isa. 57:15). The only time that eternity is mentioned in the scriptures, God is said to fill it up. No man can comprehend the length of eternity.

Billy Sunday used to have an interesting way of illustrating his thoughts about eternity. He said suppose that a bird took a grain of sand from earth to a distant planet, taking a million years to move a grain. Suppose that he continued to do this until the earth was moved to that planet. Then suppose that at the same speed he returned all the grains to their original position. By then it still would not even be breakfast time in eternity.

The Bible clearly tells us, "There shall be no night there; and they need no candle, neither light of the sun; for the Lord God giveth them light: and they shall reign for ever and ever" (Rev. 22:5).

THOUGHT: Eternity is not just a long, long time; it is longer than time.

July 7 -- Matthew 28:16-20
A Great Appearance

We will have several days of devotions based upon this passage of scripture. This is a familiar passage that is loved by many people, but it is practiced by few. Some of the passage is encouraging and some of it is challenging.

In verse 7 of this chapter you will note that certain women were told to tell the disciples to go into Galilee and that the risen Lord would meet them there. In verse 16 we see that the disciples came to Galilee because they expected to see the risen Lord there.

In Matthew 18:20 Jesus says, "Where two or three are gathered together in my name, there am I in the midst of them." God's people should have a great expectancy when they meet together to worship Him. Jesus has said that He would be there.

When you go to church, do you go to see and to be seen? Do you go just to sing or just to teach or just to fill some office, or do you go expecting to have vital contact with the Lord Jesus Christ?

Jesus has promised to meet with His own. It is a thrilling thought that God Himself will meet with and will mingle with people. Just as these disciples could expect to see the risen Savior in Galilee at the appointed place, even so we can expect Him to meet with us when we meet together in His holy name.

Let us make it our practice to be as the psalmist was when he said, "I was glad when they said unto me, Let us go into the house of the Lord" (Ps. 122:1).

THOUGHT: What greater expectancy can one have than to meet with Jesus?

July 8 -- Matthew 28:16-20
A Great Claim

The word used in verse 18 for power is the word for authority. It is power, yes, but it is also authoritative power. Jesus Christ is the one with all authority.

What could have been more encouraging to these disciples than this? They had feared that the Lord was dead and was not to rise again. Now they have found Him alive with all authority in heaven and earth! This must have put to rest their fears. It must have given them the desire to carry out the great commission that He is soon to give them. They then knew that Jesus had already exercised His authority to command death to release Him.

He has all authority in heaven. He has authority to purge sins with His own blood. He has authority to enter into the presence of the Father and to intercede for His own. He has authority to give all spiritual blessings in heavenly places. He has authority to restore life and to renew power within the lives of His own.

He has all authority on earth. He has authority to forgive sins and to set a person's conscience at peace with God. He has authority to give rest to troubled souls and to give victory over the enemy. He has authority to shield His children with the power of His love. He has authority to keep us by the power of the Holy Spirit and to instill within us the authority of His witnesses.

This is a great claim that can be fulfilled only by the Holy Son of God. "Not by might, nor by power, but by my spirit, saith the Lord of hosts" (Zech. 4:6).

THOUGHT: With God's help you can do anything that you ought to do.

July 9 -- Matthew 28:16-20
A Great Commission

Jesus said before He ascended into heaven, "Ye shall receive power, after that the Holy Ghost is come upon you: and ye shall be witnesses unto me" (Acts 1:8).

The Lord did not say that it was His hope that we would be His witnesses. He did not say that we *could* be His witnesses. He said that we *would* be His witnesses. This is simply a statement of fact.

Remember that we do not prove that we are His witnesses by proclaiming Christ to someone. We are already His witnesses. The big question is, what kinds of witnesses are we being for Him?

In verse 19 of today's reading Jesus is saying, "As you go, teach," or make disciples of people. There is no thought that God's people will not be going as witnesses. He is here telling us what to do as we go. We are to give out the gospel-- the gospel that will convert and make disciples out of people.

Then His Word further instructs us that we are to baptize people and are to teach them how they can serve God more faithfully.

What kind of witness are you? Are you faithful? Don't forget that you are His witness. Are you being an honest and good witness? As you go about your daily living, whether it be at school or at the shop; at the office or in the home; or wherever you are, remember that you are His witness.

Let us pray that God will help us to be the kind of witnesses that will be busy going and making disciples for Him as we go.

THOUGHT: A witness tells what he knows, but only what he knows.

July 10 -- Matthew 28:16-20
A Great Promise

There probably is no greater promise than the one given here in verse 20 by our Savior, "I am with you alway, even unto the end of the world." We are sent out as sheep among wolves, but we are not sent out alone. The Bible also tells us in another place, "I will never leave thee, nor forsake thee" (Heb. 13:5).

What a promise this is! This promise could not have been possible without the death, burial, and resurrection of the Lord Jesus Christ.

The tears of Mary Magdalene that she shed when she learned that His body was gone could not have been dried without His manifestation.

The doubts of Thomas on that day could not have been erased if Christ had not risen from the dead. So many doubts of people in our day could not be settled if He had not been raised from the grave.

There could have been no breaking of bread in Emmaus and no eating of fish by the sea if He had not risen. There could have been no appearance to the disciples in Galilee without the truth of the words, "He is risen."

There could be no promise of His presence with His own as we go on witnessing for Him if He had not been raised from among the dead. Praise God that He is risen and that He has all authority. He is with us as we go about our business of being witnesses for Him.

THOUGHT: Great, full, and true are His promises.

July 11 -- John 14:1-6
Heaven Is Really a Place

There are people today who think of heaven as just an influence or a condition. This is hard to understand. How can one have any kind of condition without a place for it to exist? For example, you may ask about the condition of the weather. We know that in order for us to have weather there must be a place for it to exist.

Someone may ask about the condition of the economy. We know that there must be a place for it to exist, or there could be no economy. It does not require a genius to reach this conclusion because it is just plain common sense to understand it this way.

The story is told of the traveling man who came home a couple of nights sooner than expected. When he arrived at home he unlocked the door and walked inside. He immediately sensed that something was amiss.

He asked his wife, "Who is here?" "No one," she replied. "Yes, there is someone else in this house," he answered. "No, there is not," his wife answered. "Have you been gone two or three days only to come home and cause trouble?"

The husband walked over to the closet, opened the door, and there he found a man backed up against the clothes. "What are you doing here?" He demanded. The reply came back, "Man, everybody has got to be somewhere."

It is true that everybody has to be somewhere. In eternity all of God's people are going to be in the place called heaven. Jesus said that He was going to prepare a place for us, not a condition.

THOUGHT: Jesus said that if He went away, He would come again and receive us.

July 12 -- Hebrews 12:18-24
Heaven

Heaven is mentioned many times in the Bible, but we are only given a very brief description of the place.

The Bible speaks about the Lord of heaven and about the wrath of God revealed from heaven. It speaks about the bread of heaven and about the power of heaven. It also speaks about angels from heaven. However, we have such a little told to us about heaven itself and what it is like.

As I look back over my life and count God's blessings upon me, I look more and more to my departure from this life and my stay in eternity with my Lord. We can look toward heaven. Whatever it is like, it will be far superior to this world because we will be out of the presence of sin forever.

An older preacher told of the idea he had of heaven as he was growing up. He said that his father went to the store and bought sugar, flavoring, ice, and other things that he needed to make ice cream. His mother made a chocolate cake. He said that the children were not given all they could eat because there were too many children and not enough ice cream and cake. They were told that when they got to heaven they could have all the ice cream and cake they wanted. He grew up with the idea that heaven was a place with plenty of ice cream and cake. As he grew older and studied the Bible, he came to realize that there was more to heaven than plenty of ice cream and cake.

We don't know all that we would like to know about heaven. We do know one thing, however. In heaven we will be in eternity with our Savior.

THOUGHT: Wherever Jesus is, it surely will be heaven there.

July 13 -- I Corinthians 2:14-16
Human Wisdom Cannot Know Things of God

Even the child of God who looks to something apart from the Holy Spirit cannot know the spiritual things of God. Apollos is an example of this.

Apollos was a very godly man. He was serving God and he was a very intellectual person. The Bible says that he was eloquent. No doubt he could hold an audience spellbound with his preaching. Yet, he did not have all of the truth.

A couple named Aquila and Priscilla heard him speak in the synagogue. They took him aside and instructed him and helped him in his ministry. He had been preaching that Jesus was the Christ but he knew nothing about the Holy Spirit. Read Acts 18:24-28.

Not even an educated child of God can properly understand the Bible if he depends upon his education rather than upon the Holy Spirit. Under no circumstances and at no time can the natural man understand the Bible. Not even the spiritual man who depends upon his human knowledge can understand the teachings of the Bible. This understanding is spiritually discerned. Neither scholarship nor ecclesiastical authority gives a person the insight into the Word of God. Human wisdom by itself cannot know the things of God.

Paul said, "For the wisdom of this world is foolishness with God. For it is written, He taketh the wise in their own craftiness" (I Cor. 3:19).

Human wisdom is completely unable to discover and achieve salvation. The way to be wise in spiritual matters is to surrender to the Holy Spirit and let Him teach you.

THOUGHT: The wise cannot manufacture God out of their thoughts.

July 14 -- Daniel 1:1-8
A Young Man Who Made His Decision

Young people need to make some strong decisions today and then not be ashamed to follow through with them. For one thing, they must make some decisions about social habits. What is going to be your standard on social matters? Are you going to be an easy catch whom everyone knows and exploits? You and you alone must make this decision.

Young people, you must decide about smoking, using drugs or alcohol, church attendance, salvation, and serving God. Each of these choices is very important and no one else can decide for you.

Daniel faced some hard problems in his decision but he decided that he would stand with God. His was a clear-cut decision. He purposed in his heart that he would not sin against God. He purposed that he would not let Satan and the enemies of God have the victory.

We are called upon to make definite decisions. Joshua said, "Choose you this day whom ye will serve" (Josh. 24:15). He told the people that they could not continue as they were. They could not serve other gods and expect God to forgive them. He called upon them to make their decision.

It is the same with us today. If God be God, we should follow Him. If Baal or some other false gods are what you choose, you may follow them to destruction. Let us have some convictions and let us come to some definite decisions. Follow the one true God. Don't fear the enemy and what he threatens to do to you.

THOUGHT: It takes a real man of faith to step out for God.

July 15 -- Daniel 1:8 and 6:4-9
Daniel's Decision Was a Hard One

Daniel had purposed not to sin against God long before he was tested with the den of lions. His mind was made up and his way of life was established long before the decree of the king was issued. If we have certain Christian principles laid out in our life, we will find that it is not too hard to walk with God in the pinch.

Daniel was a captive in a foreign land. He was away from home and he had no parents there to help him. There was no priest to whom he could go for counsel and encouragement. Yet, when he was challenged to defile himself and to follow the course of the world, Daniel refused.

Many others have done the same thing down through history. Joseph, when he was in Egypt, refused to become entangled with Pharaoh's wife. Moses refused to compromise with the morals of Egypt. He turned from a great office and chose to be afflicted with the people of God. The apostles forsook boats, nets, office, and father and mother in order to follow the Lord Jesus Christ.

Young people today must forsake good times, fun, money, friends and anything else that might mean compromising their Christian testimony.

There is no easy way to serve God. If we are going to please Him, we must determine that we are not going to "defile ourselves with the king's meat." Then when it comes our time to be thrown into the den of lions, we will be ready to face it.

THOUGHT: Remember your Creator in the days of your youth.

July 16 -- Daniel 1:1-8
A Holy Decision

Daniel decided that there were some things that he would not do. These things were defiling and he was not going to defile himself for the king or for anyone else. Daniel belonged to the people of God. He had come to have some real moral convictions. When the king's meat and wine were offered, Daniel said no. That is also a good word for us to learn how to say.

Daniel put God to the test and God showed that it was the best thing to do. Daniel asked for a vegetable diet rather than the king's diet. At the end of ten days Daniel and the three Hebrew children looked better than the other prisoners that had been on the regular diet.

Daniel was not afraid of being called a sissy or a wallflower or any other name that some people might have wanted to call him. He was just determined that he would not defile himself with the devil's crowd.

No decent young man wants to take as his wife a girl who has been defiled in the world. No decent young lady wants to choose a dope addict, a drunkard, or someone who is guilty of loose living as her husband.

We need to take some vows today to stay clean from the defilement of this world. The devil is out to trap every person that he can and to bring reproach upon Jesus Christ. A wise young person will do as Daniel did. He will determine not to be defiled with that which is going on today that is contrary to the teaching of the Bible. Remember, Daniel "purposed in his heart" to do as he did. Let us do the same.

THOUGHT: We need to see a crusade of purity in our land today.

July 17 -- Daniel 1:9-15
Happy Decisions

George Washington was not born a great general and president. He took a vow when he was still young to stand for the truth. When I was growing up, all school children knew of the occasion of his cutting down the cherry tree. George's father asked him if he cut it down and he answered, "I cannot tell a lie. I cut it down."

From there he went on to become a great general and to lead the armed forces of this country. He was a great political leader and he became the first president of our nation.

Abraham Lincoln saw the plight of the slave trade in America and he vowed to do something about it. After many failures in running for public office, he became the president of our nation and as president he emancipated the slaves.

These men had great determination and they stuck to their guns and were happy to see their goals reached.

We know that Daniel had great favor with the ruler of that day. King Nebuchadnezzar looked to Daniel for the interpretation of the dreams he had. The scriptures also tell us, "So this Daniel prospered in the reign of Darius, and in the reign of Cyrus the Persian" (Dan. 6:28).

No man will make a decision to serve God and then later in life be sorry that he did. However, those who do not make this decision to serve Him will regret for eternity that they did not make it.

God's children will rejoice with Him forever.

THOUGHT: It always pays to serve God.

July 18 -- Mark 12:28-34
Dying on Third Base

Some years ago the Detroit Tigers and the Cleveland Indians were playing for the pennant in the American League. It was the last game in the series of seven games. The games were all tied up at three each and at the time the score in the seventh game was tied.

The headlines in the paper the next morning read "MORIARITY AND TIGERS DIE ON THIRD." The Tigers had failed to get their man home in the bottom of the ninth inning and the Indians had come back to score the winning run in the tenth inning.

Many Christians are willing to die on third base. They get on base and their life could count for God, but they really fail to serve Him and they have no testimony to give for Him.

Many people die on third base because of their lack of dedication. They really mean to do something about it but they never get around to it. Their life never means anything to themselves or to anyone else.

Some people die on third base because of their lack of church membership, their lack of baptism, or their failure to fully surrender to God. Don't let Satan trip you as you run. Don't let him "slip one by you." Make certain of your commitment to God and don't be left stranded on third base. Be sure that you reach home plate and score that run.

Jesus said, "Why call ye me Lord, Lord, and do not the things which I say" (Luke 6:46)? Think about those words for a moment. Are you still waiting on third base?

THOUGHT: Only the runners that touch home plate count in the final score.

July 19 -- Matthew 26:36-49
Gethsemane

It has been my joy to visit the Holy Land on two occasions. There are many places of interest. Some are of more interest than others. Calvary and the empty tomb are of interest to all of His children. However, I believe the place that held the greatest interest for me is the garden of Gethsemane.

Gethsemane is a place of suffering. Here is where our Savior came face to face with the death that He was to die. He said in verse 41, "The spirit indeed is willing, but the flesh is weak." No one knows the weight of our sin that bore down upon Him there. Too often with us sin is a matter of slight importance. With Him it is a great burden. He made the decision to take my sin and your sin upon Himself when He was there in the garden. He sweated great drops of blood as He decided to become our substitute.

Gethsemane is a place of loneliness. The tender and heavy heart of Jesus yearns for fellowship but it finds none. His disciples sleep while He prays. Is it true that the church does the same today?

Gethsemane is a place of agonizing. In verse 39 we read, "O my Father, if it be possible, let this cup pass from me: nevertheless not as I will, but as thou wilt." He faced our sins and He headed to the cross to bear them.

Gethsemane is a place of commitment. Jesus Christ left the garden committed to the work of the cross. This great commitment closed the gap between God and man forever and made salvation available for the entire world.

THOUGHT: Not my will but thine be done.

July 20 -- I Samuel 20:18-27
Out of Place

There is a place of service for every child of God. No one is called without being given something to do in the Lord's service. If we are not faithful to our call, that portion of the service of God will go undone.

In our scripture for today David is missing from his place. He had a little better reason for his absence than most of us do. King Saul had come to dislike David because he thought David would replace him as king. David's life was at stake and he was missing for his own safety. Nevertheless, he was missing from his place.

The New Testament tells us of another person who was absent from his place. When Jesus appeared to the disciples in the upper room for the first time, Thomas was not there. Through the ages since then he has been referred to as "doubting Thomas" because, not having been there and not having seen Jesus, he did not yet believe that Jesus had been raised up from the dead.

Do you absent yourself from your place of service? Do you serve in an office of the church or Sunday School and take care of it well, or do they have to get someone to replace you often because you are absent?

The Lord has promised to meet with His own when they meet in His name. We expect Him to be at that gathering. Should we not be in our place as well?

There is a place for all believers in God's service. Let us all make ourselves available to fill the place that is ours.

THOUGHT: Having a responsibility is one thing, but carrying it out is another.

July 21 -- James 4:1-3
Why Prayers Are Not Answered

Many people seldom see prayers answered. There are many reasons for this and the scriptures point them out to us.

The psalmist said, "If I regard iniquity in my heart, the Lord will not hear me" (Ps. 66:18). If we are going to live like the devil, rather than serving the Lord, we should not expect God to answer our prayers. The Bible says, "He that covereth his sins shall not prosper" (Prov. 28:13).

James tells us that many people do not have answers to their prayers because they are selfish and are interested only in themselves. We cannot spend all our time praying for ourselves and leaving out others. We need to be interested in each other and to pray for one another.

James also tells us that there is too much envy, jealousy, and fighting among ourselves for us to expect God to honor our prayers. He says that this practice of lusting and warring in our members is not the way to get things from God.

An unforgiving spirit hinders our prayers. Jesus says that if you bring your gift to the altar and there you realize that someone has something against you (for example, you have offended someone), go to that person and be reconciled to him. After you are reconciled you should then come and make your offering. See Matthew 5:23-24.

Any person who will hold something against others is in no position to receive forgiveness from God. Let us be on good terms with our fellow men if we expect to receive answers to our prayers.

THOUGHT: He who approaches God must have clean hands and a pure heart.

July 22 -- Genesis 32:22-32
Divine Wrestling

We see much wrestling today that we believe to be largely fake. Today's scripture tells us of a match that is not fake. This is for real and it has a better outcome than anything you might watch on television or go to the coliseum to see.

Jacob had a very spotted life. He had deceived his father into thinking that he was Esau, the other son, and he had been given the blessing of his father. He had followed the direction of his mother and he had left home. He went to Haran to live at the home of his uncle Laban.

Jacob led an interesting life. When he reached Haran, he fell in love with Rachel. He worked seven years so that she might be his wife. However, he was tricked and he was given Leah to be his wife. He worked another seven years before he was finally given Rachel to be his wife.

During the process of time, through his cunning and conniving, Jacob increased his own belongings tremendously. When God finally moved him out of Haran, he had a large family and a large number of servants and large flocks.

As Jacob began his journey, he realized that he had to face Esau. He was frightened about this. He was frightened as he thought of meeting Esau so he sought God about this matter. God prevailed upon him to surrender completely and Jacob was a different man after this. Afterwards there was an outward sign in his life of this surrender. There will also be an outward sign in your life after you surrender to God.

Pray that He will help you to be completely submissive to Him and to His will.

THOUGHT: Do you talk about commitment, or are you committed to God?

July 23 -- I Corinthians 2:9-11
The Source of Spiritual Knowledge

Man, if left to himself, could never understand the things of God. The natural man cannot understand God or how He works.

Our eyes have seen certain things. We look around us and we see the beauty of the universe, but the natural eye of man has never seen God. When spiritual truths are revealed, man is amazed that he just never could receive them before.

The ear has heard some wonderful things. Men of eloquence and wisdom can amaze us with facts that we have not discovered, yet these same men may completely overlook the spiritual things in life.

The Holy Spirit waits with words of tenderness, love, and affection. He waits with spiritual truth to instruct us in the ways of God. Man would never have known of God's great love if the Holy Spirit had not called it to our spiritual attention. Forgiveness of sin, the high priestly work of Christ, and His second coming would mean nothing to anyone apart from the ministry of the Holy Spirit.

There are spiritual truths that the human heart has never experienced. It never will experience them without the help of the Holy Spirit. Psychiatry has some wonderful conceptions of the human soul. There are wonderful truths discovered by human observation. However, the deeper and higher truths are taught by the Holy Spirit.

"For what man knoweth the things of a man, save the spirit of man which is in him? even so the things of God knoweth no man, but the Spirit of God" (I Cor. 2:11).

THOUGHT: The Spirit of God is our teacher.

July 24 -- Ephesians 6:18-24
The Beginning of a Prayer List

Pray for the sick. James tells us that it is good to pray for the sick. Not only are the sick healed but often the lost are saved. God has a special process for His children to follow for healing. Few people choose to follow it so many people continue to be afflicted.

Pray for the lost. The Bible says, "Let him know, that he which converteth the sinner from the error of his way shall save a soul from death, and shall hide a multitude of sins" (Jas. 5:20). All of us know of lost souls and we see them every day. Let these people have a big part of your prayers.

Pray for one another. We talk about and criticize one another. We would be better off to pray for one another and not to criticize so much. We usually do not help other people by criticizing them and we certainly do not help ourselves. Praying is a much better way.

Pray for your church. The entire program of the church needs bathing in prayer. Paul reminded all the churches of his love and of his prayer for them.

Pray for the ministry. There are many programs of ministry that people have organized. Many groups are competing with one another, each trying to outdo the other. The ministries of our churches should be directed by the Lord but I am afraid that many of them are not being so directed.

Confess sin in prayer to the Lord. This is what we all need to do. The Bible says, "If we confess our sins, he is faithful and just to forgive us our sins, and to cleanse us from all unrighteousness" (I John 1:9).

THOUGHT: Pray without ceasing.

July 25 -- I Corinthians 2:12-16
We Are Given the Mind of Christ

Once I had a little dog whose name was Sandy. I could talk to him and he would turn his head from side to side, but he really did not understand. The reason I know that he did not understand is that he did not do many things that I asked him to do. He understood some things but his understanding was very limited. The only way that I could get him to understand me fully would be to take my brain and put it into his head.

This is what the Holy Spirit has done. He has taken the mind of Jesus Christ and has put it into me. I have the mind of Christ, and now I can know the things that are freely given to me of God.

He does not destroy our mind. He takes the mind of Christ and restores life to our own minds and fuses them together until old things pass away and all things become new. He gives us the power to put off the old thoughts and to put on His thoughts. He gives us the grace and enables us to grasp, feel, understand, and remember the things of God. This is the illuminating work of the Holy Spirit of God.

Before the Holy Spirit lived within me I could pick up the Bible and read it, but it would mean no more to me than the morning newspaper. Now He makes the pages of God's Word live. I can read those pages and see Jesus Christ and understand His message for me. He has given me the mind of Christ so that I can understand what he wants to say to me.

THOUGHT: The work of the Holy Spirit is to make Jesus Christ known.

July 26 -- John 16:12-15
The Holy Spirit Is Our Teacher

When a child of six begins school, she expects her mother to lay out the clothes that she will wear to school every morning. She even expects her mother to help her get these clothes on every morning.

When she gets to school, she expects the teacher to direct her in her studies. The teacher tells her what she will study at a given time.

The Holy Spirit is our teacher. If we will listen to Him and follow His leadership, we will learn much that will help us to grow spiritually.

The Holy Spirit reveals to us the mind of Jesus Christ. He must often be disappointed that we learn so little and that we learn so slowly.

Paul said, "Now we have received, not the spirit of the world, but the spirit which is of God; that we might know the things that are freely given to us of God" (I Cor. 2:12).

The Lord had many things that He wanted to teach the disciples, but they could not understand them at that time. We can understand them now because we have the Holy Spirit living within us to teach us all that God wants us to know.

He will guide us into all truth, and that truth is Jesus Christ. In verse 14 Jesus said, "He shall glorify me; for he shall receive of mine, and shall show it unto you."

Let us yield to the indwelling Holy Spirit so that we might come to know the Lord Jesus better and be able to serve Him more fully.

THOUGHT: The Holy Spirit of God teaches us important spiritual things.

July 27 -- Isaiah 6:1-8
Man as He Is

Uzziah was a great king in Judah. He was successful in war and he did much to cause Judah to prosper. He did much that was right in the sight of the Lord, but he was not completely obedient in some areas of his life. He wrongly took upon himself the priestly duties and as a result God punished him with dreaded leprosy.

Isaiah had a great liking for King Uzziah. He looked to him for leadership. He perhaps leaned too heavily upon the king instead of going directly to God. The scripture tells us that it was when Uzziah died that Isaiah saw the Lord. Do we often have people or things in our life to the point that we cannot see beyond them?

The scripture tells us that when King Uzziah died, Isaiah saw the Lord high and lifted up and he saw His holiness. Immediately Isaiah saw himself as he really was and he did not like what he saw.

Isaiah did not describe himself or his people as very good people. In verse 5 he said, "Woe is me! For I am undone; because I am as a man of unclean lips, and I dwell in the midst of a people with unclean lips."

Isaiah's thoughts of himself, and of man, must have been higher than they should have been. After a glimpse of God and His holiness, Isaiah began to see man in his hopeless unholiness before God. May God help each of us to see how utterly hopeless and helpless we are without the Lord and His grace and love.

THOUGHT: He who knows who God is will know who he himself is.

July 28 -- II Timothy 2:7-15
Spiritual Growth

Man has many ways of pacifying himself and making himself feel extra good about his activities. Christian people are no different in this respect. Churches and pastors become caught up in this because everybody likes to be praised.

It becomes quite amusing to me sometimes to see how some churches go all out for entertainment, rather than for the ministry of the truth of God's Word. On one Sunday the church might have as guest a great baseball player. On another Sunday they might have a clown for the youngsters. On still another Sunday they might have horseback riding for all children and a cowboy to teach the adults. They might have everybody from politicians to race car drivers as special guests in the church. This sort of thing may draw a crowd but it will not instruct them in the Bible.

The Bible says, "Preach the word" (II Tim. 4:2). Anything else we do is not conducive to Christian growth. It is well to use literature in our Sunday School and other areas of church teaching. There are many good methods of teaching. However, any literature or method that departs from the Bible is a time waster and will not help to grow strong Christians. Our Sunday School teachers should be trained to teach the Word of God. Any time that we find that a tool is used to replace the Bible, we should immediately get rid of that tool.

It is good at times to be entertained and to be made to laugh, but the church is not the place for that. The church is a place to seriously study the Word of God. It is through the study of the Word that we are able to have spiritual growth.

THOUGHT: The Bible is God's instruction book for His children.

July 29 -- I John 5:11-21
Only One Way

In my thinking, the purpose of an ordination council is to examine a person to determine his fitness for the gospel ministry. At the same time, the council is in a position to help and to instruct the person being examined, when this is needed.

Once I was serving on a minister's examination council when the question was asked of the candidate, "If there was a person living in a country that had not been evangelized, and that person dies without ever having heard the name of Jesus Christ, do you believe God would make another way for him to be saved?"

To begin with, I do not think that this is a very good question to ask a young man who is beginning in the ministry. One thing this question will do, though, is to send a person out looking for some answers. I know of no place better than the Bible to find answers to this and to all other questions. So let's see what the Bible says.

Romans 2:12 tells us: "For as many as have sinned without law shall also perish without law: and as many as have sinned in the law shall be judged by the law."

Acts 4:12 tells us: "Neither is there salvation in any other: for there is none other name under heaven given among men, whereby we must be saved."

John 14:6 tells us: "I am the way, the truth, and the life. No man cometh unto the Father, but by me."

The Bible speaks of only one way of salvation and that is Jesus Christ. What about those who have never heard? They will "perish without law."

THOUGHT: The law of God is surely written in their hearts.

July 30 -- Hebrews 12:1-8
The Besetting Sin

Ask the question, "What is the greatest besetting sin in the life of God's people today?" You would get as many different answers as the people you ask. First of all, besetting is defined as "constantly attacking or tempting."

Shy people might say that their besetting sin is the fear of people. Those who are slack in church attendance might say that their besetting sin is sleeping late on Sunday mornings. Others might answer that such things as going to the mountains, or going to the beach, or doing a number of other things was their besetting sin.

All these things and many other distractions take their toll on people. After giving much consideration to the question, I believe that the sin that so easily besets so many of God's people is the sin of prayerlessness.

One outstanding thing that we see in the lives of great men of the Bible is that of prayer. Abraham was a man of prayer. There may have been many faults in the life of Abraham, but he knew how to pray. When God wanted to destroy Sodom, Lot was told to get out of the city because nothing could be done as long as he was there. This is because Abraham was praying for him.

David was a man of prayer. Read the book of Psalms and you will find that David was almost always in prayer. He was constantly praising God and thanking Him for His goodness and he was seeking to have a closer walk with the Lord. He was praying for his family and he was praying for the nation of Israel.

Let us be like these men in our prayer life.

THOUGHT: Is the lack of prayer the sin that so easily besets you?

July 31 -- I Samuel 12:16-23
The Sin of Not Praying

Israel was the nation of God. He had set them apart from the surrounding nations. However, Israel was not pleased and they asked for a king so that they might be like the other nations around them.

At times God will allow us to have the things that are not pleasing to Him in order to teach us a lesson. Psalm 106:15 says, "And he gave them their request; but sent leanness into their soul." It is dangerous to rebel against the direction of God.

In our scripture for today Israel is beginning to see something of the error of their way. They realize now that they should never have asked for a king in order to be like the other nations. However, it is too late to do anything about it. The king has already been installed.

It is always best to try to walk in the directive will of the Lord, but there is always the danger of missing the mark. Samuel knew that Israel needed prayer lest they slip even further from the Lord. He covenanted to pray for them, and he even counted it a sin if he failed to do so.

Job was a man who believed in prayer. Even though nothing is said about his children doing anything wrong, he made burnt offerings on their behalf. Job said, "It may be that my sons have sinned, and cursed God in their hearts" (Job 1:5).

Let us not sin against God, or against ourselves, by failing to pray for His direct leadership and power in our lives.

THOUGHT: Prayer gets things from God.

Chapter Eight

•••

August

•••

Verse to Memorize

Ephesians 4:32

"And be ye kind one to another, tenderhearted, forgiving one another, even as God for Christ's sake hath forgiven you."

August 1 -- Acts 4:31-35
God Answers Prayer

The book of Acts records many answers to the prayers of the early church. After the ascension of the Lord Jesus, the disciples prayed. As a direct result of this they were ready for Pentecost, as we are told in the second chapter of Acts.

The Bible also tells us that the disciples "continued steadfastly in the apostles' doctrine and fellowship, and in breaking of bread, and in prayers" (Acts 2:42).

As these people prayed, there were definite effects upon both the saved and the lost people. The saved people were continuing daily walking with God and many of the lost were being saved each day.

Perhaps our problem today is not so much a lack of organizing as it is a lack of agonizing. Maybe we have too much action and too little unction. Organizing is necessary and action is an absolute must. However, neither one of these will get the job done without there also being proper prayer to strengthen them both.

In several places in the book of Acts we find that the church met together in agonizing prayer. God heard their prayers. He filled the people with the Spirit of God and with courage. After that, they went out and preached the Word of God with great boldness.

May God lay the burden of prayer upon us and may He work through us so that His will may be done on the earth.

THOUGHT: Organize, yes, but agonize so that our action will be filled with unction.

August 2 -- Luke 11:5-13
Jesus Gives When We Ask

Jesus tells us to ask, seek, and knock. The first letters of these three words form the word "ask" and this is what a lot of prayer is about. Asking is not the only element in prayer, but it is one of the most important elements.

Our Lord told us that if we ask, it will be given to us. If we seek, we shall find. If we knock, it shall be opened unto us. With encouragement like this, we should spend much time in asking, seeking, and knocking.

Jesus also asks us what kind of father would give his son a stone if he asked for bread. He asks who would give his son a serpent if he asked for a fish. He asks who would give his son a scorpion if he asked for an egg.

It is very reasonable to think that a father would give to his own son the things that would be good for him. It is likewise reasonable to think that God would give to His children those things that are good for them.

The Bible says, "Let us therefore come boldly unto the throne of grace, that we may obtain mercy, and find grace to help in time of need" (Heb. 4:16).

We are told that we have a high priest who knows our infirmities and our needs. He is able to supply every need. He will supply that need when we come to Him and ask. I never hesitated to ask my earthly father for anything. Why should I hesitate to ask heavenly my Father for anything in prayer?

THOUGHT: The greatest privilege that God gives His children is prayer.

August 3 -- Philippians 3:7-11
What Does It Mean to Know Jesus in His Person?

I know the governor of our state. I have read about him and I have seen his pictures in the paper. I have seen him on television. If he should ever come to my home I would know who he is.

Yet, I really do not know the governor of our state. I have never met him personally and I have never talked with him. I know nothing of his likes and dislikes. I know nothing about his habits or his recreational activities or his family life. Truthfully, I must say that I know about the governor, but I do not know him.

To know Jesus Christ in His person is to know what pleases Him and to know what hurts Him. To know Him is to be familiar with His thoughts and His actions and to know where to find Him. To know the Son of God in His person does not mean just to have a knowledge about Him as an exalted king. It means to have an inner knowledge of Him. It is to be one whom He counts as His dear friend. It is to be one with whom He shares His secrets.

To know Him means that we realize His personal presence in the time of storm. It is to realize His presence when we are in the valley of the shadow and when fear breaks upon us. To know Him is to realize His presence when sorrow and disappointment come upon us. It means that we know Him in the sympathy of His dealings with His own. It means that we know the redeeming and keeping power of His person.

May God help us to grow in our knowledge of Him in His person.

THOUGHT: To know about Him is one thing, but to actually know Him is another.

August 4 -- Philippians 3:7-11
Knowing Jesus in His Person

Let's give our imagination freedom for a moment and suppose that you are cast into an arena with a bunch of lions that have not been fed for several days. They all begin immediately to make their way toward you. Just as one of them makes a leap toward you, a figure leaps out of the darkness and kills the lions. He turns to you and says, "Don't be afraid. I have killed the lions and you are free."

Before you can ask who he is and thank him for what he has done, he is gone. You are taken to a beautiful place where you are cared for and supplied sumptuously every day with everything that would make you happy. Yet, there is a desire inside you to know who that person was that saved you from the lions and who now provides for you with such a loving care.

When you inquire who this person is, you are asked, "Why do you care who he is? He saved you, and now he provides all this for you because he loves you. Is this not enough?" However, this answer still does not settle the deep longing down in your soul to know the person.

When we think of the love of Jesus Christ and how He supplies our need daily, we want to love Him better. When we think how He has saved us and how He keeps us, we want to know Him better. When we think how that He is coming again for us, we have a deep longing inside us for that day to come. We want to know Him in His person and not just to know something about Him.

THOUGHT: We need to know Him, not just know some things about Him.

August 5 -- Psalm 34:7-9
A Cure for Anxiety

The word for fear used in this verse and in other verses in the Old Testament in the same sense means "a reverential trust with a hatred of evil." The Bible says that when we fear the Lord in this way, there will not be any wants or any unsatisfied needs with us.

Many anxieties perplex a great number of people today. All of these worries could be put to rest, if people would only fear the Lord.

Many people are anxious about the corruption in our government. Perhaps none of us have ever seen a time of greater corruption than we have today. It seems that each official is out to "get something" on the other. Our country really needs a lot of political cleaning up and our officials need to be able to trust each other.

We are often concerned in this country about inflation. The cost of living spirals upwards. Increases in salaries and wages are overshadowed by the rising costs of goods and services that we have to buy. Many people are anxiously asking the question, "What are we going to do about food?"

Fears over rising taxes cause anxieties in many areas. Likewise, fears mount over an increasing crime rate across the country. We are told that there is a major crime committed every few seconds. It is dangerous to walk the streets in many of our cities today, even during daylight hours.

These and many other fears afflict us. However, in the midst of it all the Bible says, "Commit thy way unto the Lord; trust also in him" (Ps. 37:5).

THOUGHT: Faith in Him settles our fears.

August 6 -- Revelation 22:8-21
The Last Message in the Bible

The content of the message is humbling. John reports that when he heard the message, he fell at the feet of the messenger to worship. The angel that had showed him these things said in verse 9, "See thou do it not: for I am thy fellow servant...worship God." The angel could have received the worship of John. He did not do so but in humility he directed John to worship God.

The character of the message is perfect. Verses 18 and 19 instruct all of us that nothing can be added to or taken from his message. Verse 6 of this chapter says that these sayings are faithful and true. We need to accept the Bible as the Word of God and believe what it says, and then we need to live as it teaches. Those who would change it to suit their own ideas will have to suffer its judgments.

The scope of the message is universal. In verse 17 we read, "And let him that heareth say, Come. And let him that is athirst come. And whosoever will, let him take the water of life freely." Whoever the person who hears the message is and wherever he may be, he has the opportunity of receiving it as his very own.

The call of the message is urgent. The testimony of the Lord in verse 20 is, "Surely I come quickly." We have no promise of another day. It is clear in the Bible that today is the day of salvation. If you put it off one more day, you have no assurance that another day will come and give you an opportunity to choose salvation.

The promise of the message is merciful. It is great to have the promise of the grace of the Lord as we try to live faithfully for Him here.

THOUGHT: The Lord is slow to anger.

August 7 -- II Chronicles 15:1-8
King Asa

King Asa was a good king in Judah. In II Chronicles 14:2-3 we are told, "And Asa did that which was good and right in the eyes of the Lord his God: For he took away the altars of the strange gods, and the high places, and brake down the images, and cut down the groves." There was prosperity religiously, politically, economically, and in other respects under this king.

Asa issued a warning to Judah to be strong in their work, for it would be rewarded. Judah had experienced some great victories over the enemy. Often after we have victories, Satan begins to try even harder to cause us to fall.

There had been a long season when Judah did not have a priest. They had not been taught the law and they were out of touch with God. When these things are true, people become weak in the faith and ignorant of what the Lord desires. They have no spiritual strength and it is a dangerous time for them. Satan is ready to take advantage of any people at such a time.

Asa had seen nation after nation fall. He had seen city after city destroyed. He had seen great vexation come upon the inhabitants of countries round about them. He did not want to see this happen to Judah. He warned Judah by showing them how other nations had fallen. He reminded them how Judah had turned to the Lord and had found Him. He urged them to be strong in the Lord.

That is some mighty good advice for all of us to follow.

THOUGHT: Strength for the battle can only come from the Lord.

August 8 -- II Chronicles 15:8-15
Inner Desire Will Turn Us to God

Verse 15 says that they had "sworn with all their heart." When there is a deep heart-felt thirst for God and a craving for His presence, a person is apt to walk with Him. When there is a hunger for the things of God and a deep desire for the ways of God, a person is apt to endeavor to walk hand in hand with Him.

The Bible tells us that when people humble themselves and pray, and seek His face, and turn from their wicked ways, then He will forgive their sin and will heal their land. (Read II Chronicles 7:14.)

This was true in the life of Isaiah. He had been looking to King Uzziah for leadership. Suddenly the king was taken from him. Isaiah hardly knew what to do. However, he did have the presence of mind and the desire to go to the house of God. When he came to the temple he saw the Lord, high and lifted up.

Isaiah was astounded. He had never had such an experience before. He saw the Lord as the One who could supply his own need and who could lead him as he led the people of Israel.

David speaks of his thirst for and his longing after the living God. He said, "As the hart panteth after the water brooks, so panteth my soul after thee, O God" (Ps. 42:1). David mentions in several of the psalms his hunger and his thirst for the living God.

The need in the life of most Christians today is the consciousness of the presence of God. This consciousness of His presence will become a reality when we have a deep desire for Him.

THOUGHT: An inner desire will turn us to God.

August 9 -- Revelation 6:9-17
Prayer without Repentance

Whatever your views of Revelation are, you will agree that there are many demonstrations and times of destruction revealed there. Suffering is the order of the day in almost all the book. Famine, war, anarchy, chaos, and death are reported throughout the book.

In our reading today the sun refuses to shine and the moon becomes a great clot of blood there in the sky. There is an earthquake and the stars begin to fall to the earth. The heavens seem to roll away. The islands of the sea and the mountains disappear. What a scene!

This should bring any people to their knees, regardless of who they are. We hear many people crying out in prayer. Listen to the voices of the large and the small as they cry out in despair. Listen to the famous and the infamous and the wise and the foolish as they cry out in despair. Listen to the captain and the bondman and the good and the bad as they cry out in despair. They all cry out to the rocks and the mountains to fall upon them and destroy them from the face of God.

I would have thought that they would pray to the God of heaven. No, they pray to the devil's rocks and mountains. They pray not for deliverance but they pray for destruction. It is not a prayer of repentance but it is a prayer for death.

This isn't all. As the judgment of God grows more intense they become more impenitent. Revelation 9:21 says, "Neither repented they of their murders, nor of their sorceries, nor of their fornication, nor of their thefts."

Thank God, simple repentance and calling upon God does bring deliverance.

THOUGHT: **The wrath of God can only be averted by true repentance.**

August 10 -- Philippians 1:18-21
Look Up and Rejoice

The Word of God is filled with expressions that point us upward, such as "Look up...look unto the heavens...look unto God...lift up your eyes...behold." These and many other expressions should cause us to look "unto Jesus the author and finisher of our faith" (Heb. 12:2).

Once I heard of a boy who had found a five dollar bill. After that, he always looked down thinking that he would find more money. When he was an old man, it was said that he had found 54,172 pins, 29,519 buttons, 32,411 paper clips, eight dollars and nineteen cents, a crooked back, and a very bitter personal disposition.

Paul said, "Rejoice in the Lord alway: and again I say, Rejoice" (Phil. 4:4). Paul certainly had the right philosophy. God's people ought always to be rejoicing people. We have light in a dark world and we have strength in our weakness. We have forgiveness of sins and we have companionship in our lonely days.

Often the expression is heard, "I am amazed that so few are faithfully following the Lord." I suppose, really, that the thing that is more amazing to me is that any people at all are faithful to follow Him.

People look for an exciting time. If we are not well off physically and financially and if we do not have crowds at church, we tend to be despondent. Let us be rejoicing people in everything. Let us be looking upward rather than looking downward. Let us always trust Him rather than worry about circumstances. Remember, we are saved by Him. We are kept by Him and we are supplied by Him.

THOUGHT: Don't just rejoice in things, but rejoice always in Him.

August 11 -- II Peter 1:3-11
The Christ We Serve

He is the Christ of power. By His power we are given everything that pertains to life and godliness. Whatever ought to be done and however love ought to be expressed, He has the power to do it. In Matthew 28:18 He says, "All power is given unto me in heaven and in earth."

He is the Christ of generosity. He gives all things that have to do with life and godliness. He gives divine life itself, and He gives what it takes for each of us to live as we should. What is your need today? Is it peace, contentment, or companionship? In Him all your needs can be met. Paul said, "My God shall supply all your need according to his riches in glory by Christ Jesus" (Phil. 4:19).

He is the Christ of exceeding great and precious promises. It is by His promises that we have forgiveness of sin. It is by His promises that we have the indwelling Holy Spirit. It is by His promises that we have all spiritual blessings in heavenly places in Christ. Because of His promises we have comfort in sorrow; we have peace in trouble; and we have companionship in loneliness.

He is the Christ by whom we escape the world's corruption. There is such a great temptation from the world today. We need His grace and power in order to escape the world and its corruption. We do have this power, for Christ "gave himself for our sins, that he might deliver us from this present evil world" (Gal. 1:4).

He is the Christ who makes us partakers of the divine nature. When we are saved, the Holy Spirit Himself comes to live within us.

THOUGHT: Every child of God has the Lord Jesus Christ living within him.

August 12 -- Matthew 11:28-30
All Ye, Come

A few years ago everyone knew of John Dillinger. He was a notorious criminal. No doubt, many stories have been told about this man that are not true, but he was a wicked person. Some of you who read this may remember him.

He was on the FBI's most wanted list. He was declared an outlaw, which meant that anyone could shoot him on sight. His pictures were everywhere and he was hunted like a rat. He peeled the skin from his fingers, trying to destroy his fingerprints. It is said that he had facial surgery to disfigure himself and to make it less likely that he would be recognized. Yet, with all the changing that he did, he never changed his heart and turned to God.

John Dillinger was no worse than Saul of Tarsus, whom God saved. He was no worse than Abraham, who was an idol worshipper. He was no worse than David, who was an adulterer. He was no worse than Mary Magdalene, who was a harlot. He was no worse than James R. Thompson, who also was a poor lost sinner. God saved all of these and He would have saved John Dillinger if only he had called upon the Lord Jesus Christ.

When Jesus said in Matthew 11:28, "Come unto me, all ye," He meant just that. He is "not willing that any should perish, but that all should come to repentance" (II Pet. 3:9). The Bible says, "He is able also to save them to the uttermost that come unto God by him, seeing he ever liveth to make intercession for them" (Heb. 7:25).

If you have never done it before, call upon Him now and He will save you.

THOUGHT: The blood of Jesus Christ cleanses us from all sin.

August 13 -- II Peter 1:5-10
Are You a Maturing Christian?

The word "add" in verse 5 is an interesting word. Let's look at it for a moment. The Greek word is "epichonegia" and it means "to furnish besides; to fully supply."

Someone has defined virtue as "manly effort." The effort is on our part as we study and strive to grow in the Lord. We are to work at fully supplying the Christian graces mentioned in these verses.

In the amphitheater days of the Greeks, there were many great performances and much preparation was necessary. A great number of things were necessary, such as performers, costumes, lighting, judges, food, lodging, and other props and other necessities. These were to be acquired and cared for by a "leader of the chorus" or an "epichonegia," the person who was responsible for all of this.

This is true in our life. We are the ones responsible for our own Christian growth. We need to make sure that virtue, as well as knowledge, temperance, patience, godliness, brotherly kindness, and love are added to our basic faith.

The person who lacks in his Christian growth is not able to properly understand the things of God. This scripture says that he "cannot see afar off, and hath forgotten that he was purged from his old sins."

Paul talks about the same growth in Ephesians 4 when he says for us to put off the old man and to put on the new man. There is something for each of us to do to stimulate our Christian growth.

THOUGHT: The proper diet aids growth.

August 14 -- Ephesians 2:1-10
Do You Remember When You Were Saved?

There are many people that I talk with who tell me that they hope that they are saved. Most people tell me that they try to be a Christian or that they do nobody any harm. There is a way we can know that we are saved and we ought to know it for a certainty.

There are perhaps some people who are saved and do not know it. This would come about by not knowing the teaching of God's Word. On the other hand, there are some who think that they are saved but they are not. This would also come about by not understanding the Word. It could come about by depending upon feeling or by depending upon some experience that has long since passed away.

The Bible says, "Believe on the Lord Jesus Christ, and thou shalt be saved" (Acts 16:31). Many other passages in the Bible tell us the same thing in different words.

Jesus said, "I am the way, the truth, and the life; no man cometh unto the Father but by me" (John 14:6). Since He is the only way and since we receive Him by faith, when we trust Him as Savior we are saved. Joy and assurance come when we trust Him to do what He says He will do.

Can you point to the time and place when you received Christ as your personal Savior? Do you know the time of your new birth? This answers a lot of questions and gives definite assurance. It helps you to move forward in sanctification, or Christian growth. Write in the fly-leaf of your Bible the date of your salvation. If you do not know the exact date, write "on this date I know that I am trusting Jesus Christ as my personal Savior." Then write today's date and your name.

THOUGHT: **It is a great joy to know the time when you were saved.**

August 15 -- John 3:16-18
Provision Enough for the World

A wealthy lawyer from a mid-western oil town went to Korea for a visit with a missionary. While traveling along one day they saw a man and his son plowing in the field. The man pulled the plow and the boy guided it. The lawyer thought that this was rather amusing and he asked that they stop and get a picture of it.

As he made his picture and talked of how much fun he would have with it back home, the missionary explained that the man had owned an ox. However, he had sold it so that he could give the money to the building fund of his church. The lawyer said, "That was a real sacrifice." The missionary replied, "They did not count it a sacrifice, but they thanked God that they had an ox to sell."

It is my understanding that the English speaking people make up about nine percent of the world's population. Ninety-four percent of the offering plate dollar is spent on them and six percent is used to minister to the remaining ninety-one percent of the people of the world.

God's provision for a lost world is sufficient for the entire world. Our reading today says that God gave His Son "that whosoever believeth in him should not perish, but have everlasting life."

Christ did not die just for a few people or just for the worthy people or just for the exceedingly bad people. He died for the whole world. The promise of a redeemer is fulfilled in Jesus Christ. We can add nothing to Him and we can take nothing away from Him. We must accept Him as He is, God's provision for the whole world.

THOUGHT: We accept Him for who He is, and God accepts us as we are in Christ.

August 16 -- John 3:16
The Greatest

Today's reading is perhaps thought by the greatest number of people to be the greatest verse of scripture in the Bible. This was the first verse that many of us ever learned. It is probably known by more people than any other Bible verse. Yet, it is not believed by most of the people who can quote it.

This verse has been the means of introducing many people to the Savior. It was called by Martin Luther "the miniature Bible." Dr. W. B. Riley said that he had been pastor for twenty-five years before he ever preached on this verse. Even then he said that he did not feel qualified to preach on such a great verse.

Someone has very appropriately described the verse as follows:

- It speaks of the greatest lover--God so loved.
- It speaks of the greatest love--God loved.
- It speaks of the greatest number loved--the world.
- It speaks of the greatest giver--God gave.
- It speaks of the greatest gift--God's Son.
- It speaks of the greatest salvation--everlasting life.
- It speaks of the greatest escape--should not perish.
- It speaks of salvation for the greatest number--whosoever.
- It speaks of the greatest method--whosoever believeth.

All of this is true because Jesus Christ willingly laid down His life. What a joy to know that One loved man enough to die in man's stead. Have you received Him?

THOUGHT: The greatest knowledge is to know Jesus Christ as Savior.

August 17 -- II Corinthians 11:13-15
The Devil Is Real

We read and hear much about the devil today. Devil worship is on the increase. Demon activity abounds around us today. Yet, there are still those who do not believe that there is a real and personal devil.

A French scientist was crossing the Arabian Desert. At the close of the day his Arab guide knelt to pray. The scientist said, "I have watched you do that several times today. What are you doing?"

"Praying," answered the guide.

"Praying? Praying to whom?" He asked.

"Praying to my God," the guide replied.

When the scientist asked if he had seen God or heard Him speak or touched Him, the guide answered, "No."

The next morning the scientist said, "There was a camel around the tent last night," to which the guide responded by asking, "Did you see him or hear him or touch him?" The scientist answered, "No." The guide then asked, "How can you believe in a camel you have not seen or heard or touched?" "I see his tracks," the scientist answered. "So I see the tracks of God in every sunrise, in every sunset, and all around me," replied the guide.

You and I can also see the tracks of the devil as we look around us today. We can even recognize his tracks in our own lives as we are sometimes tempted by him to stray away from a closeness to God.

THOUGHT: Only the power of God can conquer the devil and his allies.

August 18 -- II Peter 3:10-18
We Need a Refuge from the Power of Sin

Many Christians are held in the clutches of some sin. Some habits are very hard to break. Jeremiah said, "The heart is deceitful above all things, and desperately wicked: who can know it" (Jer. 17:9)? This is just another way of saying that it is easier to do wrong than it is to do right.

Some time ago I had a person to come by my study and ask to talk to me. The person was not a member of my church but he did not want to go to his own pastor about the matter. A story was unfolded before me, and then came the question, "Preacher, why did I do it?"

I can answer the question for that person and for many more of you who ask the same question from time to time. It is because of the power of sin.

The alcoholic is looking for an escape from the bondage of alcohol. The person with a hot temper is looking for a refuge from anger. The one who has a bitter disposition is looking for a way to escape from himself. Many people are searching for an escape from the bondage of gossiping, lying, envy, jealousy, and hatred. They are looking for an escape from the many other habits that have them tightly bound in their clutches.

Jesus Christ is the refuge that we need. Paul said that He "gave himself for our sins, that he might deliver us from this present evil world" (Gal. 1:4). Whatever your need, it can be met in the person of Jesus Christ. Look to Him this very day and enjoy the deliverance that He alone can give you.

THOUGHT: The power of God delivers from the power of sin.

August 19 -- John 6:15-21
The Watchful Eye of Our Lord

Jesus had taken the small lunch and had multiplied it and then He had fed the five thousand. He had then departed into a mountain to pray. His disciples got into a boat to go to the other side of the sea. On their way across the sea a storm arose and they were very much afraid.

Mark tells us that Jesus "saw them toiling in rowing" (Mark 6:48). Jesus always sees His own, no matter where they may be. He has them written on His heart and He never lets them out of His sight. He may let a battle rage for a while. He may seem to leave His own to themselves for a while but He always comes to the rescue. The Bible tells us that the Lord said, "I will never leave thee, nor forsake thee" (Heb. 13:5).

Job thought that he had been forsaken. He had lost all that he had, including material possessions, friends, and family. He was stricken with boils and sat in ashes. In despair he cried, "Oh that I knew where I might find him! That I might come even to his seat" (Job 23:3)! God was there all the time. At the appropriate time He made Himself known to Job.

Our Lord always watches over His own. He has us in the range of His watchcare at all times. We see in history that He watched over the three Hebrew children in the fiery furnace. He watched over Daniel in the den of lions and He watched over Job on the ash heap.

Even so He watches over you and me in all of our everyday activities.

The psalmist said, "When I said, My foot slippeth; thy mercy, O Lord, held me up" (Ps. 94:18). Yes, God always watches over and cares for His own.

THOUGHT: Our heavenly Father watches over us.

August 20 -- Philippians 2:5-8
The Humility of Jesus

Jesus Christ is the Son of the living God. He is the creator of the world. In Colossians we are told that all things were created by Him and for Him and that by Him all things hold together. (Read Colossians 1:16-17.) He is the Redeemer and He is the greatest person ever to live upon this earth. He is truly worthy of all the praise and honor that is given to Him. Yet, all through His life and even in His death on the cross He displayed such a great humility.

Jesus said, "The Son of man came not to be ministered unto, but to minister, and to give his life a ransom for many" (Matt. 20:28).

He was born of a poor woman. He spent years working in a carpenter's shop. His followers were always the poor people. They were never the rich people or those who were highly recognized.

He lived all of His earthly life without a place to call His own. He said, "The foxes have holes, and the birds of the air have nests; but the Son of man hath not where to lay his head" (Matt. 8:20).

He preached to people from a borrowed boat. He rode into Jerusalem on a borrowed animal. He was buried in a borrowed tomb. Paul said, "Though he was rich, yet for your sakes he became poor, that ye through his poverty might be rich" (II Cor. 8:9).

In humility the Lord Jesus Christ is our great example. Let us all diligently try to be more like Him.

THOUGHT: The way up is down.

August 21 -- John 3:14-16
The Cross and God's Love

Paul said, "God was in Christ, reconciling the world unto himself" (II Cor. 5:19). This is a perfect illustration of real love.

The cross is a direct proof of God's love and that He was in Christ reconciling the world unto Himself. Let's look at Christ on the cross for a moment.

There we see His head of love, pierced with a crown of thorns from the hands of man, in order that we might wear the crown of life from the hands of God.

There we see His mouth of love parched from ill treatment and lack of water, in order that we might freely have the water of life.

There we see the hands of love torn by spikes driven by the cruelty of man, in order that we might have hands to point people to Him.

There we see His feet of love pierced with the spikes and covered with blood, in order that we might have feet to take us along our way as we obey Him.

Paul said, "For scarcely for a righteous man will one die" (Rom. 5:7). Yet, when we look at the cross, we do not see someone dying for a righteous man. We see Jesus Christ the righteous One dying for the wicked people everywhere.

When He came to earth there was no room for Him and wicked King Herod tried to kill Him. All through His earthly ministry He was attacked by every conceivable evil plot. Still, in love He gave His life for every person. He even gave His life for those who were His enemies and who had been plotting endlessly against Him.

THOUGHT: Love cannot be rebuffed.

August 22 -- I Kings 18:25-39
Revival in Elijah's Day

Let us look at three areas of importance surrounding revival in Elijah's day.

1. There was a nation looking down. Politically the nation was divided and all around there was bloodshed and war. Several corrupt kings had been on the throne, and some of them had been guilty of killing the others. At this time Ahab, perhaps the worst of them all, reigned with his wife, Jezebel. Ahab made a grave mistake economically when he made a league with Phoenicia. Religiously, the country was in shambles. Jeroboam had set up the golden calf worship and Ahab was determined to take the people much farther away from God.

2. There was a prophet looking up. Elijah saw the sins of the people and the spiritual degeneration in their midst. He saw the people undecided on whether to follow God or to serve idols. Several verses in this chapter show Elijah pointing to God as the only way of deliverance. Elijah not only knew God, but he stood firmly on God's side against the eight hundred and fifty false prophets.

3. There were some people looking on. They see sin defeated. Elijah goes all out to give God His place in Israel. He puts his complete dependence in the God of Israel. Everything is on the altar. If God does not prove Himself now, Israel and Elijah will be through as a religious force. They saw Jehovah magnified. When the fire fell, the people began to praise and honor Him by saying, "The Lord, he is the God." They saw refreshment upon the land. Verses 42 through 46 explain the rain that came upon the dry land. This pictures the spiritual refreshing that comes as we are committed to God.

THOUGHT: The fire of God's judgment always falls before a refreshing comes.

August 23 -- I Timothy 4:12-16
Young People Today

"Young people are the leaders of tomorrow" is a statement that we hear very often today. I disagree with the statement. It is my belief that young people are the leaders of today and that they will be replacing us tomorrow.

Some folks think young people are just necessary evils. We must put up with them until they grow up. Well, this just is not true.

Young people fill our armies and fight our wars. Young people fill our Christian colleges and are preparing to take our place when we move off the scene. Young people have a place to fill in society and they should be recognized. In many cases they have something to say that should be heard.

A friend of mine once had his infant son in the hospital. I remember that he was critically ill. There were many doctors attending to him. They were at a loss as to what to do for the infant. Finally they told my friend that they could not help and that the baby was going to die.

A young intern, to whom no one had paid any attention up to this point, asked if he could try his remedy. He was given permission by the older doctors. What could they lose? They thought that the child had no chance. Soon after the young intern tried his remedy the young son recovered. Today the son is a twenty-three year old man who is serving the Lord.

Somewhere I read this statement: "Don't say modern youth is wild, just exercise forbearance; the faults might come from problem parents."

THOUGHT: J. Edgar Hoover said that our young people were our most priceless asset.

August 24 -- Matthew 16:21-28
Your Soul Is Valuable

There are some things in this world that are valuable. I have a piece of money that is worth about three hundred times its face value. It is an Indian Head penny, so I still do not have a lot of value there.

Recently I saw a 1926 Model T Ford advertised for sale for $600.00. This is more than twice what it sold for when brand new. In the same paper there was also advertised for sale a 1931 Model A Ford for $1,950.00. This is about five times the cost of the automobile when it was new.

These things are considered to be valuable items to some people, but I can tell you of something that is far more valuable than any of these things. It is your never-dying soul that has such value. The Lord asked the question, "For what shall it profit a man, if he shall gain the whole world, and lose his own soul" (Mark 8:36)?

Jesus Christ gave Himself for the world, but He gave Himself for each of us individually. It has been said, "If you had been the only person in the world, Jesus would have given His life for you." It is a known fact that your salvation could have been purchased with nothing less than His blood.

God thought that your life was valuable and that is why He allowed His only begotten Son to die for you. Have you ever received Him as your Savior? "For there is none other name under heaven given among men, whereby we must be saved" (Acts 4:12).

THOUGHT: Your soul is of such a great value that the Lord Jesus Christ died for it.

August 25 -- Joel 2:28-32
What about the Future, Young Person?

Our young people can be a force for good in the future. They can preach and teach and sing. They can find so many ways to reach people with the Word of God. Young people who know Christ and who are dedicated to God are some of our best witnesses today. Praise God for each one of them. Let's pray that we will have many more of them to answer the call to service for God.

By giving themselves to Christ, young people can set the course of this world. More than fifty percent of the population of America is under the age of twenty-five years. This means that there is a host of young people who need to be reached for God. The best people to reach them with the gospel are the Christian young people.

In order to be qualified to do the job, people must seek the Lord while they are still young. Don't be ashamed to be a Christian and to have some firm standards. Most young people who live it up in the world will secretly wish that they had what it takes to live as you do, if you live by these high standards.

Take a stand based upon the teaching of the Word of God. Have some real moral convictions and let neither friend nor foe ever cause you to forsake those worthy convictions.

Give yourself to God and step out for Him. Lead others rather than waiting for others to lead you. Always be aggressive for the Lord. Let everyone know exactly where you stand. Lead others to your position of faith. Don't ever backslide and go to a position of unfaithfulness.

THOUGHT: We should practice living HOLY rather than living HOLEY.

August 26 -- Ecclesiastes 12:1-6
What Is the Problem with Youth?

Many problems faced by the youth of today are not problems of their creation, although they now have to face these problems. Let's look at some of the problems that others make for our youth.

1. They have wrong publicity. There are only a few hippies, dope addicts, sex fiends, gutter bums, and outlaws who get most of the publicity, but then all of the young people have to take the rap. This is not fair to them. You will seldom find the news media at a church service conducted by young people. You won't find them at a Youth For Christ rally or at some other worthwhile activity of the young people. That which is usually reported by the media and that which usually makes the headlines is the smut and dirt. Such things tend to tarnish or destroy the name and reputation of young people.

2. They have the wrong training. Billy Graham once said that the beer drinking, wife swapping, dancing, movie going, cursing, and church-ignoring parents are training a generation of young people to be criminals. No one will deny that this is true. Let's get the home life cleaned up and it will be a tremendous help to our young people.

3. They have wrong influence. Many of our young people that go wrong today are following some older person. They just simply get in the wrong crowd. It is a shame that an adult would take psychological advantage of a young person and then lead that person into sin, but it happens all the time.

4. They have wrong desires. Young people, this is where you must be on the lookout. Get into a good church where you can be active and stay close to God.

THOUGHT: Train our youth; they have a whole life before them.

August 27 -- Matthew 8:23-27
Safe with the Lord

In my boyhood days we used to have sand storms. I have been in sand storms when you could not see the road in front of you. Where I lived we used to have one or two of these storms each year.

I remember that once my brother and I had started to go out to a swimming hole one Sunday afternoon. This had been strictly forbidden by my mother. We had left home to go to some other place, not to go swimming. To make matters even worse, we had stopped by a neighbor's watermelon patch and had helped ourselves to some of his watermelons.

As we made our way to the swimming hole, loaded with our watermelons, a sand storm overtook us. The only place of safety that we could find was an old barn that was nearby. We made our way there, being careful not to drop the watermelons. We were very frightened and we did quite a bit of praying while the storm was howling. We promised God that if He would let us escape harm from the storm we would be good and would not disobey Him or our parents again.

Now this story, although it is true, may seem to you to be just a little far fetched to illustrate our scripture for today. We should always walk close to our Savior and be conscious of His presence. Whatever our circumstances may be, we should be close enough to Him so that we can lean upon Him and be at rest and at peace in His care. He knows us and He knows our need. Read Psalm 103:14 and Matthew 6:31-32. He is able and He is ready to meet that need at once. We are indeed safe with the Lord.

THOUGHT: We may forget His presence, but He never forgets us.

August 28 -- Isaiah 40:28-31
Our Great God

His power is limitless. He created the universe and He holds it all together by His power. Moses could not lead Israel from Egypt, but God's power brought them out in due time. Joshua's power could not conquer Jericho and Canaan, but the power of God delivered them into Joshua's hands.

His presence is universal. The psalmist said that he could not hide from God. Whether he made his bed in heaven or in hell, he said that God was there. God is omnipresent, which means that He is everywhere at all times. This being true, He can help us no matter what our problems.

His knowledge is perfect. God knows everything that can be known. This means that He knows all facts, causes, operations, relations, and purposes. He knows fully all of the past, all of the present, and all of the future. Paul said, "O the depth of the riches both of the wisdom and knowledge of God! How unsearchable are his judgments, and his ways past finding out" (Rom. 11:33).

His holiness is infinite. God has never done any wrong and He has never been touched or defiled with evil or with wrongdoing or wrong motives. The holy creatures continually cry out in His presence, "Holy, holy, holy, Lord God Almighty" (Rev. 4:8).

His love is past understanding. It is eternal, matchless, and indescribable. It is not emotion or sentiment but it is the eternal outgoing of Himself toward His creation. "But God commendeth his love toward us, in that, while we were yet sinners, Christ died for us" (Rom. 5:8).

THOUGHT: The living God is my Savior.

August 29 -- Ephesians 1:1-6
Accepted in Christ

One of the sweetest truths in the Word of God is our acceptance with God. This is the real basis of our joy and happiness. We must never lose sight of Jesus Christ.

Satan always attempts to discourage God's people. He constantly reminds us of our past failures. He tells us that no person could do some of the things that we have done and still be a Christian. He keeps us looking at our sins.

We must keep looking to Jesus Christ. Our sins were laid on Him. Paul tells us that we are "accepted in the beloved." The Beloved is the Son of God. He has made a way to God for us through His own blood. Satan wants us to get our eyes off Jesus and upon what we do or what we don't do.

Let us keep looking at what God sees. He looks at Christ and not at our past sins. We know that our sins are great, but we must remember that we have been made the righteousness of God in Jesus Christ.

First Peter 2:24 says, "Who his own self bare our sins in his own body on the tree, that we, being dead to sins, should live unto righteousness: by whose stripes ye were healed."

Isaiah said, "All we like sheep have gone astray; we have turned every one to his own way; and the Lord hath laid on him the iniquity of us all" (Isa. 53:6).

God has only one basis upon which He can accept us, and that is in the person of Jesus Christ. That acceptance is made possible by our faith in Him.

THOUGHT: We must never lose sight of the Lord Jesus Christ.

August 30 -- Ephesians 6:1-9
Folding at the Foundation

Our whole society is founded upon the home. The home is the basic unit of our society. The home began in the Garden of Eden and it also fell there. Since the fall of Adam and Eve in the garden, the home has been in trouble and so has all the world.

Today we point to many needs around us. There is the need for revival in our churches and the need for holiness among our people. There is the need for honesty in our business and the need for sobriety in society.

All of these are very much needed, but the basic unit largely responsible for our ungodly world today is the home. It is sad to say that life in the average home today promotes indifference, coldness, unconcern, and a bitter disposition. Unfortunately many homes are hotbeds of drinking, use of drugs, and sexual perversion.

The Bible tells us of a man by the name of Lot who strayed from God and as a result he lost his home, his wife, and his children. King David also let sin come into his home and he had to pay an awful price. One son died and a daughter was abused by another son. Another son took the life of that particular son. Yet another son rebelled against him and tried to take the throne from him.

It is our homes and the life in the homes today that is shattering our nation, breaking down society, and bringing disgrace to the cause of Christ.

Chances are that our nation will never be destroyed from without. However, unless there is a definite change in the home, the basic unit of our society, there is a great possibility that our nation may crumble from within.

THOUGHT: Homes that are for God mean a nation that is for God.

August 31 -- John 8:12-19
Following Jesus

To the lost the Bible says, "Believe on the Lord Jesus Christ and thou shalt be saved" (Acts 16:31). To the saved the Bible says, "Follow me" (Matt. 8:22). The Bible also says, "He that saith he abideth in him ought himself also so to walk, even as he walked" (I John 2:6).

A common failure with Christians is following the life pattern of a good man, rather than following the Lord Jesus Christ. How can we follow Him? There are many things that could claim our attention, but there are four main things that we will consider today.

1. We can follow Him in Bible study. We never can really know Christ apart from Bible study. The Bible tells us about Him and His will for our lives. We should make it a practice to read the Bible every day. Some people will be able to read it more than others, but no Christian can grow and follow the Lord without proper Bible study.

2. We can follow Him in prayer. He is given as our great example in prayer. The disciples saw Him in prayer and asked Him, "Teach us to pray" (Luke 11:1). The Bible tells us, "Pray without ceasing" (I Thess. 5:17), and again, "Men ought always to pray, and not to faint" (Luke 18:1).

3. We can follow Him to the house of God. We are told that "as his custom was, he went into the synagogue on the Sabbath day" (Luke 4:16). God has ordained that we should fellowship together and He tells us to meet together regularly for this purpose.

4. We can follow Him in witnessing. Jesus never missed an opportunity as a witness. Others should be able to see Jesus in us.

THOUGHT: Follow Him and He will make you become fishers of men.

Chapter Nine

•••

September

•••

Verse to Memorize

Acts 4:12

"Neither is there salvation in any other: for there is none other name under heaven given among men, whereby we must be saved."

September 1 -- I Corinthians 10:1-13
Help When Needed

A little boy named Johnny was very inept in his daily habits. He was not obedient to his parents. He often talked disrespectfully and he was always getting in trouble because he just would not listen to his parents.

His mother, very afraid that he might grow up to become a real problem, decided something must be done about it. One day she set Johnny down and talked at length with him about things that he should do and things that he should not do to bring joy in the home. She told him that she and his father loved him very much and wanted him to be a nice boy. This would bring joy to them and would cause others to like Johnny, to say nothing of keeping him out of trouble. From then on the whole life of the young fellow began to change. He was not disobedient and disrespectful as he had been in the past. He stopped doing things that displeased the parents. Johnny was a different boy. His mother's talk had been a great help to him.

Jesus Christ is our help. He wants us to live a life that will bring joy to us and that will honor Him. He has given us the instruction that we need in the Bible and He lives within us so that He can work through us.

Through Christ's crucifixion we have pardon and peace. Through His resurrection we have everlasting life and daily victory over sin. Through His indwelling we have constant leadership of the Holy Spirit. He has made a way for us to escape the power of temptations. Jesus already has victory over all sin and He is always ready to give help to us when we need it.

THOUGHT: Our sins are great, but we are righteous in the Lord Jesus Christ.

September 2 -- Galatians 1:1-9
Good News from God

Everywhere we look today we find bad news. On the local front we are confronted with crime. News reports in the newspapers and on the radio and television are full of drug and alcohol abuse, stealing, maiming, and killing. On the national scene the situation is not better. The rioting in the streets and on college campuses of a few years ago has for the most part been replaced with deep chaos and confusion in the government. Yes, there is plenty of bad news everywhere.

However, I am glad that there is good news from God, even in a day when so much seems to be so bad. That good news is the gospel of Jesus Christ. Paul talks about this gospel and says that there is nothing to take its place. He says that if anyone preaches another gospel, we are not to pay heed to it. The one who preaches it is to be accursed.

Usually that which is newsworthy is bad. Most people are attracted to bad news. It seems that fallen man is just inclined to be that way. If I mention Adam and Eve, what is it that comes to your mind? Probably most of you would think of the fall of man and the depraved nature that man has as a result of his fall. This just seems to be the natural leaning of man. I want us to look at the good news connected with Adam and Eve. True, they sinned and we are all sinful. Along with this bad news God gave us good news. By shedding the blood of innocent animals and taking their life, He took their skins to make a covering for Adam and Eve.

Praise God for this good news, which is a picture of the death, burial, and resurrection of Jesus Christ. May God help us to turn our eyes to the good news.

THOUGHT: Do you tend to starve on bad news when you could feast on good news?

September 3 -- Psalm 24
Looking at Revival

Many great things have taken place in America because of revival. Let us look at some of them.

Colleges and universities have been born out of revival. Some of our leading schools, such as the University of Pennsylvania, as well as Princeton, Columbia, and Rutgers universities were born in revival. Church members have come from revivals. In 1800, one person in sixteen belonged to a church; in 1900, it was one person in four; and by 1950, half of the people were church members. Drunkenness, gambling, and crimes have been halted by revival. Prison reforms, Bible societies, Sunday Schools, Bible institutes, rescue missions, and orphanages have come as the result of revival.

There are certain characteristics that will bring about revival. A spirit of prayer on the part of faithful Christians and a spiritual hunger by the people of our churches will bring revival. Preaching of the Word of God by our preachers and soulwinning by our people will bring revival.

There are also certain obstacles to revival, such as a lack of concern and compassion for lost souls. Liberalism in our schools and pulpits is an obstacle. Stubborn and hard hearts that refuse to repent and turn to God are also obstacles.

Until our people are ready to turn from sin in repentance to God we will not see revival among us. We need to have clean hands and pure hearts so that we can stand in His holy place.

THOUGHT: You can have revival when you want it sincerely.

September 4 -- I Peter 1:1-9
What Christ's Resurrection Did for Me

The resurrection of Jesus Christ brings justification to believers. Paul said that He "was delivered for our offenses, and was raised again for our justification" (Rom. 4:25). Justification is an act of God whereby the believer is declared just. Had there been no bodily resurrection of Jesus Christ, there would have been no basis for justification.

The resurrection of Jesus Christ secures eternal life. The Holy Spirit goes to great lengths in Romans 6:5-11 to tell us that Jesus Christ died unto sin and lives unto God. We are to likewise reckon ourselves to be dead unto sin and alive unto God. This means that the believer has already died and now has that resurrection life of Christ, which is everlasting.

The resurrection of Jesus Christ assures us of sanctification. Jesus Christ is victorious over sin and the grave and in Him the believer shares the same victory. When one receives Christ, he is at that moment set apart unto God. As we study the Word of God, we are being set apart for the service of God. When Christ comes again, we will be completely set apart unto God. We have been saved from the penalty of sin, we are now being saved from the power of sin, and we will some day be saved from the very presence of sin.

The resurrection of Christ procures our glorification. The Bible says, "When he shall appear, we shall be like him; for we shall see him as he is" (I John 3:2). To be like Him is the desire of every child of God.

THOUGHT: The resurrection of Jesus Christ is the fulfillment of the gospel.

September 5 -- I Corinthians 15:51-57
The Power of His Resurrection

Paul wanted to know Jesus Christ in the power of His resurrection. What did he mean? Did he mean that he might know that Jesus arose bodily from the grave? No, he knew that already. Did he mean that he might know that he might be raised from the dead? No, he also knew that already. Then what did Paul mean?

Paul meant that he wanted to experience in his own body the very power that the living Christ experiences in His resurrection body. He wanted to experience daily the power of the life that arose from the grave of sorrow and bitterness that had imprisoned it.

Paul is thinking of a life that has escaped from the bondage of corruption that had held it. Jesus is not held by the bonds of death. By the resurrection He has moved into the glorious liberty of the Son of God. Paul himself also wants to experience the entirely new atmosphere that comes with the resurrection life.

Paul is saying that the resurrection life of Jesus Christ has a quality of power about it that he wants to know. He is talking about a life that has faced sin, has died to sin, and now has victory over sin. Romans 6 tells us that Christ died unto sin once, but now He lives unto God. Paul wants a life that accepts all the resurrection life of Christ.

A Frenchman became an English citizen. He was very happy about it and when someone asked him why, he answered, "We did not lose the battle of Waterloo, but we won it." He had accepted all of England's victories. We should also accept all of Christ's victories.

THOUGHT: All my failures are in me, and all my victories are in Christ.

September 6 -- Romans 10:5-13
The Message of Missions

Paul describes two ways of life, the law way and the faith way. He says that whoever takes the law way must live by the law. You and I know that no one ever lived without breaking the law except the Lord Jesus Christ. Paul has several things to say about the faith way.

The faith way is an easy way. It is unveiled in the Lord Jesus Christ. He came to earth and lived a sinless life. He took our sins to Calvary and paid the sin debt. He arose from the dead and He gives life to all who believe in Him.

The faith way is a new way. No one has to descend into the deep or ascend into heaven in order to bring Christ to us. In verse 8 we see that the message is "nigh thee, even in thy mouth, and in thy heart." This is the word of faith that Paul preaches.

The faith way is a planned way. Paul says that we are to confess with our mouth what we have believed in our heart. The message that we have believed is that of the death, burial, and resurrection of the Lord Jesus Christ.

The faith way is an effective way. Paul says that a person has salvation when he confesses what he believes. The Bible says in verse 13, "Whosoever shall call upon the name of the Lord shall be saved."

This is the message of missions, whether it be missions in our own home or in our own city. The message of faith is to be carried to the uttermost part of the earth. The message of the death, burial, and resurrection of Jesus Christ is the message that God has provided His plan of salvation.

THOUGHT: Mission plus message gives a man a great opportunity.

September 7 -- Romans 10:14-21
The Urgency of Missions

Most of us think of millions of people dying without Christ as personal Savior when we think of the urgency of missions. This, of course, is a principle upon which urgency is based. People are dying, hopeless and helpless, having never heard the message of the gospel.

Paul seems to look beyond the need of the lost to see the inactivity of the saved, and there is where he places the urgency. Yes, an urgency is brought about by the state of the lost, but an even greater urgency is brought about by the failure of the Christian to respond with the gospel.

Paul says that the lost cannot call upon one in whom they have not believed, or believe in one of whom they have not heard, or hear without a preacher. Neither can one preach unless he is sent. Paul is saying that there is an urgent need that we send preachers to the field with the gospel.

We, as the church of Jesus Christ, need to send forth those preachers who have already been sent by the Lord of the harvest. These preachers need to be sent out with the gospel message, "Whosoever shall call upon the name of the Lord shall be saved" (Rom. 10:13).

These preachers need to be sent out with a strong inner impulse to tell those in other lands that Jesus Christ has provided the way to eternal life.

These preachers need to be sent out with the power to preach, to teach, to write, to visit, and to bring the lost people to salvation in Jesus Christ.

THOUGHT: Win the lost at any cost.

September 8 -- II Chronicles 7:12-18
God's People Consecrated

Lord, my greatest is so little, and my most is yet
    so small,
When I measure it with Jesus there is nothing left at all,
And I hesitate to answer when I hear Thee call.
Can the Lord, One who owns the cattle on a thousand
    fertile hills,
He who speaks in voice commanding and the angry
    water stills--
Can the Lord, who died for sinners on the cross of
    Calvary,
Use me even in my weakness? Yes, for He demands
    of me
Perfect strength, and then He gives it in His all-
    sufficiency.
Take my greatest, Lord--it's nothing--and my
    strongest, though it's less.
Thou canst use the little, Father, and the humble
    offering bless;
And I'll serve Thee, Lord, forever, and Thy blessed
    name confess.
                               -Author Unknown

It is God's committed and consecrated people through whom He will work to bless the entire nation.

Jonathan Edwards said that he was going out to preach with two things in mind. First, every person ought to give his life to Christ. Second, whether or not any other person gave Christ his life, Jonathan Edwards would give Him his.

THOUGHT: A life totally consecrated to God accepts all tasks as God-appointed.

September 9 -- Luke 11:1-13
Prayer

Prayer is not always asking God for something. It may be just talking to Him. Dr. John R. Rice wrote a book entitled, "Prayer: Asking and Receiving."

A small boy knelt by his bed for his evening prayer, while his mother sat on the bed. When he had finished his prayer, he remained on his knees for a minute or two.

His mother then decided to question him, "What did you ask God for?"

"I didn't ask God for anything. I just told Him I love Him," the boy answered.

Isn't it true that most of the time when we pray we are asking God for something? We should also spend time in our prayer praising God and thanking Him for all His mercies to us. The Psalms are filled with the songs of praise to a loving and merciful heavenly Father.

Matthew Henry said that praising and blessing God is work that is never out of season. He said that nothing better prepares the human mind for receiving the Holy Spirit than holy joy and praise. Praising God silences fears, sweetens sorrows, and keeps hopes up.

At times when your heart seems troubled, but it is really troubled over nothing in particular, try spending a little time in God's presence. Tell Him of your love for Him and thank Him for all that He has done for you. Thank him for all that He is now doing for you and for all that He is going to do for you in the future.

It is a good thing just to spend some time with Him, not in asking Him for something, but just in talking with Him.

THOUGHT: Prayer is the highest use to which man's speech can be put.

September 10 -- Jeremiah 29:10-14
The Need in America

People in all walks of life are asking the question in one way or another, "What is America going to do; where is the stopping place?"

People in all walks of life are also trying to answer that question. The philosopher has given us his answer and the chemist has given us his answer. The geologist has given us his answer and the theologian has likewise given us his answer. Perhaps all of them are right in their sphere of thinking, but most of them fall short of the real answer. They don't seem to know the sure cure for our country's problems.

Some people say that we should pour billions of dollars into the slums for putting up new buildings. They say that we should give every family a guaranteed minimum yearly income. They say that this would stop the riots and chaos that exist in some of these places. By doing this, they say that the great need in America will be met.

Some people say that the politicians should confess up. They say that the drinkers, the drug abusers, and the immoral people should clean up. They say that the gamblers and the thieves should straighten up. Then we would have real revival and America would soon be heaven on earth.

Someone asked the great evangelist, Gypsy Smith, "How can we have revival?" His answer was, "Take a piece of chalk and draw a circle on the floor; then step inside the circle and ask God to send a revival inside that circle."

He was probably right!

THOUGHT: This world needs a one world revival.

September 11 -- Ephesians 2:1-7
The Object of God's Love

"For God so loved the world" (John 3:16). God loves man. Man is the object of God's love and this is proven by the fact that man is the object of redemption.

God slew the animals in the Garden of Eden so that man might be provided clothing and so that we might be shown a picture of the coming Savior.

God had Noah to build the ark so that He might further show His love and, again, that we might be shown a picture of the coming Savior.

God gave His people the many sacrifices and offerings to constantly remind them of His love and of the promise of the coming Savior.

Israel constantly turned aside from following God, but God kept calling them back. He continually reminded them of His love for them and He pointed them again and again to the coming Deliverer.

God sent the prophets to remind the people that He has loved them with an everlasting love. One after another He sent the prophets to warn them of the enemy and to remind them of the coming Messiah.

Jesus Christ, God's Son, came to prove God's love for man. Read Romans 5:8. He who knew no sin became sin for us. He did not come so that He might better Himself. He did not come because He needed redeeming grace for Himself. He came because God loves man and man had no way of salvation apart from Jesus Christ. This is God's way of commending (or proving) His love toward us.

THOUGHT: Love forgets all other things for the sake of the loved.

September 12 -- Acts 2:42-47
Unity in Purpose

The church in Jerusalem had many principles that would be good for us to adopt in our world today. They had the preaching of the Word of God and they had the faithful attendance of the members. They also had a unity of purpose. This is shown particularly in verses 46 and 47 in our scripture reading for today.

They continued in attendance and in fellowship. They continued in rejoicing and in praising God and in favor with the people. They also continued in having large numbers of people being saved and joining the church.

The Bible said of our Savior, "He steadfastly set his face to go to Jerusalem" (Luke 9:51). He did not falter or change His mind. This is real purpose.

The church needs purpose and it needs unity in purpose. Unless the members of the church agree on the purpose and unless they are united in that purpose, there will be little happening of any value.

The following lines have a message for many of us.

> A horse can't pull while kicking, this fact we merely mention,
> And he can't kick while pulling, which is our chief contention.
> Let's imitate the good horse and lead a life that's fitting;
> Just pull an honest load, and then there'll be no time for kicking.
>   -Author Unknown

THOUGHT: It will cost something to be loyal to our church, but it will pay great dividends.

September 13 -- Hebrews 10:19-25
Church Attendance

Acts 2:1 tells us, "And when the day of Pentecost was fully come, they were all with one accord in one place."

It is amazing to think of any church having all its members present at any one time for any service. If this happened the pastor would probably die of shock. Yet, this is what is said about the church here in the book of Acts.

The story is told of a little girl whose parents did not go to church. She attended a church that was close enough so that she could walk to it. Eventually she received Jesus as her personal Savior. One day her father said to her, "You never miss a service at that church. Why?" She replied, "I do not want to miss anything."

It is great for anyone to be able to say that about his church. It can be rightly said if the church teaches and preaches the Word of God.

We should attend church as a matter of testimony. A deaf woman attended regularly a church that had no special ministry for the deaf. She was there for every service with her Bible in her hands. Someone asked her why she did this and her answer was, "I want people to know which side I am on."

Many people get out of the habit of church attendance and once they do this they find that it is very hard to become active again. We should never allow Satan to talk us out of being in the House of God. Let us never forsake the assembling of ourselves together.

THOUGHT: "I was glad when they said unto me, Let us go into the house of the Lord" (Ps. 122:1).

September 14 -- Romans 10:1-4
The Desire for Missions

The Apostle Paul was one of the greatest missionaries of all time. This is clearly disclosed in this tenth chapter of Romans. Paul had spent much of his ministry going about the country seeking to lead the lost to Christ and to establish churches. In his letter to the church at Rome, he has something to say about his desire for his own people.

Paul expresses his real heart's cry for Israel. He is not asking that they might stop drinking or desecrating the Sabbath or living immorally. He gets to the real need of all lost people by saying that their need was "that they might be saved."

He has a deep desire for them because he sees them as they are. Paul says that Israel's zeal of God is not according to knowledge. They are groping in the darkness. He says that they are ignorant of God's righteousness and that they are trying to establish their own righteousness by their works. They are not submitting themselves to God and they are not receiving the righteousness of God, which is Jesus Christ.

Thus, Paul is spending himself in intercessory prayer for the people who are his brethren in the flesh. This is missions in the first degree. So often churches give missionaries money and send them off to a foreign field. After that, they never think of them again until they return home on furlough. There is a better way than this.

Our hearts should be so burdened for missions and missionaries that we would regularly spend time in prayer for them. We should pray continuously that the lost would be saved and that the workers would be encouraged to be strong and faithful in their work.

THOUGHT: Did God call you to stay at home, or to go to the foreign field?

September 15 -- John 3:16
The Purpose of God's Gift

"That whosoever believeth in him should not perish, but have everlasting life." This is the purpose of God's gift.

God gave His only begotten Son so that you could have everlasting life. This is the gift that He offers. Have you accepted it? His gift is a perfect manifestation of His love. Let's see what this verse of scripture says about it.

God's love, as manifested by His gift, is universal in its scope. The Bible says "whosoever believeth in Him." This includes the millions upon millions of Chinese, Indians, Russians, and others throughout the whole world.

God's love, as manifested by His gift, is individual in its application. Someone has said that the death of Jesus Christ is sufficient for all, but that it is efficient only for those who receive Him. This is entirely true and whenever the Bible says "whosoever" it is making an individual application. Each person can believe and each person must believe for himself.

God's love, as manifested by His gift, is God-like in its compassion. Who but our loving God would shed the blood of His own Son for the salvation of His enemies? "For Christ also hath once suffered for sins, the just for the unjust, that he might bring us to God" (I Pet. 3:18).

God's love, as manifested by His gift, is endless in its duration, "everlasting life." Do you have this life? You can have it right now by receiving Jesus Christ as your very own personal Savior.

THOUGHT: He gave His all for my nothing.

September 16 -- II Corinthians 5:17-21
What Paul Said about God's Gift

Paul said, "Thanks be unto God for his unspeakable gift" (II Cor. 9:15).

Perhaps neither you nor I know of a man who had a better education than Paul. He was a man of letters. He had sat at the feet of a man named Gamaliel, one of the greatest educators of his day. Yet, Paul says that the gift of God is unspeakable. Even under inspiration of the Holy Spirit, Paul cannot adequately describe the gift of God.

Paul said, "Unto me, who am less than the least of all saints, is this grace given, that I should preach among the Gentiles the unsearchable riches of Christ" (Eph. 3:8). There is the peace of God that passes all understanding. There is the love of God that overlooks the insignificance of man. There is the grace of God that overlooks the unworthiness of man. There is the keeping of God that overlooks the weakness of man. The depth of His great riches can never be fully comprehended.

Paul says that He is an unchangeable gift. We live in changing times. Everything all about us is constantly changing, except for the basic need of all men. The Bible says, "Jesus Christ the same yesterday, and to day, and for ever" (Heb. 13:8). He is ever capable of meeting our needs.

Paul also said that He is an unequaled gift. Paul is persuaded that there is no one, no thing, or no creature that can separate us from the love of God in Christ Jesus. Read Romans 8:38-39. We have known great men and women of deep love in this life. We have seen many indications of love expressed but there is no equal to the love of God as expressed in Christ Jesus.

THOUGHT: Christ is the Gift of all gifts.

September 17 -- Galatians 1:1-5
The Gift of God's Love

We have heard the question, "If you had to give a member of your family for the lives of the rest of your family, which one would you give?" This is an unfair question. Chances are almost nil that this choice would ever have to be made. Besides, we can spend our time thinking along more productive lines.

Yet, our heavenly Father had to face this very thing. Man had sinned against God. Man could do nothing about it because he had lost his prerogative to choose. At one time he had the right to choose, but he had chosen evil and as the result he lost contact with God.

God's love must reach down and do something for man or he would be eternally lost. God did not just send an angel to come into this world to redeem man. He did not just send cherubim or seraphim or any of the other holy creatures. He gave the best that He had, which was His only begotten Son, to redeem fallen man. The Son is known as the Word of God and He is known as God the Son. He is also known as the second Person of the Godhead.

This was truly a gift of love. God saw a guilty world. He knew how man had rebelled against Him. He knew of the corrupt, depraved, and defiled heart of man. He knew that man had absolutely no hope whatever if left to himself. In His love God sent His Son to redeem that man.

Hallelujah! What a gift He gave!

THOUGHT: God's Gift is sufficient for man's sin.

September 18 -- John 3:18-21
Why Is It Important to Receive Jesus as Savior?

Our acceptance before God depends entirely upon what we do with Jesus Christ in this life.

In the sport of basketball, a person must have the ability to take the basketball down the court and to fake his opponent out of position. He must be able to shoot a basket or to pass the ball to someone else who is in a better position to shoot. Then he must be able to get back down the court and take the ball away from the opposing team or keep them from scoring a basket. It is very important that he play both good offense and good defense in the game. If he can do all these things well, then he is acceptable and will in all likelihood be given a position on the team.

Salvation is different. It is important that a person live a life acceptable to God after he is saved, but he cannot live such a life before he is saved. Thus, he is not accepted by what he does but he is accepted by what Christ has already done.

Our scripture reading for today tells us that a person is condemned "because he hath not believed in the name of the only begotten Son of God." It is important that a person receive Christ so that he will not be condemned.

John 3:36 says, "He that believeth on the Son hath everlasting life: and he that believeth not the Son shall not see life; but the wrath of God abideth on him." It is important that a person receive Jesus Christ so that he can escape the wrath of God. Have you received Him?

THOUGHT: Born once and die twice; but, born twice and die once.

September 19 -- John 5:19-24
Who Decides What I Will Do with Jesus?

Have you noticed how direct the words of Jesus are in our verse for today? He says, "Verily, verily, I say unto you." This could be no more personal and individual than it is. This directness is to be found throughout the New Testament. God's Word is meant for each of us individually.

Suppose that a child is out at night and he hears a strange noise. Who decides what he will do about it?

Suppose that the children come home from school and find that their mother has made a pie before she left for the store. Who decides whether or not they will sample a piece of the pie while she is gone?

In both of these cases the child decides what he will do about the prevailing circumstances. Each person also decides for himself what he will do with Jesus Christ. Parents cannot decide for the children and brothers cannot decide for sisters. Mothers cannot decide for fathers and friends cannot decide for friends. This is always a personal and individual decision that must be made.

The matter of choice is one of the greatest dignities that God has left to man. I can choose things for myself and I do choose things for myself. I may choose to ruin my life or I may choose to surrender my life to Christ. I may choose to receive Him as my Savior and to serve Him and to glorify the Father in my life. Or, I may choose to push Him aside and make a mess of my life by rejecting the only way of salvation.

I have received Him as my Savior. Have you?

THOUGHT: Choosing to receive Jesus is the greatest choice anyone can make.

September 20 -- Ephesians 6:18-22
Prayer

Recently I was in a meeting with a committee that was dealing with a person who had been somewhat derelict about his responsibilities. After we had discussed the situation for two hours, a member of the committee summed the problem up by saying, "I believe our whole matter of difficulty is a lack of communication."

This is true in the life of many Christians. The Bible tells us, "Ye have not, because ye ask not" (Jas. 4:2).

When Gypsy Smith was saved, he immediately wanted to see the conversion of his uncle. It was not proper for a gypsy to address his elders on the subject of duty, so the young fellow began to pray for his uncle.

One day the uncle saw a hole in the boy's pants. He said, "Rodney, how is it that you wore a hole in the knee of your pants faster than in the rest of them?"

"Uncle, I have worn them out in praying for you, that God would save you," was his answer.

The older gypsy began to cry and he put his arms around the boy, pulling him to himself. Soon he received Jesus Christ as his Savior.

The Bible says, "Men ought always to pray, and not to faint" (Luke 18:1). Are you being faithful to continue in prayer and to not lose heart?

THOUGHT: Prayer is like the weather; people talk a lot about it, but do little about it.

September 21 -- Philippians 2:5-8
Humility

It is so easy for us to make more of ourselves than we should. The Bible says that one ought to take heed when he thinks that he is standing, lest he fall. See I Corinthians 10:12.

Jesus said that it is not good to take a high seat when you are invited to dinner. A more noble person than you may come in and you may have to be asked to take a lower seat. He advised that we take a low seat, then if a person comes in to whom we are superior, we will be asked to take a higher seat. This is very good advice.

It is said that Queen Elizabeth visited a hospital ward one day, where she spoke to a little girl and asked where she lived. The child said, "I live in Battersea." This is a rather poor section in the city of London.

The child asked the queen, "Where do you live?"

"Oh, I live just behind Gorrigne's Department Store," the queen replied. The queen did not lie, but neither did she want to embarrass the child.

Paul said, "Unto me, who am less than the least of all saints, is this grace given, that I should preach among the Gentiles the unsearchable riches of Christ" (Eph. 3:8).

No person is more humble than our Savior Himself. He was willing to turn apart from all that was His with the Father and to take upon Himself the form of a servant. He was willing to be made in the likeness of man and to be obedient to death, even the death of the cross. Just think about it. He did it all for you and me!

THOUGHT: The person whom God would exalt He first humbles.

September 22 -- John 1:6-13
What Can I Do with Jesus?

Pilate asked the screaming mob, "What shall I do then with Jesus which is called Christ" (Matt. 27:22)? We have heard people who were distressed by certain problems ask themselves, "What can I do?"

The most serious question that anyone can face is this question, "What shall I do with Jesus?" This is a question that everyone does face. This question will lead to another one, "What can I do with Jesus?" A person cannot evade this question. Whoever we are and wherever we are, we are faced with this matter of what we will do with Jesus.

There are two alternatives from which we *must* choose. We can receive Jesus Christ as personal Savior and let Him have our life as we serve Him or we can reject Him and have nothing to do with Him. We cannot ignore Him and evade the question. We must either receive Him and crown Him King and Savior, or by doing nothing we reject Him and crucify Him in our heart.

Notice very carefully, there are not four things that we can do, or even three things, but there is one of two things that we must do with Jesus. We must either receive Him or we will reject Him. We will either make Him our friend or He will be our foe. We will either follow Him or we will turn away from Him. We will either say yes to Him or we will say no.

We began with the question, "What can I do with Jesus?" We conclude with the question, "What have you done with Him?"

THOUGHT: Actions speak louder than words.

September 23 -- Matthew 27:15-22
A Good Question to Consider

Moses told a relative once, "Come thou with us, and we will do thee good" (Num. 10:29). Can we tell people with whom we come in contact the same thing? We cannot help other people in respect to eternal life unless we are in the family of God.

Have you ever considered the question, "What shall I do then with Jesus which is called Christ?" Have you considered it sufficiently enough to do something about it? All of us must face it and we must do something about it.

It is interesting to look out over a congregation and to see the faces of people. I have done this often and have wondered just what particular expressions meant.

I have watched the older folks. Some of them had white hair and wrinkled faces and bodies bent from the toil of the years. I have watched the middle aged people with their strong determination and their family oriented demeanor, most of them generally presenting the picture of health. I have watched the young people who are beginning to accept responsibility and who know something of the seriousness of life. I have watched the boys and girls with smiling faces and who do not have a care in the world.

The thought always comes to me, "What have they done with Jesus?" This question must be answered by them all, whether they are the aged, the middle-aged, the young adults, or the youth. Every one of them will either receive Him or will reject Him.

What have you done with Him?

THOUGHT: Salvation is yours for the asking.

September 24 -- Jeremiah 31:1-3
The Fact of God's Love

The story is told of a great missionary who had spent many years in China. One day, dressed in his Chinese garb, he stood by the river waiting for a boat to take him to the other side. As the boat approached, a Chinese man ran up and knocked the missionary to the ground. He jumped into the boat, and ordered the boatman to take him to the other side.

By this time the missionary had pulled himself from the mud where he had fallen and was beginning to wipe the mud from his clothes. The Chinese man then saw that the man he had knocked down was not one of his own countrymen but was a foreigner instead, whereupon he began to apologize very sincerely to the missionary.

The missionary got into the boat that he had ordered and asked his assailant to ride with him to the other side. The missionary frankly forgave the man for his act of violence and began to tell him about the Savior. Because of this manifestation of love, this man was saved.

The Bible tells us a great truth, "But God commendeth his love toward us, in that, while we were yet sinners, Christ died for us" (Rom. 5:8).

There is no better way to prove love than becoming sin for your enemy, paying his sin debt, and purchasing him for yourself so that he might be with you in eternity. This is just what Jesus did on the cross.

Praise God, His love is a fact!

THOUGHT: God does not love us because Jesus died, but Jesus died for us because God loved us.

September 25 -- Hebrews 12:1-14
The Message of the Cross Meets Human Needs

Every person who has lived since Adam, except Christ, has had a depraved nature and has needed a Savior. Jesus Christ said, "I am the way, the truth, and the life" (John 14:6). There is no way to God except by Him. There are certain organizations that can do much to help people. Some of these will help them to kick the alcohol or drug habit. Through certain group therapy and one-on-one counseling, they can help people find themselves and help them break many bad habits. Breaking a bad habit does not meet the complete need that a person has and it is not a way to God.

There are many good social clubs that are committed to helping people in various ways. In their own area of operation, they may do a fine job and they are to be commended for doing so. The fact is that even though you may help a family that is at the point of breaking, the main problem of the person still has not been resolved. You may help someone who has emotional needs or you may help educate and refine a person. You may help a person obtain his social needs, but the main problem still has not been resolved. The main problem is that the person needs a way to God.

On the cross at Calvary, Jesus Christ took all the sin of all mankind and paid the sin debt. He paved the way to God in His own blood and He met man's greatest need.

Only the message of the cross can overcome all the problems of man. Only it can lift him from the miry clay and set him upon the Rock. Only it can give him a new song and establish his goings. Only the message of the cross points a man to God, and then takes him there.

THOUGHT: Why should you guess about things when you can be sure?

September 26 -- Galatians 6:14-18
The Cross of Christ Is Necessary

The cross of Christ is necessary because of the power of sin. The blackest page in the history of the world is the entrance of sin into man. Sin is more deadly than cancer eating away at a man's body and bringing a certain death. Man can send a rocket to the moon and he can put a laboratory out in space. He can destroy a whole city in one giant blast but he cannot equal the power of sin.

The cross of Christ is necessary because of the tragedy of sin. Sin cursed the life of Adam and Eve as it took the tree of life from them and caused their dismissal from the beautiful Garden of Eden.

Sin brought the great destruction of the flood. It wrecked the cities of Sodom and Gomorrah. It sent the mighty man David reeling in defeat and shame.

Sin today is filling the jails and penitentiaries. It is creating poor-houses and bread lines. It is breaking up homes. It is sending children to orphanages and it is sending the parents to insane asylums.

The cross of Christ is necessary because sin is a dangerous thing. Sin ruins all that is good and pure and holy. It brings physical death and it brings spiritual death. Worst of all it brings eternal death.

It has been said that we would be better off to play with a diamond back rattler or with forked lightning or with twenty thousand volts of electricity than to play with sin. Sin is much more dangerous than most people can even imagine.

THOUGHT: The message of the cross is the only match for sin.

September 27 -- Romans 5:1-11
What the Resurrection Life
Will Do for Us

Romans 5:9 tells us that we are released from the guilt, penalty, and stain of sin by Christ's death on the Cross. Verse 10 tells us that we have the power of His resurrection life to conquer sins in our daily life. This power enables us to live a life of holiness here.

The resurrection life will sweeten up a bitter disposition and it will correct a critical attitude. The fruit of the Spirit will be seen in the life of one who allows Christ to live through him. The Bible explains to us that the "fruit of the Spirit is love, joy, peace, longsuffering, gentleness, goodness, faith, meekness, temperance: against such there is no law" (Gal. 5:22).

The resurrection life will bring deliverance from habits that produce guilt and defeat in our lives. Jesus Christ "gave himself for our sins, that he might deliver us from this present evil world" (Gal. 1:4).

Paul again tells us, "Not that we are sufficient of ourselves to think any thing as of ourselves, but our sufficiency is of God" (II Cor. 3:5).

The resurrection life will give us victory over our besetting sin. Now that we are "dead indeed unto sin, but alive unto God" (Rom. 6:11), we are not to let sin reign in our members. We have the privilege of surrendering the members of our body to God so that they may be the instruments of His righteousness.

The believer has the mighty power that raised Jesus from the dead working in him. It can keep him from sin and enable him to live the Christ-honoring life.

THOUGHT: Remember that man's extremity is God's opportunity.

September 28 -- Philippians 4:10-13
Knowing Him and Doing His Will

Two people who had not seen one another for several years met and each asked the other, "Where are you now working and how are things with you?" In time, they gave their answers. One man said that he was working with a chemical company. He said that his work was really out of his line and that he did not understand it and that it was chore for him rather than a joy.

The other man said that he was happy in his work as Christian education director in a church in a distant city. He said that he loved the people and that he believed in his work and that he was having the time of his life.

We need to find God's will for our life and then we need to follow Him in it. Whenever He leads us, He will direct our activities to His honor and for our encouragement.

Because Abraham knew God, he left his home, his people, and his country to go to a land about which he knew nothing. Because Moses knew God, he gave up the place of leadership in Egypt and the pleasures of sin for a season. He chose instead to follow the leadership of God. He became a "nobody" on the back side of the desert so that he might become a "somebody" in the will of God. Because Paul knew God, he traveled around the country. He was abused by his own people and he was imprisoned by those to whom he preached. Yet, he rejoiced that he was counted worthy to suffer for Jesus' sake. Because we know Him, we can love Him and serve Him and win the lost to Him.

THOUGHT: To know Him is to love Him sincerely and to follow Him.

September 29 -- II Timothy 1:12-14
Illustrations of Knowing One in His Person

Several of us were going on a tour of the mission field in South America. We met at the air terminal in Miami, Florida. I did not know any of the people at the time but after I was introduced to them, we came to know each other somewhat on the trip. On the other hand, I had a cousin whom I knew very well. Every time I had the opportunity to do so I went by to see him and to spend some time with him. Because of this I knew him quite well. What makes the difference?

We know a person when we recognize him. Do you recognize the Lord Jesus Christ in everything you do? Is He there to guide you and to direct you in your decision making and to give you strength for the task before you?

We know a person when we know something about what he does. Do you have a personal knowledge of the one who gave you the forgiveness of your sin, the cleansing from your guilt, and your deliverance from the power of sin? Do you know the Lord by looking to Him daily for your spiritual food so that you might grow in His grace?

We know a person when we are on speaking terms with him. Can you imagine having a close friend with whom you do not talk? If you know the Lord you need to talk to Him. We need to pray to Him without ceasing.

We know a person when we visit in his home. It is hard to believe that a person can love God and never attend services in His church. When we know Him, we will want to be with His people and to study His Word in His house.

THOUGHT: To know Him is to want to spend time in His presence.

September 30 -- Ephesians 5:21-28
Wives in Submission

Once I knew of a man that required his wife to go to the field and to work along with him. She also had the responsibility of keeping the house in shape, preparing the meals, and caring for the children. This mother had given birth to twenty-one children and the oldest child was still under twenty years of age.

God said that the woman was to be in submission to her husband. However, He did not say that she was to be a slave to him or that she was to be used only for the man's pleasure. We know of homes today where there is not the normal submission to the husband, but the husband has become a beast to make inhuman demands of the wife.

Many heartaches and broken homes come from the fact that men require too much of their wives. Many wives are required to work outside the home and to keep house and to bear children, but they get no help or sympathy from the husband. This is not what God means for the relationship when He says for wives to "be in submission."

God means for the wife to look to her husband for provision, protection, love, and companionship. She is to respect him as the head of the home and she is to allow him to make the major decisions. Sometimes the husband and the wife may not be able to agree on a specific matter that is of great importance. The husband is responsible to make the decision in these cases.

We must remember that God's instructions are for Christian homes. He has only one thing to say to the lost people and that is, "Believe on the Lord Jesus Christ, and thou shalt be saved" (Acts 16:31).

THOUGHT: Home should be a foretaste of heaven.

My Favorite Scriptures

1.

2.

3.

4.

5.

6.

7.

8.

9.

10.

Chapter Ten

•••

October

•••

Verse to Memorize

Romans 8:28

"And we know that all things work together for good to them that love God, to them who are the called according to his purpose."

October 1 -- I Timothy 5:14-15
The Woman in God's Work

God says that women are to get married, help establish a home, bear children, and be the keepers at home.

What a great place the woman has. When God wanted a man to serve as priest and prophet, He called upon the godly woman Hannah to be his mother. When God wanted a faithful helper for his servant Paul, He directed Lois and Eunice to instruct Timothy in the scriptures. When God wanted a forerunner for the Lord Jesus Christ, He chose the home in which there was a godly mother named Elisabeth.

Eve became the mother of all living and it was through her and her seed that God promised a Redeemer. When God wanted a mother for His only begotten Son, He chose a virgin named Mary. She was a humble woman who would teach the boy to be "strong in spirit" and to "increase in wisdom" and to be "in favor with God and man."

Many of us can remember good mothers. My mother was not taught in the scriptures as some people I know today are. However, she had great faith and she encouraged her children to go to church and to serve the Lord. Had it not been for her insistence that I be faithful in church, I might not have come to the Lord Jesus Christ when I did. I owe a great deal to my mother.

Women have a great part to play in service for God. I praise Him for the many women who love Him and serve Him.

THOUGHT: God has a place of service for every person who is a Christian.

October 2 -- John 14:27-31
Perfect Peace

The second grade was having "show and tell." One little girl showed the stub of a ticket and told about her family going to Disney World. She told of the different things they saw and rode. When she told about riding the roller-coaster and how high and fast it was, the other students asked her if she was not afraid. "No," she said, "my Daddy had his arms around me."

Daniel was a man of prayer. He was in a strange land. Yet, even in a strange land he was true to His God. His custom was to pray three times a day. He was told that if he continued to do that, he would be thrown into the den of lions. Daniel continued to pray as he had before and, sure enough, they threw him into the den of lions.

After having Daniel thrown into the den of lions, the king spent a sleepless night. He went to the den early the next morning and found Daniel well, because "my God hath sent his angel, and hath shut the lions' mouths" (Dan. 6:22). Daniel had perfect peace in his situation.

When Jesus was about to be crucified and to return to the Father, He told the disciples that He was leaving His peace with them.

The world can give peace that will last for a short while, but that kind of peace will soon fade away. The peace of God is a lasting peace.

The Bible says, "Casting all your care upon him; for he careth for you" (I Pet. 5:7). Let us rest in the peace that only God can give.

THOUGHT: The peace of God far exceeds all of our understanding.

October 3 -- Romans 1:14-16
The Power of the Gospel

Some years ago during World War II, the United States dropped atomic bombs on two cities in Japan. The cities were almost totally destroyed. The destruction was such that Japan, seeing what could happen to their entire country, made an unconditional surrender and laid down her arms of war.

Today even more powerful bombs have been developed. We have added to the arsenal the hydrogen bomb and the cobalt bomb, and who knows what else. These bombs are capable of destroying entire cities.

America and Russia have the power to put people on the moon. They have the power to send space ships to Mars and to keep people in space for months at a time. None of this technology is capable of saving a soul or forgiving sin.

The power of the gospel is the power of God Himself. The power of creation has placed this universe in motion. All of the stars, planets, and other heavenly bodies are so created and placed so as not to interfere with each other and to stay in position for thousands of years. The power of God rolled back the waters of the Red Sea and let the people go through on dry ground. The power of God went into the fiery furnace and kept the fire from touching the three Hebrew children.

The power of the gospel can forgive sin and break habits. It can restore homes and it can heal broken hearts. It can meet the need of every person. It is the power of God unto salvation.

THOUGHT: Our need is not the power of destruction, but the power of God unto salvation.

October 4 -- John 3:16-18
The Person of the Gospel

The gospel of Christ is more than a creed, a covenant, or a document. The gospel is a person.

Many people today say that they are following Moses. Well, Moses was a great man and he accomplished much for God. It was through Moses that the law was given. He spent forty years on the back side of the desert in preparation for delivering Israel from Egypt. He challenged Pharaoh and did indeed lead Israel out of Egypt. However, this does not make him a savior to the world.

David was a great king who did much for Israel and who left us many psalms that call our attention to God. He is called the man after God's heart, but David has no saving power. There are many who refer to David as a great man and who revere him highly, but he cannot save anyone.

The person of the gospel is the Lord Jesus Christ. Paul said that he preached the gospel. Then he defines the gospel as the death, burial, and resurrection of Jesus Christ. He says that if we have believed anything else for salvation, we have believed in vain.

The Bible says, "He that hath the Son hath life; and he that hath not the Son of God hath not life" (I John 5:12).

In our verses today, God says that a person is saved because he believes on the Son or he is lost because he does not believe on the Son.

Yes, the gospel is much more than a creed, a covenant, or a document. It is a person and that person is Jesus Christ, the only begotten Son of God.

THOUGHT: The gospel is indeed a living message because Jesus is a living person.

October 5 -- Genesis 22:1-14
Abraham's Ram

Abraham waited a long time for the promised son to be born. Just a few years later, God told Abraham to take his son Isaac to one of the peaks of Mount Moriah and to offer him as a sacrifice to God.

What would be your response if God had asked you to do something like this? Don't let anyone tell you that this is a myth. It is something that actually happened.

Abraham took his son and had his servants to get the wood. They set out for Mount Moriah, which was probably about fifty miles away. When they reached the place he took the wood for the burnt offering and laid it upon his son. He took the fire and a knife and they left the servants. They began making their way to the top of Mount Moriah.

Isaac spoke to Abraham in verse 7 and said, "Behold the fire and the wood: but where is the lamb for a burnt-offering?" Abraham said in verse 8, "God will provide himself a lamb for a burnt-offering." The altar was built, the wood was laid on it, and Isaac was bound to it. Abraham took the knife to slay his son, but the angel of the Lord stopped him. He said in verse 12, "I know that thou fearest God, seeing thou has not withheld thy son, thine only son from me." Abraham then saw a ram caught in the thicket. He released his son and took the ram and sacrificed it to God.

This is a picture of the sacrifice of Jesus Christ in our stead. We could not pay the sin debt, but He paid it for us. He became our substitute. Let us thank God for this good news and let us share it with others.

THOUGHT: The Lord Jesus Christ is both the Offerer and the Offering for our sins.

October 6 -- Psalm 85
Spiritual Awakening

We hear the question asked, "What will it take to bring a spiritual awakening to America?" I would like to suggest several things that would help to answer this.

It will take obedience to God's Word. In Nehemiah 8:1 the people said, "Bring the book." This is what we need today. People are studying almost everything except the Bible. We cannot obey the Bible if we do not know what it says.

It will take high moral standards. The morals of our beloved country are doubtless at an all time low. Alcohol and drug abuse, pleasure madness, sports mania, sexual perversion, wild entertainment, and the like are replacing the conscious need for the presence of the Lord.

It will take a reverence for the Lord's Day. To many people today, Sunday is no more than any other day. The day is spent in work and in pleasure, in buying and in selling, and in other ways to take people away from worshipping God.

It will take brotherly love. Our country is in the midst of a terrible situation now because of a lack of brotherly love. So much of the time it is evident that each person is interested in himself and in no other.

It will take honest stewardship of finances. I know of people who cannot have a spiritual awakening because they will not give to God that which is His. This thing stands between them and God.

It will take increased church attendance. God can do nothing for many people unless He does it between eleven o'clock and twelve o'clock on Sunday morning.

THOUGHT: To give a spiritual awakening, God needs man's cooperation.

October 7 -- Luke 15:17-24
Welcome of Grace

The prodigal son presents several contrasts. He left home, turning his back upon the father; he returned home seeking the father. He left with plenty; he came back broke. He left looking for pleasure in the world; he returned looking for peace with the father.

A man who was down and out came to my door today. He was destitute and hungry. When he asked for something to eat, he reminded me of the prodigal son. He was dirty and ragged and it was evident that he was having rough times. We see many people who are like this today.

The prodigal son reached the end of his rope. He came to the place that he could not bear his circumstances any longer. He said that even the hired servants in his father's house had plenty to eat, while he had nothing. He decided that he would go back to his father's house and ask not to be a son, but to be made a servant.

His father had different thoughts. When the prodigal son returned, the father embraced him and kissed him and began to shower upon him many wonderful gifts. He gave him those things that would identify him as his son.

This is what God does for the sinner that repents and returns to the Father. Only the grace of God would receive one who has turned his back upon home and upon the Father. Only the grace of God can cleanse one from the filth of sin and give him the place of a son. This is what God does for everyone who turns to Him.

Have you received the wonderful welcome of grace from the Lord?

THOUGHT: God's grace is greater than our sins.

October 8 -- Ephesians 4:7-16
Assignment or Opportunity

Many of us go about our Christian life as if it is a real chore, a task rather than a joy. The Lord never intended that it should be this way.

I heard a story about two young boys who were asked to explore a certain piece of woods and then come back and report on what they saw.

The first boy went out and was gone about ten minutes and then returned. When he was asked what he saw, he replied, "Nothing! Just a lot of trees. Woods are the same everywhere. If you've seen some, you have seen them all."

The second boy stayed past the ten minutes, twenty minutes, even thirty minutes. When he finally returned, he was asked the same question, "What did you see?" He described the beautiful scene that was his in the woods. He had looked at the blue sky and had seen little white clouds like lambs floating overhead. He had seen birds and squirrels going from tree to tree. He had run along the brook and had listened to it sing as it rolled over the roots and rocks on the bottom. He said that he wanted to go back again sometime to follow the trails that the little animals made as they went down to the brook for water.

What was the difference between the two boys? One of them had an assignment, but the other had an opportunity.

Many Christian workers do not have the joy that God wants them to have. They do not see the Christian life as a golden opportunity, but they see their Christian life as a very difficult assignment.

THOUGHT: Cheerfulness makes a great difference in the service you render.

October 9 -- II Chronicles 15:12-15
Seeking

One reason why many people make so little of their Christianity is that they are only half-hearted in their service.

Amaziah was a man like that. He was king over Judah for twenty-nine years. The Bible says, "And he did that which was right in the sight of the Lord, but not with a perfect heart" (II Chron. 25:2). Do you know some people like that? They want to have a hand in the world, but at the same time they want to be called faithful Christians. The two do not mix and if we try to mix them, we get into trouble.

Amaziah failed to follow the Word of God. He ended up as a defeated king and died in the hands of the enemy. This happens to every person that disobeys God.

One day a rich young ruler came to Jesus and wanted to know what he must do to inherit eternal life. Jesus told him that he was not really sincere because he could not call Him good without recognizing that He was God. After Jesus told him to keep the law, the young man said, "All these things have I kept from my youth up" (Matt. 19:20).

Jesus said, "If thou wilt be perfect, go and sell that thou hast...come and follow me" (Matt. 19:21). The rich young ruler proved his half-heartedness by leaving sorrowfully because he had great possessions. He was not willing to give up his riches in order to turn to God.

If we seek to walk with God, then we must give up the world. Read what the Bible has to say in Deuteronomy 10:12-13 and in Matthew 6:33. Proverbs 8:17 tells us, "Those that seek me early shall find me."

THOUGHT: Seeking people find God.

October 10 -- John 7:1-13
Why Is Everybody Talking about Jesus?

Today we hear many remarks about Jesus Christ. The Son of God is brought into every walk of life. However, it is not in a way that recognizes Him as the only begotten Son of God, the Savior of the world. He is being thought of and talked about as the jolly-good-fellow who causes us to have good fortune in everything we do.

Jesus is often the subject of conversation, singing, and jesting. Why do they use Him? There are many famous men who have had more acceptance with the world than He ever had. Why do they not use Napoleon, Plato, Washington, or Kennedy? All of these were more widely accepted in their day than Jesus of Nazareth was.

Jesus was born in a stable in the little town of Bethlehem. He grew up in the home of poor and humble people. He spent His early years in a carpenter's shop. He never was more than a hundred miles away from His home. Of course, He also never saw a television set, heard a radio, flew in an airplane, or rode in an automobile.

Yet, the Son of God has the most revered name of any person who ever lived. "Thou shalt call his name JESUS: for he shall save his people from their sins" (Matt. 1:21). Paul says that He has been given a name that is above every name. He says that one day everyone will bow before Him and proclaim Him Lord. They will give glory to God the Father. Read Philippians 2:9-11.

Yes, people get very religious sometimes and talk much about Jesus, but He did not come just to be the subject of conversation. He came to be received and to be the Savior of all those who will call upon Him. Have you called upon Him to save you?

THOUGHT: There is life for a look at the Savior.

October 11 -- Proverbs 29:1-18
We Need a Vision of God

To many people God is just a good influence. To them He is not a person who has a right to us and to all we own. We need a better understanding of who God is and how He works. We need to understand our responsibilities to Him.

We need a vision of God's sovereignty. Some people today feel that they are their own boss and that no one has any authority over them. They feel that God has no right to require anything of them. However, God made us all and He gave us all life. He sustains us all and He has complete sovereignty over each one of us.

We need a new vision of God's power. There are many people who feel that for them there is no deliverance from their habits and their problems in life. God is all powerful and we miss much by failing to look to Him. Job said, "I know that thou canst do every thing, and that no thought can be withholden from thee" (Job 42:2).

We need a new vision of God's love. God is love and He loves His creation. He who loved us enough to die on the cross in our stead surely loves us enough to give to us His best in this life. People often feel that they are not loved because everything does not always go their way. It is best for us to have things the way God knows we need them.

We need a new vision of God's holiness. Holiness is a lost word with man, yet God is still holy and He requires you and me to be holy also. The Bible says, "Thou art of purer eyes than to behold evil, and canst not look on iniquity" (Hab. 1:13). In Isaiah, God is said to be holy more than thirty times. We need a vision of God as He is.

THOUGHT: He who knows God walks with God.

October 12 -- Romans 6:1-10
Remember

You probably have read these ten verses before. They may be rather familiar to you but I hope that you will go back and read them again and again. Their message is so very important. These verses give us truths that we must remember if we are to have assurance of salvation.

These verses here speak of the death, burial, and resurrection of the Lord Jesus Christ. Verse 3 speaks of the Christian being baptized into the death of Christ. So, we know that Christ died. Verse 4 speaks of us being buried and raised with Him. So, Christ was both buried and raised from the dead. Verse 9 tells us that Christ was raised beyond, or on the other side of, the grave. He is not on the same side of the grave as we are. We are facing the grave but He is looking back upon the grave. He lived, He died, and He was buried; now He is risen. He does not have to go through death and the grave again. We still have to go through them unless He returns before our time to die. Verse 10 says that He died unto sin once and now He lives unto God.

Did you notice that these verses merely state the facts about the death, burial, and resurrection of Christ? They do not ask us what we think about the facts! They only tell us that these are the true facts about Jesus Christ.

Now, remember that our Savior has already completely paid the sin debt. It was paid by Him shedding His blood. That is why He died on Calvary. We need to remember these things as we daily serve Him. It will make us more profitable as we serve Him.

THOUGHT: Believe what God says, not what you want to think.

October 13 -- Romans 6:1-11
Reckon

We have already discussed the fact of the death, burial, and resurrection of Jesus Christ as it is reported in the first ten verses of Romans 6. Just to review briefly, in verse 3 we have His death and in verse 4 we have His burial and resurrection. In verse 9 we see that He was raised beyond the grave and that He is not on the same side of the grave as we are now. Also, in verses 9 and 10 we see that He died once and He does not need to die again for sin. Thus, the sin question is completely settled in Him.

Now we come to the word we will study today. Reckon is a bookkeeping term. When a bill is paid, that payment is reckoned to your account. When the business manager looks over your account, he sees that what you owed has been paid in full.

Verse 11 tells us to reckon all the truths of verses 1 through 10 to our own account. "Likewise reckon ye also yourselves." Just as they apply to Jesus Christ, apply them to yourselves. This means that by faith we have all the benefits of the death of Jesus Christ. Verses 3 and 4 tell us that we died, we were buried, and we were raised again. Verse 5 tells us that we were raised like Him. Verse 6 says that the old man, the sinful nature, is destroyed and now we do not have to serve sin. Verse 7 says that we are freed from the sinful nature. Verses 9 and 10 tell us that we will die no more, but we are alive to Him.

This will not become real to us unless we reckon it to be so as we are told to do in verse 11. Let us be sure to do that very thing.

THOUGHT: By faith we have all the benefits of the sacrificial death of Christ.

October 14 -- Romans 6:1-12
Reign

Back again we go to our study in Romans 6. Don't let our dwelling on this passage cause disinterest on your part. We are dealing with some very important matters to us. They are important to us if we want to have assurance and peace and if we want to be a good testimony to others.

It is great to know that the work of Christ on the cross has been accepted completely by the Father and that the sin question is now settled forever. It is also great to reckon this to ourselves personally, that is, to apply to ourselves all that Christ has done.

Now, as those who are saved by faith in Christ and as those who are delivered from the dominion of sin, we are not to allow sin to reign in our mortal bodies. What does this mean? It simply means that those of us who know Jesus Christ as personal Savior do not have to commit sin. Verse 12 gives us specific instruction that we are not to allow sin to have control over our activities.

Why should I allow an evil tongue to continue to control me when my evil tongue has died? Why should I let an immoral mind continue to control me when I have been delivered from immoral things? I died when Jesus Christ died and I was raised when Jesus Christ was raised. All that He did on the cross has been applied to my account. Because of this I am delivered from the old sinful nature. Because of the reality of these truths, I am not to allow the old nature to reign over me any longer.

We will continue our study of this passage later by discussing how to regulate ourselves in this regard.

THOUGHT: My victory over sin is Jesus Christ.

October 15 -- Romans 6:1-13
Regulate

By this time you may be beginning to wonder about reading these verses for the last several days. Again, let me emphasize to you the importance of this passage of scripture and the necessity of our being familiar with its teaching.

My favorite word of this series of study is the word regulate. We are to regulate our activities. Verse 13 tells us that we are not to yield to sin, but we are to yield to God. Thus, we regulate our lives by yielding the members of our body to God so that they will be used to glorify Him.

We will never be able to do this unless we remember that we have died and have been raised again in Jesus Christ. The victory that He has over sin we are to reckon as our own victory. In order to keep sin from reigning in our lives, we must regulate the usage of the members of our body by yielding them to our heavenly Father. How can this be done?

In James 4:7 we are told, "Submit yourselves therefore to God: Resist the devil, and he will flee from you." If we are to expect victory over sin and the devil, we must submit to God. We regulate our lives as we pray and read His Word. We regulate our lives as we attend services in His house and as we tell others what He has done for us. When we follow the directions He gives to us in His Word, we will be able to regulate our lives so that we can live them for His honor.

THOUGHT: Don't try to do for yourself what Christ has already done for you; rely upon it.

October 16 -- Matthew 21:28-32
Doing It Now

So many people plan to serve God, but they plan to do it later on in life, not now. Can you remember some things that you have planned to do as a Christian service but you have put them off until you finally forgot to do them? Many people are still unsaved today simply because they have carelessly put off their own salvation.

Some of you who are reading this today may have planned to read the Bible through but you never did get started. Some of you may have thought about talking with a neighbor about the Lord, but you just never got around to doing it. Some of you may have thought about visiting that widow or that sick person, but other things have taken your time and you never got around to making that visit.

One of the sons in our scripture reading for today said that he would not work. Later he repented and did the task that he had been asked to do. The other son said that he would work, but then he did not do what he had been asked to do. Which of the two sons do you suppose pleased the father?

Have you taken a look at your life recently to see which of these two sons you are like? If so, what did you find?

In the hustle and bustle of life it is often very easy to think of many good things that we would like to do tomorrow. Then when tomorrow comes, if it does come at all, there are things that prevent us from doing those good things that we had thought about doing. Let us give some thought to doing those things now rather than waiting for a tomorrow that may not come.

THOUGHT: Obedience is better than sacrifice.

October 17 -- Matthew 28:1
The Fate of the Sabbath

Jesus Christ came into the world and grew up into manhood. He began his priestly work at about thirty years of age. He went into the synagogues on the Sabbath day to teach and to preach. The Lord said, "The sabbath was made for man, and not man for the sabbath" (Mark 2:27). Any time the ox was in the ditch on the Sabbath, it was lawful to get him out of it. When one was hungry on the Sabbath, it was right for him to prepare food and to eat it. These things are illustrated in the work of the Lord Jesus and His disciples. The Pharisees and the scribes were opposed to the teaching of Jesus because His teachings contradicted their own teaching.

Our verse for today says two things that are significant. First, it says that the Sabbath came to an end. Up until the time when our Substitute arose from the grave, worship on the Sabbath day was recognized and practiced. Then, upon the resurrection of Jesus Christ, the day of worship was no longer Saturday, the Sabbath day. The scripture for today says, "In the end of the sabbath," and it not only speaks of that particular day, but it speaks of worship on the Sabbath day.

Second, it says that Sunday, or the first day of the week, became the day of worship. It was upon the first day of the week that Jesus arose from the dead. It was upon the first day of the week that He began to appear to His disciples. It was upon the first day of the week that the disciples began to meet. It is upon the first day of the week that every one is to "lay by him in store, as God hath prospered him" (I Cor. 16:2). Our day of worship is no longer the Sabbath, the last day, but it is Sunday, the first day.

THOUGHT: We are to serve God, not days.

October 18 -- Matthew 28:1-8
The Resurrection

All four gospels give us a detailed account of the crucifixion of the Lord Jesus Christ. All four gospels give us an equally detailed account of the resurrection. Both the crucifixion and the resurrection are important and both are proven by the Word of God.

Our verses for today tell of two of Christ's disciples, Mary Magdalene and that other Mary, thought by some to be Mary the mother of Jesus, coming to the tomb. They did not expect to see Jesus. They did not expect Him to be risen from the dead. We are told that they came to "see the sepulcher." However, when they arrived there at the tomb they found something very different.

The angel of the Lord had come in the midst of an earthquake. He had rolled the stone away from the door of the tomb and had sat upon the stone. Is it not a strange thing that the angel said nothing to the keepers of the tomb, but that he spoke to the women? The angel said, "Fear not ye...he is not here, for he is risen." There is no need to try to teach to the lost the great doctrines of the Bible. One must know Christ as Savior before he will be very interested in the resurrection or in any other doctrinal teaching.

These women who came to the tomb were given the message of the resurrection. They saw the place where He lay and quickly they went to tell it to the other disciples.

We should ask ourselves two questions. Am I a child of God? Am I faithfully taking the message of salvation to others? We must answer both of these questions affirmatively if we are going to be faithful to His will for our lives.

THOUGHT: "Seeing" the resurrection will make "servants" out of Christians.

October 19 -- Matthew 28:10-15
The Devil's Attempt at Cover-up

We have heard much in recent years about attempted cover-ups that have plagued our federal government. Our scripture tells us that these modern events are not the first attempts at cover-ups.

Guards were placed around the tomb of Jesus to keep Him from escaping or to keep someone from stealing away the body. When they heard that Jesus was risen, they were in deep trouble. They went to the chief priests and elders and reported that Jesus was not in the tomb. These religious leaders, rather than being happy that Jesus was their Messiah, were very much upset. They paid large sums of money to the keepers of the tomb to tell people that while they were asleep the disciples came and stole the body of Jesus away.

If they were asleep, how would they have known that the disciples came? Besides, there were four rows of soldiers around the tomb. They were facing both toward the tomb and away from the tomb. All of them would not have been asleep at the same time. It would have been impossible for someone to come through their ranks and to steal away the body of Jesus. This is just another attempted cover-up by Satan's forces that failed.

The devil never will get away with his false claims. We know that Jesus arose from the grave. The devil lost that battle and he has lost the war with the Son of God. We know that one day the Almighty God will cast him into the lake of fire. There he will be tormented forever.

THOUGHT: We can hide nothing from God. You can be sure that your sin will catch up with you.

October 20 -- Matthew 28:16-17
A Great Appearance

The disciples had walked with the Lord and had been taught by Him for over three years. With one exception, they were with Him in Gethsemane. They were with Him when one of their number betrayed Him into the hand of the enemy. They forsook Him and fled. Afterwards they followed Him afar off as He was led from one official to another. They were afar off as He endured the mock trial that ended in His being condemned to death, the death on the cross.

The disciples were there when He was crucified. They were there when His body was taken down from the cross and laid in the tomb that had been borrowed from Joseph of Arimathea. The One whom they had loved, whom they had followed, and whom they had depended on as a teacher, was now gone. Their hope had been shattered.

Once again, they see Him! He appears to them in Galilee, just as He had told them that He would do. All hope had been gone and their hearts were lonely and broken. Then, in their midst there appears the One whom they thought that they had lost.

Have you ever had such a great appearance in your spiritual life? Has there been a time when to you it seemed that there was no hope? With disappointments and heartaches and loneliness showing their ugly faces, did you feel that there was no hope? Then, Jesus appeared! Maybe it happened while the preacher preached or while the Sunday School teacher taught. Maybe it happened while a friend talked to you or while you read your Bible. What a great appearance it was!

The disciples worshipped Him. Let us do the same.

THOUGHT: All our hope lies in the arms of faith in the Lord Jesus Christ.

October 21 -- Matthew 28:18
A Great Claim

What a statement is made in this verse! Only Jesus Christ who had been crucified and buried and was now risen again could truthfully make such a statement.

The Lord did not tell the world how long we would need this great power of God. He just said, "All power is given unto me in heaven and in earth." He is the One who existed with the Father before the foundation of the world. He is the One who came into this world by way of a virgin birth. He is the One who lived here a sinless life. He is the One who went to Calvary and died a victorious death and who is now risen from the dead. He is the One who has been completely obedient to the Father. Now all power is given to Him.

Is He your Savior? He has power to forgive sin. Our sin is removed as far from Him as the East is from the West. Read Psalm 103:12. He has put our sin behind His back and He will never remember it against us again. Read Isaiah 38:17 and Jeremiah 31:34. He is the only one who can forgive sin.

Is He your Comforter? He has the power to give you peace and comfort in the midst of your heartache and trouble. He can bring peace to your soul when your friends and your loved ones fail you.

Is He your daily Guide? He wants you to surrender to Him so that He can guide you around the many pitfalls that would bring unpleasant experiences your way.

Is He your constant companion? He wants to be and He will be if you will let Him. Remember, "All power is given unto me in heaven and in earth."

THOUGHT: Jesus meets every need.

October 22 -- Matthew 28:19-20
A Great Commission

These verses have been used many times down through the years to challenge the faithfulness of the children of God. They have been called the Magna Charta of the Christian faith. Much instruction is here given to the people of God, but the sad truth is that so many people do little or nothing to carry out these commands. Let us now look at verse 19 and the first half of verse 20.

First, we are told to go. The way that God has chosen to reach the world with the gospel is by having people going and telling others as they go. We are not asked whether we would like to go or not; we are commanded to go. We should all be faithful to this call.

Second, we are told to evangelize. The word "teach" in verse 19 is not the word for instruction; it is the word for getting people saved. We are to go with the gospel with the purpose of getting people in all the nations of the world saved.

Third, we are to baptize those who trust Jesus Christ as Savior. Baptism is meant to be an outward sign of an inner cleansing. We can see then that baptism clearly is something that comes after salvation, not before it.

Fourth, we are to teach them, or instruct them, in all the things that He has commanded us. What a great plan Christ has given to us! He has ascended back into heaven. He is there at the right hand of the Father. However, He has left the great work of evangelizing the world to us. We are His "disciples" for this day and time.

He has very clearly told us what we are to do. As we read these verses, surely we can understand them. Now, what are we going to do about it?

THOUGHT: Souls are crying! Men are dying!

October 23 -- Matthew 28:20
A Great Promise

How wonderful God is! He never gives us work to do without giving us all we need in order to get it done. He has told us in these verses to go with the gospel and to get people saved. He has told us to baptize them in the name of the Father, Son and Holy Spirit. He has told us to instruct them in all His wonderful teachings.

This is a big job, isn't it? Not one of us is able to do this on our own. Jesus has also told us here, "And, lo, I am with you alway, even unto the end of the world." What a great promise this is from the Savior to His servants.

We should understand that there are at least two ways for us to expect the presence of the Lord Jesus Christ. One way is the presence of His person. The other way is the presence of His power.

We are told that we have the presence of His person when we receive Him as our personal Savior. He comes to live within us in the person of the Holy Spirit. The Bible says that if we have not the Holy Spirit we are none of His.

We have the presence of His power in our life only as we are faithful to Him in carrying out the great commission in our life. Are we going out and evangelizing, baptizing, and instructing? If we are not, then we have no right to expect His power in our life.

Let us purpose in our hearts that we will be faithful to Him. When we do this we can expect His great promise to become real to us.

THOUGHT: Practice the presence of Jesus Christ.

October 24 -- Psalm 8
How Excellent Is His Name!

Did you ever go out at night and look up into the heavens and try to count the stars that fill the sky? Of course, man cannot begin to number them. We have sought out certain designs and we have tried to find certain star groups. When we look at the Milky Way, we just have to stop counting. It is utterly amazing. We are told that there are many, many galaxies that are much more complex than our own galaxy, the Milky Way. God placed them all there. How excellent is His name!

I am also amazed when I go out into the woods and study the different kinds of trees and other growth there. Here is a pine tree and there is an oak tree. Over there is a maple tree, or a gum tree, or a cypress tree. When I go out into the cultivated fields and find potatoes, peanuts, cotton, and so many other kinds of plants growing from the same soil, I am again amazed. Who directs all this growth? It is the One of whom the scripture says, "How excellent is thy name."

The Person we are speaking of is my God and my Father. Is He also your God and your Father? I can very well remember the time when I came to receive Jesus Christ as my own personal Savior. For a long time I had wanted to be saved, but I was afraid that my "crowd" would laugh at me and call me a sissy. I am glad that I finally realized that salvation was the greatest need of my life. Then I surrendered my heart to Christ and He saved me. Now the great God of creation is also my Savior.

How excellent is His name!

THOUGHT: His name is above every name.

October 25 -- John 10:1-21
I Am Glad that God Knows

How wonderful it is to be safe with Jesus Christ as Savior, keeper, and Lord. The great hymn writer must have understood this when she wrote, "Safe in the Arms of Jesus." In Isaiah 43:1 the Lord says, "I have called thee by thy name; thou art mine."

There are homes in which the children are not safe and wanted. There are homes in which the husband and wife do not love each other. There are some tragic situations in this world where there is no love or concern for those who should be closest together. But God knows and He cares.

In verse 14 of today's scripture lesson we read that He knows His sheep. Here in this verse we are told that those of us who are saved are called sheep. We are told that our dear Savior knows us and that we know Him.

In Nahum 1:7 we are told, "He knoweth them that trust in him." Sometimes we forget the most important things. I know of a pastor who was scheduled to preach a funeral at three o'clock one afternoon. At the appointed time, he was not there. Someone called his home and found that he had forgotten and was out mowing the yard. Yes, we do forget. However, God does not forget.

In Job 23:10 the Bible tells us, "He knoweth the way that I take." Someone has said that there is nothing that can be known that God does not already know. Psalm 103:14 tells us, "He knoweth our frame." Isn't it great that He does know all there is to know about us?

Since He does know all about us, we can safely leave ourselves in His loving care and under His direction.

THOUGHT: God knows my name, my life, and also my eternity.

October 26 -- I Thessalonians 4:13-18
It Is True

In fulfillment of the Old Testament, Jesus came and gave Himself a ransom for the sin of the world. It had been predicted by the prophets that He would come and "when the fullness of the time was come" He did come (Gal. 4:4).

The New Testament tells of His coming and about His death at Calvary. It tells about His resurrection from the dead and about His ascension back to the right hand of the Father. It also promises that He will return to this earth.

There are many people today who are asking the same thing that many people of past years have asked, "Where is the promise of His coming?" People do not want to believe what they do not understand. So many of them do not understand these things because they do not read the Bible. Even as Jesus told the Pharisees, they can tell the seasons but they cannot discern the times.

If a person is willing to accept the promises from God's Word about the second coming of Jesus, he should also be expecting His soon return. All things point toward His soon coming. For example, Israel is a nation again. The European Common Market is looking like the Roman empire. There are wars and rumors of wars all around the world. There are reports of earthquakes in many places. The morals of the world appear to be about the worst they have ever been. Even modern communication and transportation and breath-taking developments in technology seem to be working hand in hand to help set the stage for His return.

Is it true that He is coming again? Yes, my friend, you can rest assured that it is true.

THOUGHT: Yes, praise God that He is coming. Are you ready for Him?

October 27 -- Isaiah 6:1-7
Sterilizing the Tongue

Read again verses 6 and 7. This is speaking about some sin of the lips or tongue. The tongue is perhaps engaged in more sin than any other part of our body. What other member of our bodies needs such purifying or sterilizing?

There is the lying tongue. "All men are liars" (Ps. 116:11). There is the quick speaking of self-confidence in Luke 22:33, where Simon Peter had to "eat his words." There is the proud tongue. King Nebuchadnezzar said, "Is not this great Babylon, that I have built" (Dan. 4:30)? Of course, we can read about what happened to him and to his great Babylon.

There is the gossiping tongue. What a curse the tongue proves to be in this regard. Too many people are involved in such things. There is the unclean tongue. Paul said, "Put off...filthy communications out of your mouth" (Col. 3:8). There is the questioning tongue of doubt. Thomas said, "Except I shall see...I will not believe" (John 20:25). He had missed the fellowship with the disciples and he had missed seeing the Lord on that historic occasion.

There is the angry tongue. How often we say things to people and about people that we should not say. Paul says, "Let not the sun go down upon your wrath" (Eph. 4:26). There is the dumb (silent) tongue. So many people fail to witness because too many of the other things are wrong with their tongues.

Have you had your tongue sterilized lately? "If we confess our sins, he is faithful and just to forgive us our sins, and to cleanse us from all unrighteousness" (I John 1:9).

THOUGHT: The tongue is a small member, but it is a burning fire.

October 28 -- Ruth 2:17-19
What Will Your Day Be?

Let us think about the question that is asked in this verse, "Where hast thou gleaned today?" You may remember this account from the book of Ruth. Naomi and her husband and two sons had left Israel and had gone into Moab several years before this time. While there in Moab, Naomi's sons had married two of the Moabitess women. Then Naomi's husband and her two sons had died in Moab. One of her daughters-in-law had decided to stay in her own country but the other daughter-in-law, Ruth, returned with Naomi to Israel. In order to get food enough, Ruth was going behind the reapers and was gathering up that which they had left behind in the fields. When she came home with such an abundance of grain, Naomi asked, "Where hast thou gleaned today?"

Does anyone ever ask you where you have been gleaning in reference to the Word of God? Is there such a growth in your Christian life that it attracts the attention of others and moves them to inquire about it? Where have you been gleaning lately? Have you been reading the Word of God? Have you been faithfully attending Sunday School? Have you been faithfully attending the preaching services? Have you been getting spiritual food from other church ministries so that you might be better prepared to be a good witness for Him?

Does your gleaning reflect favorably on your Christian life? Or, do you need to change some of the places where you do your spiritual gleaning so that your gleaning will be more in abundance?

THOUGHT: Gleaning in the Word will produce an abundant fruit in the life.

October 29 -- Romans 1:18-23 and 2:11-16
Living in Darkness

You may have heard of people living their entire life in an area where there are no electric lights, no running water in the homes, no bathrooms, no automobiles, and no modern farming tools. Are these real people? Do they have souls that will live somewhere forever? It is rather hard for most people in America to have any real understanding of what this means. However, it is true. Many, many people in our world live and die without ever seeing an electric light bulb, a mouth-harp, an automobile, or a yo-yo.

What about these people? Where do you think they will be in eternity? The verses that we have read tell us that they are all responsible to God and that they are without excuse. There is the law "written in their hearts" that some things are right and that some things are wrong. The very creation itself tells them that Someone is responsible for making the world and that man could not have done it himself. There is a God and the people have a desire to know that God. This is the "Light, which lighteth every man that cometh into the world" (John 1:9). These verses also tell us that if they never know that God, then they will "perish."

It is necessary for us to do all that we can to get the gospel to the ends of the world. Jesus said, "No man cometh unto the Father, but by me" (John 14:6). Those people who are living in darkness can never call upon One whom they do not know. They cannot know Him unless someone tells them about Him. Are you giving to the work of missions so that these people might have a chance to know Him?

THOUGHT: No preaching means no hearing and no sending means no preaching.

October 30 -- Jeremiah 31:34; Hebrews 8:12 and 10:17
Gone Forever

Someone reported passing a highly ritualistic church a few days before what is called "Good Friday." Outside the church was a big bulletin board with these words upon it: "This is the day--Good Friday--when we come together to remember the sins for which Christ died."

Why should we want to remember that which God does not remember against us? God said, "I will forgive their iniquity, and I will remember their sin no more" (Jer. 31:34). That is good enough for me! Of course, it is not as easy for me to forget my sin as it is for God to do so. I remember them all too well. At times I catch myself remembering my sins and holding them against myself. God does not do that, for He forgives and He forgets those sins.

Do you have assurance that your sins are forgiven? Have you come face to face with Jesus Christ and taken your sins to Him and left them with Him? Even though you may remember them at times, do you rejoice that He does not now, nor will He ever, remember them against you again?

It is such a wonderful thing to be saved and to know it. If you know that you are saved, you have reason to rejoice. My friend, I tell you that you should rejoice. If you do not know that you are saved, get on the telephone and call your pastor or some other Christian today. Tell him that you need some help in order to be saved. Then, when the Lord saves you, your sins will also be gone forever.

THOUGHT: Gone, gone, gone, gone; yes, my sins are gone.

October 31 -- Ephesians 4:1-6
There Is Just One Way

"All aspirins are alike." Is that statement true or false? How many times do we hear such a statement? Some people want to prove that all aspirins are alike and other people want to prove that they are not alike. Whether all aspirins are alike or not, we will leave that to the druggists to prove or disprove.

There are other statements that are heard many times, such as, "We are all working toward the same goal," or, "We are all going to the same place but we are just traveling different roads." We have even heard it said, "We are all children of God."

It should be understood by each of us that there are not several ways to God. There is only one way. Jesus Himself said, "I am the way, the truth, and the life; no man cometh unto the Father, but by me" (John 14:6).

We are also told in Acts 4:12, "Neither is there salvation in any other: for there is none other name under heaven given among men, whereby we must be saved."

Often people who may mean well will take scripture out of its context and make it say something that it does not mean. By doing this they deceive many people into believing that there are many ways of salvation. Let us be very careful to whom we listen and be alert to what they say to us.

A great habit for one to have is that of reading a portion of scripture each day. This is how God talks to us and this is how we will know His will. Don't let anyone deceive you. Study the Bible so that you can know it for yourself.

Acts 16:31 says, "Believe on the Lord Jesus Christ, and thou shalt be saved."

THOUGHT: Begin the day with God and He will end the day with you.

Chapter Eleven

•••

November

•••

Verse to Memorize

Psalm 100:4

"Enter into his gates with thanksgiving, and into his courts with praise: be thankful unto him, and bless his name."

November 1 -- Titus 3:1-8
Not by Good Works

Years ago Dr. M. R. De Haan gave a very good allegory about "Bill Dollar," a five dollar bill. The story will not be repeated exactly as he told it, but the meaning will be essentially the same.

Bill Dollar was a very proud five dollar bill because of all that he had done. His fine deeds were well known and were lauded by many.

Soon after he was born he was given to the grocery man in payment for groceries. The grocery man gave Bill to the paper man for delivering the morning paper. He was then given to the department store for a pair of shoes. The man at the department store gave him to the farmer in exchange for vegetables. The farmer gave Bill to the mechanic for working on his tractor.

The mechanic gave Bill to the poor man who did some work in his yard. The poor man gave him to his landlord for rent on his house. Bill eventually made his way into the missions fund of the local church.

Then suddenly it happened! The teller at the bank detected the fraud. Bill was a counterfeit five dollar bill. He was immediately taken out of circulation and set aside to be thrown into the fire and burned.

Let us learn this well. No matter how much good a person thinks he is doing, every one of us is born a counterfeit and we must be born again. We are not genuine unless we are sealed with the Holy Spirit.

THOUGHT: Is your life counterfeit, or is it real?

November 2 -- Mark 8:34-37
How Much Is Enough?

The wealthiest man in town had just died. Many friends were coming by to pay their last respects to "Cap'n Jack." In the group were a father and mother and their eight year old boy. As they left, the mother said to the father, "How much did he leave?" The father replied, "I really don't know." The little boy said, "He left all he had."

The Bible says, "Lay not up for yourselves treasures upon earth, where moth and rust doth corrupt, and where thieves break through and steal: But lay up for yourselves treasures in heaven, where neither moth nor rust doth corrupt, and where thieves do not break through nor steal: For where your treasure is, there will your heart be also" (Matt. 6:19-21).

There is nothing wrong with us getting some great possessions in this world. The danger comes when we let our possessions get us and when we put them before the Lord.

> There was a man in our town, and he had good health,
> But recklessly he squandered it accumulating wealth.
> And when he saw his health was gone, with all his
>   might and main
> He squandered all the wealth he'd won to get his
>   health again.
> And when with neither health nor wealth, he in his
>   coffin did lay,
> The preacher couldn't say a thing except, "Friends,
>   let us pray!"
>   -Author Unknown

Let us use wisely what we have been blessed with here.

THOUGHT: Do you own your wealth or does your wealth own you?

November 3 -- Jude 14-19
Real or Unreal

The Bible says, "For that which I do I allow not: for what I would, that do I not; but what I hate, that do I...For I know that in me (that is, in my flesh) dwelleth no good thing: for to will is present with me; but how to perform that which is good I find not" (Rom. 7:15,18).

Paul was honest with God, with himself, and with everyone else. He was aware of his own sinful nature and the lust of the flesh. He was aware of his inability to do anything about it. He would agree completely with our Savior when He said, "For without me ye can do nothing" (John 15:5).

Many people make claims of holiness that are not proven by their lives. Verse 16 of our scripture for today says, "These are murmurers, complainers, walking after their own lusts; and their mouth speaketh great swelling words."

Do you make claims about your spiritual life and your own goodness that you know are not true? Everyone else knows the truth about it, so there is no need for you to make boasts about a holy life that you are not living.

You may remember Ananias and Sapphira. In Acts 5 they made claims about themselves that were not true. Their report was that they were giving to the church all the money they received for a piece of property. God knew that they were lying and he struck them dead.

Let us not try to make others believe that we are what we are not.

THOUGHT: Let God do His work in your life and you will not have to pretend.

November 4 -- Psalm 37:1-10
Commit Thy Way unto the Lord

Someone told the story of a ship that was caught at sea during a storm. The ship was being tossed about and was in danger of being destroyed. The furniture had been tied down securely. All the passengers had been confined to their rooms for their own safety.

One man, frantically afraid, made his way along the handrails to the pilot's quarters to get any information that he could about their fate. The pilot knew that he could not make himself understood above the roar of the storm. He knew that he would not be able to tell the passenger his plans to guide the troubled ship between two rocks and into the bay ahead. He simply turned, looked at the man, and smiled. The passenger turned, went back to the other passengers and said, "Don't be afraid, all is well. I have seen the pilot's face."

Through the admonition of the Word of God, we can see our Pilot's face and be aware of His presence. He can always make Himself heard above all the rumble and roar of the evil of this world. The Bible says in various places, "Fret not thyself...trust in the Lord...delight thyself in the Lord...commit thy way unto the Lord...rest in the Lord and wait patiently for him..."

> I will commit my way, O Lord, to thee,
> Nor doubt Thy love, tho' dark the path may be,
> Nor murmur, for the sorrow is from God,
> Yea, there is comfort ever in Thy rod.
>
> -Author Unknown

THOUGHT: Have you seen the Pilot's face lately?

November 5 -- Galatians 6:7-9
Never Give Up

Do you ever become discouraged? Do you ever feel like saying, "I might as well give up; I just cannot hold out any longer?" Everyone has times of despondency. We all face the times when we do not feel as if there is any use trying. Dr. Bob Jones used to say, "Just keep on keeping on."

Paul became weary about a physical problem that he called a thorn in the flesh. He said that this thorn was given to him "to buffet me, lest I should be exalted above measure" (II Cor. 12:7).

When Paul then begged the Lord that this thorn be removed, the Lord said to him, "My grace is sufficient for thee: for my strength is made perfect in weakness" (II Cor. 12:9). Paul went on to say, "Therefore I take pleasure in infirmities" (II Cor. 12:10).

A missionary returned home on the same ship with a president of the United States. Upon reaching New York, he saw great crowds of people and a brass band. It turned out that the band and all the people were there to welcome the president home. No one came to meet the missionary. He was discouraged and said, "Lord, I have given my life on the mission field. Crowds of people come to welcome the president; no one welcomes me home. Is my work for Thee not worth it?" Then it seemed to him that the Lord answered, "Son, you are not home yet."

Remember especially verse 9 of today's reading, "And let us not be weary in well doing: for in due season we shall reap, if we faint not."

THOUGHT: Every pay day does not come at the end of the week.

November 6 -- Hebrews 9:16-22
Anything Costs Something

Someone has made the statement, "Salvation is free, but it is not cheap." Someone else has changed the words of the second part of that statement, so that the statement reads, "Salvation is free, but Christianity costs you something." Both statements are true.

God gives to us salvation by faith in His Son, but salvation cost God His Son. Who would want to give up a child or another loved one for the life of another? None of us would want to face that test. Yet, our heavenly Father faced it knowing that there was no other way for His fallen creation to be redeemed. He gave His only begotten Son so that we might be saved. Our salvation cost God His Son.

My Christian life costs me something. I cannot be pleasing to God and live a selfish, greedy, and lustful life here. I must deny myself, take up my cross, and follow Him. This simply means that I will say "no" to the desires of the old self and say "yes" to God and His will for my life.

Once there was a young man who wanted to become a doctor. He knew that there would be a lot of money coming his way if he went into the medical profession. God did not want this, but He wanted this young man to be in the ministry. The young man turned his back upon all the financial gain that could have been his and he followed God and His leading into the ministry. He went to a foreign mission field where he would have the bare necessities of life. It cost him to serve God. However, there is coming a day in which he will reap what he has sowed. Read Galatians 6:7-9.

THOUGHT: God gave me His salvation; I ought to give Him my life.

November 7 -- Matthew 8:23-27
Jesus and the Storm

"Peace, be still" (Mark 4:39).

This is what a well-known song quotes Jesus as saying. When He spoke those words the sea was stilled and the storm was quieted. This is the way Jesus works in our lives if we will only let Him.

Jesus had been busy. He had recently preached the sermon on the mount, which is recorded in Matthew 6 and 7. In chapter 8 we read that He had met and healed the leper. He had healed the servant of the centurion and He had healed Peter's wife's mother. He had also preached the message concerning discipleship and He had issued the call to the people, "Follow me."

Now Jesus and His disciples enter a ship and start across to the other side. Jesus goes to sleep. Suddenly there arises a storm on the sea, as often happens in that area. The disciples are afraid and they call the Savior and say, "Lord, save us: we perish."

It would be easy for us to rebuke the disciples for not having faith in Jesus. He does seem to rebuke them for being of "little faith," but I think that I see another angle to what He says. The disciples did not try to plow through the storm by themselves. They called upon the only one who could help them in such a time as this.

As long as you and I are willing to commit our all to Jesus Christ, we can have peace. As long as we rely upon Him and trust in Him, we can have peace. This is the peace of God that passes understanding, even in the time of storms.

THOUGHT: Relax in the Lord Jesus Christ and you can relax in the world.

November 8 -- Mark 2:1-12
Forgiving Sins

This man in today's reading could do nothing for himself for he was completely helpless. He had palsy, a disease that is a type of paralysis. Not only was he paralyzed, but he was shaking and could not control the movement of his limbs. You may have seen people like that. The only way that this man could ever hope to get to see Jesus was for someone else to take him to the Lord.

There were those men who cared enough to do something about it. They came to where the sick man was and they put him on a small pallet. They brought him to the house where Jesus was and they made arrangements for him to be put before the Lord. When they got him to Jesus, He cared enough to heal the man physically and to forgive his sin. Jesus said to him, "Thy sins be forgiven thee." Don't you know that these were wonderful words to this man! Then, to prove to the people that He could do this, He told the palsied man, "Arise, and take up thy bed, and go thy way into thine house." Indeed, joy must have flooded the soul of this man.

Are you saved? Can you rejoice in complete salvation in Christ Jesus? If so, what are you doing to bring those who do not know Him to where He is? Do you have as much concern for those around you as these four men had for the man with palsy?

There are many people who need our concern. Just as Jesus was moved with compassion for this sick man, even so let us ask God to cause us to be moved with compassion for the lost souls around us today.

THOUGHT: God is not looking for men of ability, but men of availability.

November 9 -- Mark 8:1-9
God Will Provide

What are we going to do? We all ask this question from time to time. With some of us, it is just a habit; with others of us, it becomes a part of fear.

Did you notice how Jesus said that these people did not have enough food to last them until they could get home? They had eaten their last meal but they were now loosing their strength fast. They were some distance from their home and they would faint before they could reach home.

The disciples had some food but it was not much and it was not nearly enough for a crowd of people this size. Someone has said, "Man's extremity is God's opportunity." When these disciples brought what they had to Jesus, He made it what was needed. There were even seven baskets full left.

What do you suppose that we can do about the crises that we face from time to time? Somehow, I believe that God will provide for us that which we need.

First, He wants us to commit ourselves to Him. Second, He wants us to commit what we have to Him. When we have done this, He will make what we have sufficient to do what needs to be done.

It has been said, "You have everything you need to do what God wants you to do right now." Do you believe that? Commit your all to Him and He has promised that He would direct your paths.

THOUGHT: A little becomes a lot when it is fully committed to God.

November 10 -- Mark 2:1-12
Healing the Sick

In a recent study we read these verses and saw how four men were concerned for another man. We saw how they brought him to Jesus and how Jesus forgave his sins and sent him back to his own house carrying his own bed.

Today I want us to see something else in this passage. Jesus healed the sick man, but these four men had a big part in the healing. If they had not shown their concern by giving their time and making the effort to get the man to Jesus, chances are that Jesus would not have seen this man. The man would not have been healed.

How much time do we give to help Jesus in His healing ministry? Just tonight someone called me and requested prayer for herself and for a brother and sister. This afternoon I called a family to inquire about their physical condition. Earlier today I went to the hospital to visit with and pray for some people. How often God uses our visits and our prayers to bless the lives of others.

In this day in which we live we are too little concerned about our neighbors. Few people visit and offer assistance any more. Few people offer to run errands or do little jobs around the home for those who are in need. Few people offer to make themselves available so that the Lord might bring healing through them.

There are many people around us who need either physical healing or spiritual healing. Let's ask our heavenly Father to make us more concerned about these people.

THOUGHT: He does the blessing, but we can be the channels through which the blessing flows.

November 11 -- Mark 9:14-29
Power over the Devil

Many people do not know what you mean when you mention demon possession. There is much more demon possession today than many people want to believe.

Our verses today tell us of an evil spirit that had possessed a young man and was doing some terrible things with him. He could not speak or hear and he had seizures. He was tormented by this demon.

No one, including the disciples, had been able to give the poor man any relief from the demon. Jesus cast the demon out but not before the young man had been thrown to the ground, foaming at the mouth and crying out in pain. Yes, demons are very real. They possess the lost people and they oppress the saved people.

How often do we think of someone who is a drunkard or who is otherwise living a very filthy and degraded life when we think of demon possession or demon oppression? This is not always the case. Some of the worst cases of demon activity is among those who outwardly seem to be very pious. Selfishness, stubbornness, envy, jealousy, an antagonistic attitude, a bitter and mean disposition, and many other things of this nature are all the result of demons.

We should be very careful to avoid demonism. It cannot be conquered just by relying on our own power. We should stay close to the Lord Jesus Christ and be committed to Him and rely upon His power.

THOUGHT: Submit yourselves to God. Then resist the devil and he will flee from you.

November 12 -- Matthew 6:19-24
Seeing Single

To have single vision means that both eyes see the same thing. God has so created the eyes that they both transmit what is looked upon to the brain at the exact same time. If this is not true, your eye is not normal and you need to visit your eye doctor. Sometimes this perfect balance is distorted and a person has "double vision."

If one is going to serve the Lord Jesus Christ, he must see the same thing that Jesus sees. In our scripture for today our Lord says, "No man can serve two masters." If the eye is single, we will be busy laying up treasures in heaven where moth and rust do not corrupt. Only the one who "walks with the Lord" is laying up treasures in heaven. The person who follows the world system is laying up treasures on earth and all of this will end up being wasted effort. Remember that sin is very, very deceitful.

Once a man came home drunk. His wife had waited up for him until she could wait no longer and then she had gone to bed. She left a candle burning for him. When he came home in his drunken condition, his eyes told him that there were two candles. He thought, "No use to waste a candle." So he blew out one of the candles he saw, but he was then left in the dark. He had been deceived.

Sin is very deceitful and it will leave you in the dark. People desperately need to have their spiritual eyes opened by the Lord Jesus Christ. Read Matthew 20:32-34.

Is your eye seeing single or is it seeing double? Watch and pray so that you will not be deceived.

THOUGHT: How can two people ever walk together except they be in agreement?

November 13 -- Revelation 3:7-13
Open Door

Every Christian ought to look to God for leadership. All too often we make plans and ask God to bless them. We should seek God's leadership in our planning. If He is not in the planning, He will not be in the carrying out of the plans. We should seek His will in all our plans.

The Lord has set before you an open door. Do you know what it is? Some of you work in an office. Some of you work in a mill or in some other place of service. You should be as convinced that God has placed you in the work that you do as the pastor is convinced that God has placed him in the ministry. Whatever we do, we should do it according to His holy will.

Yes, God has set before you an open door. It is an open door to pray and to be a good witness. It is an open door to study the Bible and to be an example of the believer. Have you seen this open door in your place of service? Do you take every opportunity you have to step through the door that He has opened for you?

God has also given you this day as an open door. Let us go out today and let others see that He is in us. Let them hear about Him from our lips and see Him in how we live our life today.

The Lord has set before us many open doors. No man can shut the doors that God opens, just as no man can open the doors that God shuts. Let us step through the open doors while they are still open to us.

THOUGHT: May God help us to know when a door is open before us.

November 14 -- Numbers 13:26-33
"Fraidy" Cats

This whole chapter tells about the twelve spies that Moses sent to spy out the land. Ten of them gave bad reports. They said that they were like grasshoppers in the sight of the people in the land. They agreed that the land was beautiful and that there was plenty of food. However, they were just "fraidy" cats and would not say let's go and take the land. Two of the spies were brave and trusted God. They were Joshua and Caleb, who said, "We can take it. God has given us the land; let's go get it." Israel listened to the ten other spies and they did not go into the promised land. Out of that group of twelve spies, only Joshua and Caleb lived to enter the land forty years later.

Where I grew up down on the farm my dad raised strawberries. We used to put up scarecrows to keep the birds away. Some of the birds would stay out in the woods, but it was hard to frighten away the mockingbirds. They would sit on top of the scarecrow and sing at the top of their voice and advertise the fact that they were full of strawberries.

God has placed many fruits of blessing in this life for you and me to enjoy. Do we let the "fraidy" cats scare us away from these blessings? Do we allow the scarecrows of fear, doubt, laziness, self-interest, and worldliness to rob us of these blessings?

Let us this very day feast upon God's blessings that He has so graciously provided for us to enjoy. Why should we wait for forty years to enjoy His blessings? Or why should we risk not even enjoying His blessings at all?

THOUGHT: You and God make a majority in the community where you live.

November 15 -- Exodus 3:1-5
Holy Ground

Moses was born in Egypt. When he was just a little baby the Egyptians issued a decree to kill all of the Israelite baby boys that were under two years old. His parents made a basket and put Moses in it. They hid the basket in the edge of the river hoping that he would not be killed by the Egyptians. One day Pharaoh's daughter found Moses near the river's edge among the bulrushes and she took him home with her.

Moses grew up in the palace of Pharaoh with his own mother as his nurse. God had arranged it that way. Thus, even though he grew up in the Egyptian palace, he was taught all about the God of heaven.

In later years Moses had to leave Egypt because of the danger to his own life. He then came to the land of Midian. This is where God wanted him to be so that he could be prepared to go back to Egypt and lead the people of Israel to freedom. God was able to get Moses' attention and to show him what he was to do. God said to Moses, "The place whereon thou standest is holy ground." I have often heard it said that all ground is holy ground for the child of God.

Have you let God speak to you and show you what He wants you to do? Has He spoken to you about leading people out of bondage and into the freedom from sin? The place where you are right now is holy ground. Why don't you let God speak to you about that loved one or that neighbor? Pray for that person and then go to visit him or witness to him in whatever way you can.

THOUGHT: For the Christian all ground should be considered holy ground.

November 16 -- Romans 8:28-30
Called of God

A Christian is one who has heard the call of God and who has come to follow Him. Note that the Greek word for church is the compound word "ekklesia." The first part of the word, "ek," means "out from." The second part of the word comes from the Greek word "kaleo," and it means "to call." Thus, the meaning of church is a group of people who are called out from the world, with the understanding that they are to follow the Savior.

The Christian has at least five calls from the Lord. He not only is called out of some things, but he is also called into some things.

1. He is called out of darkness (this is conversion). See I Peter 2:8.

2. He is called into fellowship (this is communion). See I Corinthians 1:9.

3. He is called to holiness (this is consecration). See Leviticus 20:7.

4. He is called for blessing (this is compassion). See I Peter 3:9.

5. He is called unto glory (this is coronation). See I Peter 5:10.

The Christian's call begins with his salvation, at which time he is washed and cleansed in the blood of Jesus Christ. This settles the salvation question forever. Next there is the call to fellowship with like-minded believers. Then there is the matter of his Christian service, which means that he is to be separated from the world. As he grows in holiness he can be a blessing to others and he can come to have sweeter fellowship with God and with his fellow Christians. When the Lord is finished with him on earth he will be called to heaven.

THOUGHT: Have you made your calling sure?

November 17 -- Ephesians 6:10-18
Prayer

Paul here describes the armor of God. He does not stop with six pieces of armor as so many people feel that he does. The seventh piece of armor, and certainly one of the most important pieces, is prayer. Six is the number of man and of failure. Seven is the number of completion and of victory. Paul gives us some good instruction when he says, "Praying always with all prayer and supplication in the Spirit, and watching thereunto with all perseverance and supplication for all saints."

No doubt the greatest privilege God ever gave His children is the privilege of prayer. We can come to Him and talk with Him about everything that concerns us in any way. What are your prayer habits?

Many of the great men of God have spent several hours each day in prayer. It is our opportunity to bring the lost, the sick, and the troubled to God in prayer. By doing this we have a part in their lives.

Pray for God's preachers. No group needs prayer more that they do. Most people would be shocked to know of the pressures that are faced by the ministers of the gospel. There is nothing that is too small or too big to be brought to God in prayer. Whatever it is, He can give His direction concerning it.

Remember the request that the disciples made to Jesus, "Lord, teach us to pray" (Luke 11:1). Let that same request be yours today.

THOUGHT: Men ought always to pray and not to loose heart.

November 18 -- Ephesians 5:1-17
Growing as a Christian

A group of babies is a beautiful sight to see. Some are large and some are small. Some are long and some are short. Some have red hair and some have no hair. Some are fat and some are skinny. Yes, they are a beautiful sight but if you were to see that same group a year later and they were the same size, they would not be so beautiful. The hair, the eyes, and the other features might be as before, but unless there had been proper physical growth, there would be very much concern about them. No parent would be happy about a child that remained the same size a year after it was born.

When people come to know Jesus Christ as personal Savior, they become babies in Christ. Many things may differ about them, but they all are the same in that they are babies in Christ. It would not be proper to expect the same growth in each one of them. However, we should expect at least some growth in each one. Just as the physical growth differs some from baby to baby, even so spiritual growth differs some from new Christian to new Christian.

There must be the proper feeding and the proper exercise and rest. There must be the proper health necessities if we are to expect the babies to grow as they should. This is also true with the spiritual growth of new Christians. There are certain necessities that they must have.

The scripture reading for today deals with the growth in the life of the Christian. We will continue to look further at the great instruction given in these important verses as we meditate on the next few devotionals.

THOUGHT: Many Christians are stricken with spiritual anemia.

November 19 -- Ephesians 5:1-17
Growing as a Christian

How long have you been a Christian? Have you grown in your knowledge of Jesus Christ and His will for your life? You might not have grown as much as others you know, but you should be able to recognize at least some growth in your life since you became a Christian.

Our scripture reading for today says, "Be ye therefore followers of God, as dear children." The first thing that a Christian must do is to follow God. What does this mean and how can we follow Him?

There is listed in these verses a series of aids or instructions to help us to follow Him. Did you notice them as you read the verses? Let's look again.

1. Walk in love, verse 2. Christ has made it possible for us to do this. He takes bitterness and hate away as we let Him. He loved us when we were sinners and were without strength. It is now our duty to love people who are sinners.

2. Avoid moral corruption, verse 3. Paul says that these things are not to be named among us. You may have seen a young lady with a certain kind of hairdo and have commented, "That just does not become her." Paul says that an immoral life is not becoming for the Christian.

3. Don't be a joker, verse 4. Paul does not mean that a Christian cannot tell funny stories and laugh. He means that we are to be serious about some things. We should not make a joke out of everything. Many people go out of their way to try to make everything funny. Paul says that this just is not commendable for the Christian.

We will continue our study of growing as a Christian next time.

THOUGHT: Growth in Christ calls for some of your personal energies.

November 20 -- Ephesians 5:1-17
Growing as a Christian

Let us begin where we left off the last time. We were pointing out in these verses the instructions that are given to promote Christian growth.

4. Don't be deceived, verse 6. As sad as it is, many people are being deceived today and they are being led astray by well-meaning people. We need to abide by "thus saith the Lord." This is one reason why it is so important to be in a church where the gospel is preached. Do not be willing to take someone else's word about things. Spend time in the Word of God and see what He says.

5. Walk as children of light, verses 8 through 10. What is the light? Light is the teaching of God's Word. We have no light from heaven except as it comes to us in Jesus Christ. We receive this light from Him as we study the Word.

I know that I am saved because the Bible tells me to "believe on the Lord Jesus Christ, and thou shalt be saved" (Acts 16:31). I know that I have everlasting life because the Bible says, "He that believeth on the Son hath everlasting life" (John 3:36). I know that I will not be lost because the Bible says that I am "kept by the power of God" (I Pet. 1:5). I know that the Holy Spirit lives in me because the Bible says that my body is the "the temple of the Holy Ghost" (I Cor. 6:19). I also know that I can live for God because the Bible tells me that "I can do all things through Christ which strengtheneth me" (Phil. 4:13).

Our light comes from the Word of God. How much light do you have? Do you have more light now than when you were first saved?

We will continue this study next time.

THOUGHT: Listen to "thus saith the Lord," not to "thus saith man."

November 21 -- Ephesians 5:1-17
Growing as a Christian

When we began this study, there was no intention that it should last this long. However, it is our desire that there be help here for the Lord's family. We will continue to point out the instructions for Christian growth.

6. Do not be identified with evil, verses 11 through 13. Today many people want to follow the ways of the world and at the same time be identified with the Lord's people. Anything that would bring reproach upon Christ is darkness and we should have no fellowship with it. The dance, the movie theaters, the use of alcoholic beverages and drugs, and many other questionable things will have to be avoided if you want to grow as a Christian. As a Christian, and because I love God and because I want to be like Him and to please Him, I must have no fellowship with the works of darkness.

The question is often asked, "How will I know what to leave off, since so many of my friends do these things that you have mentioned?"

Verse 13 says that we will know these things as we become more acquainted with the Word of God. The Bible is "light" and it is light that reveals or "makes manifest" the evil things that we call the darkness. As we faithfully study God's Word and as we grow in Him, the area of darkness will become more and more clear to us. As it becomes more clear to us we can turn from it and determine that we will "have no fellowship with it."

We will continue our study of growing as a Christian next time.

THOUGHT: The devil is the father of liars but our God is Light.

November 22 -- Ephesians 5:1-17
Growing as a Christian

Awake! Walk circumspectly! Redeem the time! These should be words that cause us to exercise great caution. They should be words that set off an alarm within us.

7. Light is available, verse 14. Today we hear so many people say, "I just cannot understand the Bible." Of course, a Christian should not say this. We have the Holy Spirit living within us to guide us into all truth (see John 16:13). He is the author of the Word of God and He wants to teach us. This verse says that the reason we do not have more light is because we are asleep. Don't be as one who is asleep or as one who is dead. Be as one who is wide awake and alive in Christ Jesus. Study and seek to understand the Word and He will give you the light that you need. This makes for good Christian growth.

8. Walk straight, verse 15. Circumspect is an interesting word. The definition is given for the Greek word as "most exact; most straitest." If a thing is exact, it cannot be more exact or most exact. Yet the Holy Spirit seems to be saying to us that we are to be very careful and exact in our walk for God. We are showing Christian growth when this straight walking is realized in our life.

9. Use your time profitably, verse 16. We need to take some time from good and worthwhile activities. We need to spend this time with our God in the study of His Word. We need to spend time in some serious meditation on the Word. We need to use our time for Him and His work rather than to use it all for self.

We will continue our study of growing as a Christian next time.

THOUGHT: Fools often waste their time, but wise people don't.

November 23 -- Ephesians 5:1-17
Growing as a Christian

One thing that is always of concern to a Christian is knowing the will of God. Verse 17 says that we should understand what the will of the Lord is. All that has been said in these devotions will help us determine what His will is for us. We must be willing to live clean lives and to avoid that which would contaminate us. Unless we are willing to study His Word, there is no way to know what His will is. We are proving that we want to know His will when we follow the instructions of the first half of this chapter. What are some areas of God's will for us?

First, it is His will that every person be saved. He clearly says that He is "not willing that any should perish, but that all should come to repentance" (II Pet. 3:9).

Second, it is His will that we let Him use us. "I beseech you therefore, brethren, by the mercies of God, that ye present your bodies a living sacrifice, holy, acceptable unto God, which is your reasonable service. And be not conformed to this world: but be ye transformed by the renewing of your mind, that ye may prove what is that good, and acceptable, and perfect, will of God" (Rom. 12:1-2).

Third, it is His will that we depend upon Him. "I will therefore that men pray every where, lifting up holy hands, without wrath and doubting" (I Tim. 2:8).

Fourth, it is His will that we become more like Him. First Thessalonians 4:3-17 gives us a list of seven things that have to do with our sanctification and His will for us.

Learn to practice these teachings. Be the Christian that God wants you to be.

We will continue this study next time.

THOUGHT: God's will for you can be known only through His Word.

November 24 -- Ephesians 5:18-20
Growing as a Christian

When a person is converted, the Holy Spirit comes to live in the body of the believer. When Jesus Christ informed the disciples that He must leave them, He also told them of the Comforter, the Holy Spirit. The Comforter would come to take His place in them, not just with them. We are told that our body is the temple of the Holy Spirit.

Paul said, "I am crucified with Christ: nevertheless I live; yet not I, but Christ liveth in me: and the life which I now live in the flesh I live by the faith of the Son of God, who loved me, and gave himself for me" (Gal. 2:20). As Paul lived by faith, he was surrendered to the Lord and the Holy Spirit directed his life. Therefore, Paul could say that his life was actually Christ living within him.

When Paul says, "Be not drunk with wine," he is not saying that it is all right to drink some wine as long as we don't drink a lot. He is saying that we are to be controlled by the Holy Spirit rather than by the things of the world. His subject is the fullness of the Holy Spirit. It is not how much wine we should drink. It is the will of God for His children that we turn from the degrading things of the flesh and the world. These things have been described in the earlier verses of this chapter. It is the will of God that we allow the Holy Spirit to fill us and to direct all of our activities.

As we grow in our Christian life, the Holy Spirit will control more and more of us. We will then produce more and more of the fruit of the Spirit that we read of about in Galatians chapter 5.

THOUGHT: To be filled with the Holy Spirit is to be controlled by Him.

November 25 -- John 1:40-42; 46
Come and See

We have two good illustrations before us of someone bringing another to Jesus. When Andrew came to know Jesus, he went out right away and brought his brother, Simon Peter, to the Savior. When Phillip was saved, he went and found Nathanael and he shared his knowledge of the Savior with him.

The normal activity of a Christian is to tell others about Jesus Christ. The Bible says that we are to go into the highways and hedges and that we are to compel the people to come. The Lord said, "Go ye therefore, and teach all nations, baptizing them in the name of the Father, and of the Son, and of the Holy Ghost: teaching them to observe all things whatsoever I have commanded you: and lo, I am with you alway, even unto the end of the world" (Matt. 28:19-20).

We find no place in the Bible that the lost are told to come to church. However, we are told throughout the New Testament to go out and tell them about the saving grace of our Lord Jesus Christ.

Andrew "brought him to Jesus." Phillip said, "Come and see." What are we doing today to get people to the Savior? These men did not try to explain some hard to understand doctrine. They simply brought them face to face with the Savior Himself. Andrew and Phillip demonstrated changed lives. Do we demonstrate changed lives? Is it evident that Jesus has done something for us? Let us share our life and our testimony with some unsaved person this week.

THOUGHT: When did you bring someone to the Lord Jesus Christ?

November 26 -- John 1:45-47
A Skeptic Saved

The name Nathanael means "the gift of God." In verse 47 our Lord said about Nathanael, "Behold an Israelite indeed, in whom is no guile!" Christ did not mean that Nathanael was already saved and that he did not need the Savior. He meant that there was no hypocrisy about him.

Nathanael had questioned whether anything good could come out of Nazareth. This city was known as a wicked city and Nathanael knew about that. He did not believe that the Savior could come from Nazareth. Thus he questioned, "Can there any good thing come out of Nazareth?" He did not believe that the Messiah had come.

Phillip said to him, "Come and see." We have looked at that phrase already. Today I want us to see how this man becomes a Christian. We will also see how anyone else becomes a Christian.

Nathanael is a skeptic. He is one who questions things and does not believe unless he can be shown. Yet, his name means "the gift of God." Does it seem a little strange that a skeptic's name should mean "the gift of God?"

Nothing needs to be made more clear to people today than the fact that salvation is the gift of God. Nathanael received the gift of salvation and in verse 49 he said, "Thou art the Son of God."

The Bible says, "The gift of God is eternal life through Jesus Christ our Lord" (Rom. 6:23). Have you received this wonderful gift of life? If not, today is a great time to trust Him to give it to you. If you have received it, then go out and tell others about it.

THOUGHT: God saves all of those who will commit themselves to Christ.

November 27 -- John 1:47-50
Chosen of God

It is an amazing thing to be chosen of God. Jesus had chosen Nathanael before he had even seen Him. While Nathanael was still under the fig tree, Jesus knew his heart and all about him. There is a sense in which we choose the Lord, but there is also a sense in which we are chosen by the Lord.

Nathanael never would have chosen Christ. He had already said that nothing good could come out of Nazareth. He was a skeptic and his mind was made up already. The Lord knew all about this but He still had chosen Nathanael to be one of His twelve disciples.

Do you realize today that the only reason that you can claim eternal life is because you are chosen by the Lord? Christ said, "Ye have not chosen me, but I have chosen you, and ordained you, that ye should go and bring forth fruit, and that your fruit should remain" (John 15:16). The Bible also says, "According as he hath chosen us in him before the foundation of the world, that we should be holy and without blame before him in love" (Eph. 1:4).

Someone asked a twelve year old boy once, "Son, have you found Jesus?" The boy's reply was, "Pardon me, sir, I didn't know Jesus was lost; I was lost, and Jesus found me."

Do you rejoice in God's salvation today? It should bring us unspeakable joy to know that He chose us to receive His great salvation. Let us rejoice today and thank Him for His eternal love for us.

THOUGHT: It brings great joy to us to know that Jesus chose us.

November 28 -- John 1:47-48
Jesus Knows All

Does this scripture passage sound strange to you? It should not, for the Bible says that God knows the end from the beginning. Let us now look at three more verses of scripture.

In Proverbs 15:3 we read: "The eyes of the Lord are in every place, beholding the evil and the good." Also, in Jeremiah 16:17 we read: "For mine eyes are upon all their ways: they are not hid from my face, neither is their iniquity hid from mine eyes." Again, in Hebrews 4:13 we read: "Neither is there any creature that is not manifest in his sight: but all things are naked and opened unto the eyes of him with whom we have to do."

These are sobering thoughts, aren't they? God knows all about you today. He has always known all about you. The Bible says, "Be sure your sin will find you out" (Num. 32:23). The psalmist cried out, "Whither shall I flee from thy presence" (Ps. 139:7)? He then mentions several places but he admits that God is always there.

Now let's just take a brief inventory. Are you saved? Do you have assurance that Jesus Christ has washed your sins away with His own blood? The Bible says, "Believe on the Lord Jesus Christ, and thou shalt be saved" (Acts 16:31). Have you believed on Him in order to be saved?

If you are a Christian, is your life pleasing to God? Do you have the kind of testimony that points people to Jesus? Do people want to be like you? Jesus said, "Ye shall be witnesses unto me" (Acts 1:8). What kind of witness are you?

THOUGHT: Praise God for the fact that He knows all about us.

November 29 -- Nehemiah 1
A Man with a Concerned Heart

Recently I have been attracted to Nehemiah. He was a great man of God. We need to have more men like Nehemiah today. Let us now notice some things about this man in our scripture for today.

First, in verses 1 through 3 he is told the condition of his people in Jerusalem. Nehemiah was cupbearer of the king of Persia. He asked certain ones from Judah how it was with those who were still in Jerusalem. The report was not good. The walls were down, the gates were burned, and the situation was not good at all.

Second, in verse 4 we see that he had compassion on the people. He wept, fasted, and prayed for several days because of their condition. How many of us have this kind of compassion? Are we burdened about the conditions that we see around us today? We need to have compassion as Nehemiah had. Do we weep and pray when we see the sin of the people around us today? Do we see the need to minister to their needs?

Third, Nehemiah prayed that God would do something about the condition of the people, as we read in verses 5 through 11. In verse 5 he speaks of the character of God. God is the God of heaven and He is great. He keeps His covenant and He is a God of mercy. In verses 6 and 7 Nehemiah confesses the sin of the people. We live in a day when sin is no longer considered to be really bad. May God help us to see our own sin and the sin of the people. In verses 8 through 10 he speaks of God's promises. God has promised to remember and to forgive. In verse 11 he asks God to hear him and to prosper him.

THOUGHT: Dear God, make me more like your servant Nehemiah!

November 30 -- Nehemiah 2:17-20
Getting the Spirit to Build

Today as we see Nehemiah, he has received special permission from the king to go to Jerusalem and to repair the city. God has heard his prayer and has given him acceptance with the king. He has letters from the king authorizing that he be given materials for rebuilding Jerusalem.

In verse 17 Nehemiah talks with the people about the destruction in the city. He has made the rounds and has inspected the walls and now he reports his findings. How are the walls around your life? Have you made a tour of inspection recently? What are the conditions around your church? Does it have the proper facilities to minister to the needs of the people?

In verse 18 the people respond and are ready to build. "And they said, Let us rise up and build. So they strengthened their hands for this good work." We are involved in a good work. Let us strengthen our hands as these people did.

In verse 19 the enemy ridicules their undertaking. There are always those who will rebel against everything that the Lord begins. Our attitude must be that of trusting in the Lord and moving ahead with His plans.

In verse 20 Nehemiah rebukes the enemy in the name of the God of heaven. "If God be for us, who can be against us" (Rom. 8:31)? The enemy has no authority to hinder the people of God as long as they follow the Lord's leadership. "The God of heaven, he will prosper us."

THOUGHT: When have you carefully inspected the walls of your life?

Things I Am Thankful For

1.

2.

3.

4.

5.

6.

7.

8.

9.

10.

Chapter Twelve

•••

December

•••

Verse to Memorize

Galatians 4:4

"But when the fulness of the time was come, God sent forth his Son, made of a woman, made under the law."

December 1 -- John 10:7-10
Is Heaven All?

Many people seem to think that all that matters is their getting to heaven. If they can just get inside the gate they will be satisfied. I am not satisfied with that and many of you are not either. Someone said, "I want all that God has for me." Every Christian should feel that way. Verse 10 tells us that we can experience abundant life. Jesus said, "I am come that they might have life and that they might have it more abundantly."

On the flyleaf of my Bible I have written several proverbs that I have collected through the years. I would like to share one of them with you: "To see Jesus crucified takes me to heaven. To see me crucified with Christ gives me heavenly life here."

Paul tells us, "Likewise reckon ye also yourselves to be dead indeed unto sin, but alive unto God through Jesus Christ our Lord" (Rom. 6:11). It is only as we do this and as we yield the members of our body to Christ that we can really grow in the grace of God. Paul says, "Know ye not, that to whom ye yield yourselves servants to obey, his servants ye are to whom ye obey" (Rom. 6:16)?

Every Christian needs to surrender his body to Christ. He needs to let Him direct what he thinks, what he says, what he does, how he feels, where he goes, and how he reacts to this life. Only as he does this will he "grow in grace and in the knowledge of our Lord and Savior Jesus Christ" (II Pet. 3:18). Only as he does this will he be able to truly live the abundant life here on earth.

To see Jesus crucified will get us to heaven. To see ourselves crucified with Christ will give us heavenly life here.

THOUGHT: Salvation is more than just a ticket to heaven; it is a life lived here.

December 2 -- Matthew 14:1-14
Sin Always Finds One Out

Herod was a wicked king. John had told Herod that he should not be living in sin. This did not please the king at all. He did not like the preaching of John the Baptist, so he had John killed by beheading him.

The king was very rich. He had a beautiful wife, whom he had taken from his own brother. He had many servants and everything seemed to be going well for Herod. He probably never gave a second thought to having John beheaded. He was satisfying his own sinful selfishness. He thought that no one would ever really care if John was put to death.

Now Jesus comes on the scene. Just as John had done, Jesus is preaching, "Repent, for the kingdom of heaven is at hand" (Matt. 4:17). Herod now remembers his sin of having John the Baptist killed. He became afraid and he thought that Jesus was John the Baptist risen from the dead. Herod's sin had caught up with him and now he was afraid. Herod never repented and he was never saved. The scriptures show that he died in his sin.

You have the opportunity to repent of any sin that you have committed. You also have the opportunity of trusting the Lord to deliver you from evil. Trust Him and let Him deliver you. Remember, your sin will find you out, or catch up with you (see Numbers 32:23), either in this life or in the life that is to come. Galatians 6:7-8 tells us, "Be not deceived; God is not mocked: for whatsoever a man soweth, that shall he also reap. For he that soweth to his flesh shall of the flesh reap corruption; but he that soweth to the Spirit shall of the Spirit reap life everlasting."

THOUGHT: You might hide sin from people, but you cannot hide it from God.

December 3 -- Matthew 16:22-27
Discipleship Calls for Self-denial

"If any man will come after me, let him deny himself, and take up his cross, and follow me." This verse falls easily into four divisions. Just to look at it quickly, we might entitle the divisions as follows: a man's desire; a man's denying; a man's delivery; and a man's distance.

No one will follow the Lord if he has no desire to do so. How is it in your own life? Is it really your desire to follow the Lord wherever He leads? If a person is satisfied with his own life as it is, he will have little desire to change it. We spend time visiting, shopping, golfing, traveling, camping, and doing many other things that we desire to do. How is our desire when it comes to serving the Lord?

A person who does not deny himself will not serve God. This does not just mean that he will deny himself to engage in certain things. It means that he will deny the old self-life from controlling his thinking and his actions. He must put self aside and let Christ sit upon the throne of his life.

A person must deliver, or take up his cross, if he is to properly fulfill a life of discipleship. The cross each one of us is to bear is the death of the self-life. It is not easy to do this, but self must be reckoned to be dead.

Finally, we must see to it that there is little distance between us and the Savior. This, of course, means that we should be side by side. We must put forth an effort in order to stay close by His side. Are you now doing that?

THOUGHT: No man pampers himself and serves God at the same time.

December 4 -- Matthew 15:1-20
Doing or Being

Jesus said that many people talk religiously and live devilishly. In verse 15 of today's reading He said, "This people draweth nigh unto me with their mouth, and honoreth me with their lips; but their heart is far from me."

He also told the disciples that what a person does is not so important as what he is. The truth is that what a person does will be controlled by what he is. Jesus said, "But those things which proceed out of the mouth come forth from the heart; and they defile the man."

Jesus had been asked by the Pharisees why His disciples ate without washing their hands. In the opinion of the Pharisees and according to their traditional teaching, this was defilement of the worst kind. That which Jesus is teaching here is that a person should be more concerned about the inner condition than the outward appearance.

Which interests you more, what people think about you or what God knows about you? Paul said for us "to be strengthened with might by his Spirit in the inner man" (Eph. 3:16). Our relationship to the Lord and our fellowship with Him will determine what we do and what we don't do.

Paul also said, "But put ye on the Lord Jesus Christ, and make not provision for the flesh, to fulfil the lusts thereof" (Rom. 13:14). This can only be done as we learn of Him and as we walk with Him.

Are you more concerned with what goes into the mouth or with what comes out of the mouth?

THOUGHT: Man does the things he does because he is what he is.

December 5 -- Matthew 5:13-16
The Christian's Relationship to the World

Too many Christians give very little thought to their influence upon the people around them. It is easy to become selfish and to fail to realize the effect our way of life has upon those people around us.

The character of the child of God is described in verses 3 through 10 of Matthew chapter 5. The relationship we are to have with the world is described in our verses for today. We are the salt of the earth and the light of the world.

Salt has several characteristics. One of these is that it is a preservative. Being a country boy, I can remember my dad applying salt to meat to preserve it so that we would have meat for the winter. Salt flavors food. I watch my wife as she puts salt in food as she prepares it for cooking and eating. Salt also induces thirst. This is the work of the Christian in the world. He is a preservative and he should give life a good flavor. As others see him they should become thirsty for the Christ that they see in his life.

Light also has several characteristics. Light travels in a straight line. It is reflected from one object to another, but it will not be reflected very well from a dirty surface. Our life must be clean and we must walk straight before the world if we are to point others to Christ. All light is from one source and that source is God. He is light and we are the light of the world as we reflect that light which God is.

As the salt of the earth and as the light of the world, are you doing the job that God expects you to do?

THOUGHT: We are our brother's keeper.

December 6 -- John 4:35-38
The Urgency of Winning the Lost Now

My father was a strawberry farmer. He always had one to three acres of strawberries. When the strawberries were ripe we had to pick them or we would lose them. My dad could not say, "The berries are ripe, but I do not have time to gather them. I will just wait until next week or next month." No, the berries would rot in the field if he had done that.

My dad used to go around the community and get help to pick the strawberries. I have seen as many as thirty or more people picking the berries at one time. I used to pick as many as a hundred quarts of strawberries a day. When they are ripe, you either pick them or you lose them.

The Lord tells us that it is this way with winning the lost. The fields are white already to harvest. You have people living next door or down the street or even across town from you who are lost and who need you to point them to Jesus Christ. Are you faithfully doing that?

We need many workers now. We have already lost many people because no one went to them with the gospel. Will you go to some lost or unchurched person and point them to Christ? Some of you are teachers or officers in the church. Are you busy in the harvest field for God? "Lift up your eyes, and look on the fields; for they are white already to harvest."

Can you sense the urgency of winning the lost now while the Lord is still extending His mercy?

THOUGHT: We are faced today with the urgency of reaching the lost.

December 7 -- John 5:1-9
Hopeless Sinners Can Be Saved

It is easy to give up on someone for whom you are praying. Many people have to wait for years before they see the person saved for whom they are praying. It is said that a great man of faith in England prayed for fifty-two years for two men. One of the men was saved just before the man of faith died and the other was saved two years after his death.

Our scripture for today tells of one who had been laid at this pool for thirty-eight years. Each day someone would bring him and leave him there. No healing came but he did not give up hope. He kept seeking to be healed. One day the Savior came along and He healed the man. The man then arose and took up his bed and went home. No one ever had to bring him to the pool again.

One time in our church we had a man to come to the Lord. Some of our people had been praying for this man for twelve years or more. It would have been easy to give up after so long a time, but there is never a time to give up when you are praying for someone. God heard the prayers of His people on behalf of this man and He brought him to Himself.

Some of you are praying for loved ones and friends. At times you become discouraged. Do not give up but just keep on praying to the Lord. In His own good time, God will do the work in those hearts.

Hopeless sinners can still be saved by turning to the God of hope.

THOUGHT: No case is hopeless with God.

December 8 -- John 5:19-24
As Simple As This

Many people think that salvation is to be achieved through trying not to do some things and trying to do some other things. Well, this is not the teaching of God's holy Word. Our verse for today tells us that salvation is available to everyone. However, it is available only on God's conditions, not on man's conditions.

In verse 24 Jesus said, "He that heareth my word." We have heard God's Word as it teaches the death, burial, and resurrection of the Lord Jesus Christ. This is made plain in our Sunday School and preaching services. Even the youngest ones in attendance often can understand this.

Then our Lord continues, "And believeth on him that sent me." This means that we take God at His Word. He said that Jesus came to save sinners and that He saves those who believe on Him. We have to either believe this or reject it. If we believe it, then we must believe that it applies to us as individuals. For example, I believe that Jesus Christ is the Savior and I believe that He paid my sin debt when He died. I believe that He came into my heart when I confessed my sin and asked Him to save me.

Jesus continues to tell us in this verse that anyone who hears and believes "hath everlasting life, and shall not come into condemnation, but is passed from death unto life."

Isn't it a great joy today to know that this is true in your life because you have heard His Word and you have believed on the Lord Jesus Christ for your salvation? What is more simple and yet what could be more profound than the fact that Jesus loves me?

THOUGHT: Have you been born again?

December 9 -- II Corinthians 5:17-21
Five Evidences of the New Birth

Turn in your Bible to I John. John gives us five evidences, or marks, of the new birth. Check these out in your own life and you can know whether you have been born again or not. Read the following verses.

1. I John 2:29. You will have the desire to do that which is right in the sight of God. If you are living the same kind of life that all the other people of the world are living, you are not born again.

2. I John 3:9. You have given up the habit of sinning and no longer live in sin. This does not mean that the old flesh no longer desires sinful and worldly things, but it means that you no longer have to satisfy that fleshly longing. God's people try to avoid sin rather than living in it.

3. I John 3:14. Do you have hatred in your heart for someone? Do you love some people that you thought that you would never learn to love? God works miracles in lives when Christ comes into them.

4. I John 5:1. Do you have any hope of salvation at all apart from Jesus Christ? He is God's anointed Savior and there is no hope apart from Him. When one acknowledges Jesus Christ as his own personal Savior, the Bible says that he has passed from death unto life.

5. I John 5:4. A Christian who is growing normally will experience victory over sin. This verse says that God's people "overcome the world." Each passing year you should experience more and more victory in your life.

THOUGHT: The condition of the person's heart is evidenced in his or her life.

December 10 -- I John 5:1-13
Certain Things God Wants Us to Know

We live in a day of insecurity and uncertainty. Unstable conditions bring people fear, anxiety, worry, and depression. However, there are some things that we can know that God wants us to know. Let's consider some of them.

1. He wants us to have assurance that Jesus Christ is our living and personal Savior. In II Timothy 1:12, Paul says, "I know whom I have believed." Paul knew the Lord Jesus Christ as a person. God wants each of us to have this same assurance that Paul had. Christ's work for me makes me safe and His word to me makes me sure.

2. He wants us to know that all our sins have been forgiven. This is not something for us to imagine; this is something for us to know. This is what God's Word plainly teaches. Do you take God at His word and are you sure that He took your sin upon Him? Ephesians 1:7 says, "In whom we have redemption through his blood, the forgiveness of sins, according to the riches of his grace."

3. He wants us to know that we have passed from death to life. When a person is born into this world he is spiritually dead. When he is saved he is made spiritually alive. He is then said to have passed from death unto life. Do you believe God for this?

4. He wants us to know that all that is happening in the world today is moving toward the fulfillment of His will. There is going to come a time when Christ will be acknowledged as King of Kings and Lord of Lords.

Regardless of the insecurity and uncertainty of the world around us, God wants us to realize that we are safe in the arms of Jesus.

THOUGHT: Faith is the evidence of things that are not seen.

December 11 -- Exodus 16:14-22
How to Become Strong Christians

When a person is saved, he is just beginning the Christian life. No one wants to remain a spiritual baby all his life. Just as there are certain laws of physical growth, there are also certain laws of spiritual growth. Let's look at some of these laws.

1. You need to eat plenty of good food. No one can properly grow, physically or spiritually, without eating. You need the right kind of food daily. Remember how God provided for the people of Israel. As the Bereans in Acts 17:11 did, even so you need to search the scriptures daily. There is no substitute for doing this.

2. You must get plenty of fresh air. Did you ever try to go for five minutes without breathing? Don't try it! If you are to grow and to be spiritually healthy, you must have the fresh air that comes to you through prayer. Our Lord spent time in prayer. He found it necessary to get alone with the Father. How we all need to do this.

3. You need plenty of good exercise. You must get some exercise or you will not be healthy. Every saved person should be in a good church where the gospel is preached and where he can serve the Lord. Preaching, Sunday School, and prayer meeting attendance are very important exercises. You also need fellowship with other believers. You need the exercise of teaching, singing, and visiting. You need to work with children, young people, and adult men and women as you all grow together.

4. You need plenty of quiet rest. There are several scripture passages that tell us to "wait upon the Lord." You need quiet time with the Lord in prayer and in the Word.

THOUGHT: Eat, breathe, exercise, and rest properly for spiritual growth.

December 12 -- Psalm 48:1-14
Directions for Godly Living

People always want to know what will help them to live godly lives. Proverbs 23:7 says about man, "For as he thinketh in his heart, so is he." We know that this is true, so we need to be very careful. Consider the following.

1. Jesus Christ is the only perfect man; follow Him. No better advice can be given to anyone. The Bible describes Him as the perfect man. He is our perfect pattern and example. We are to consider Him and to learn of Him and we are to follow Him.

2. Know the great doctrines of the church and you will become strong in serving the Lord. Study the great doctrines of faith, the virgin birth, the resurrection, grace, sanctification, God the Father, God the Son, and God the Holy Spirit. There is so much in the Word that we do not know. Let us learn these great doctrines and live for God.

3. Know and live by the principles laid down in the Bible and your life will be well pleasing to God. We should then be able to recognize our sins and shortcomings. In the Bible we find guidance for our life. We find comfort and companionship and we find plans for our life. We learn about the company that we are to keep and we learn of the joy that is given in His love. God's Word is filled with great principles for living.

4. Know and avoid the careless behavior of the unspiritual people. So many times we are influenced by those with whom we associate. We need to be very careful to choose the right friends.

5. Know what it is to be in the company of God's people. Read Psalm 1:1. Someone said, "What holds our attention determines our actions."

THOUGHT: What have you thought about lately?

December 13 -- Isaiah 6:1-9
Have You Seen What Isaiah Saw?

  1. **In verse 1 Isaiah saw Jesus Christ in His pre-incarnate glory.** He saw the glory that Jesus had before He came to earth to be our Savior. John 1:14 says that when Jesus became man and dwelt among us, "We beheld his glory, the glory as of the only begotten of the Father." Isaiah saw this long before we did.
  2. **In verse 1 he saw Him reigning.** He was sitting upon a throne. The earthly throne was empty. King Uzziah had died and Isaiah had no other way to look, so he looked upward. Which way are you looking and to whom are you looking today?
  3. **In verses 1 and 2 he saw the Lord worshipped.** The Lord was high and lifted up and the angelic host worshipped Him. He was worthy of their worship and He is worthy of our worship today. Whom are you worshipping?
  4. **In verses 2 and 3 he saw His purity and holiness.** Even the heavenly hosts covered their faces and their feet before the holy God. How careless we are sometimes when we are in the presence of our Lord.
  5. **In verses 3 and 5 he saw His power.** God is the "Lord of hosts." He is in perfect control of His universe and His will shall ultimately be done.
  6. **In verse 5 he saw His majesty.** Isaiah said, "Mine eyes have seen the King." Do you get the thrill of having seen the King, the Lord of hosts, with your spiritual eye?
  7. **In verse 3 he got a glimpse of His future glory.** "The whole earth is full of his glory." One day we will also see His glory in that future world.

THOUGHT: What you see influences your life.

December 14 -- John 9:1-7
Giving Sight to the Blind

The first time that I saw a person with a "seeing-eye dog" is something that I shall never forget. The woman was able to go up and down the street and she could cross the street. She could go into stores and do many things that a blind person normally cannot do. In a sense, the seeing-eye dog gave her sight.

Two brothers and a sister in one family were born blind. They have one sister who has sight. The blind members of the family line up behind the sister who has sight, with each person placing his or her hands upon the shoulders of the person in front of them. By doing this they are able to walk when otherwise they would not be able to walk.

Every person born of man since Adam has been blind spiritually. There has been no human cure for this blindness, but God has provided us with spiritual sight through His only begotten Son, the Lord Jesus Christ. Our spiritual blindness is removed as we receive Him as our personal Savior and He becomes our Substitute.

The Lord had been to Jerusalem to the feasts. As He was about to leave, He saw a blind man in the crowd. The Lord Jesus healed that man who had been blind from his birth. A short time later the Pharisees accused the man of being a disciple of Jesus. The man that was healed then preached a sermon to them and they excommunicated him. However, he was no longer a blind man.

I am glad that Jesus also saw my blindness one day. He invited me to come to Him for healing from my spiritual blindness and when I came He gave me spiritual sight.

THOUGHT: Spiritual sight brings spiritual light.

December 15 -- John 15:1-17
How to Have Fullness of Joy

The Lord wants each of his children to have abundant joy. In verse 11 of today's scripture we read, "These things have I spoken unto you, that my joy might remain in you, and that your joy might be full." His joy! I am so glad that He has given His joy. Let's look at some things about joy.

1. Christians ought to be joyful. Joy ought to be the prevailing characteristic of our life. Paul said, "Rejoice in the Lord alway: and again I say, Rejoice" (Phil. 4:4). This does not mean that we are never sad and unhappy. We can be unhappy and rejoice at the same time. Happiness depends upon things that happen in this life. Joy depends upon what Jesus has done on the cross. I rejoice in Jesus Christ even though I may be unhappy over my circumstances in this life.

2. What is there about this joy that Jesus gives? In verse 11 we see that it is Christ's joy. The true Christian life is simply the life of Christ being lived in man or woman. It is the fullness of joy. Christ's joy will overcome the sharpest disappointment that we may have. It is an abiding joy and it remains with us at all times and in all situations. We ought to share this joy with others.

3. How can we have this joy? We have it when we have Christ. He gives us that joy. We have it when we are in submission to Him. Whatever comes our way, we can rejoice when we commit it all to Him. We have joy because of the indwelling and infilling of the Holy Spirit. Jesus wants us to have this joy and He has given us the Holy Spirit to abide in us as the joy of the Lord.

THOUGHT: The Spirit of Christ is not only with the Christian, but in him.

December 16 -- Matthew 5:14-15 and John 8:12
The Light of the World

The story is told about a traveling man who gave a young boy a ride. As they rode along, they came to a pasture filled with mules. The man asked the boy, "Why are all the mules here?" The boy answered, "Sir, these mules work all day in the mine. They are brought up on Sundays to get light so that they will not go blind."

Jesus is the light of the world. As His disciples, we are to learn of Him and to let the world see Him in us. By doing this we become the light of the world.

It is a wonderful thought that He would use us as the vessels through which He would make Himself known to a lost and dying world. Yet, just as Jesus said, "He that hath seen me hath seen the Father" (John 14:9), we should be able to say he that sees me sees something of Jesus.

However, this can only be true in our lives as we study God's Word and come to know Jesus better and as we then allow Him to control us. The Bible is the written Word and Jesus is the living Word. We know Him as we allow the Holy Spirit to teach us through the Bible. All of these things work within us so that we can give the world around us light.

If we are the only light that some people ever see, how much light do they see? How do we affect them? "Ye are the light of the world" (Matt. 5:14). Let us pray that only the true Light will be seen in us.

After working all week in the mine of the world, do we not need to get the light at church on Sundays so that we won't go blind?

THOUGHT: Light dispels darkness.

December 17 -- Matthew 26:6-13
Cleansing

Something was called to my attention just recently that I would like to share with you in the next several devotionals. Tomorrow we will read another passage of scripture that will give us another account of the matter we are considering in today's reading.

The supper referred to here takes place in the home of Simon the leper. You remember that leprosy in the Bible is a picture of sin. Simon had been unclean and according to the Levitical law he must acclaim himself so. He was instructed in the law to cover his mouth with a cloth and to cry "unclean" when someone approached him. There is little question that he had now been cleansed by the Lord. Out of love for the Lord and for what the Lord had done for him, he prepared a supper for Jesus.

It has been suggested that leprosy is never healed but that it is sometimes cleansed. Have you been cleansed from your sin? Only the Lord Jesus can do that. We are not talking about being healed from sin and leaving the stigma there; we are talking about being cleansed from sin and leaving nothing there but the scar.

Have you been to Jesus for the cleansing power? Are you washed in the blood of the Lamb? Examine yourself today and determine if you have been cleansed. If you have not yet been cleansed, ask Jesus to cleanse you now.

We all need the cleansing that only God can give. Read Psalm 51:1-2.

THOUGHT: The blood of the Lord Jesus Christ cleanses us from all sin, leaving no stain whatsoever.

December 18 -- John 12:1-11
Fellowship

In the last devotional we talked about being cleansed from sin. This is the first thing we must do in our approach to God. Fellowship comes after we have been saved, for no one has fellowship with God until after becoming a child of God. Becoming a child of God happens when we receive Jesus Christ as Savior.

In our scripture for today Jesus is in the home of friends whom He loves very much. You will remember that Lazarus had died and had been raised from the dead by the Lord. Now Jesus has come by for a visit and to fellowship with these people.

They enjoy fellowship around the table. This we often experience with one another, don't we? We invite people to come and to have a meal with us because of the fellowship that we can have and enjoy in that way. This is a picture of the fellowship that we need with one another and with our Savior, the Lord Jesus Christ.

We experience this fellowship as we spend time with Him. We need to learn more about Him by reading the Word of God. We need to share with one another the blessing of God upon our lives. What better place is there to go than to church and what better way of promoting fellowship is there than by attendance at church? At church we sing songs of praise to His name, we study His Word, we share His Spirit, and we enter into His manifest presence in prayer.

Cleansing comes first and then fellowship follows that. Is your fellowship what it should be, or are there areas in your life that need His cleansing touch? Commit it all to Him so that your fellowship can be what it ought to be.

THOUGHT: Our fellowship should have God as the other fellow.

December 19 -- John 12:1-8
Service

We read several times about Jesus' visits to the home of Lazarus, Martha, and Mary. Martha is portrayed as always being busy. Luke 10:40 says that she was "cumbered about with many things." Luke also mentioned that Martha complained about Mary not helping her.

Serving God is good and His children should serve Him. However, we can give too much emphasis to serving and not enough attention to some other very important matters. We see many churches that are "as busy as bees," but sometimes we wonder what is being accomplished for God and His glory by all the busy-ness.

One of the first things necessary in the life of a Christian is growth in the knowledge of God. This comes about through a study of His Word. Perhaps it would be a good idea to have training periods for new Christians before they are "put to work."

In verse 2 of today's scripture there is no mention of Martha complaining as there is in Luke 10. Could it be that the resurrection had become a reality to her? We need to know that Jesus has died for our sins. We also need to know that He is risen to deliver us from ourselves and from useless service.

Some people serve tirelessly in order to feel that they are saved. Others serve willingly because they know that they are saved. Which is it with you? Paul writes about reasonable service in Romans 12:1. First John 4:19 says, "We love him because he first loved us." Perhaps we could say that we serve Him because He first served us.

THOUGHT: Let us not serve and complain, but let us recognize all that we have in Christ and serve Him and rejoice.

December 20 -- John 12:1-8
Worship

In Luke 10 Mary is seated at the feet of Jesus while Martha is busy at work. In our scripture lesson for today, Mary is anointing Jesus while Martha is busy serving. On both occasions Martha is busy while Mary seems to be doing nothing of any importance.

Here is a real lesson for us. Worship is not always seen by the outsider. In Luke 10 Jesus said that Mary had "chosen that good part." In John 12 He said, "Let her alone." Jesus knew the heart of Mary. He knew that she had a deep love for Him and that she understood His teaching about His death, burial, and resurrection.

Worship will cost you something. The first mention of worship in the Bible is in Genesis 22:5, where Abraham said of Isaac and himself, "I and the lad will go yonder and worship." Abraham knew that this was going to cost him his son. What have you given up and what does it cost you to worship God?

The last mention of worship in the Bible is in Revelation 22:8-9, when John fell down at the feet of the angel. When he did this he was told not to worship the angel but to worship God. Much that takes place in churches is not really true worship of God, but it is worship of popularity, excitement, and other things.

Let us pray that God will teach us what it really means to worship Him in the beauty of holiness. Read John 4:22-24 to see what Jesus said about worship. Let us examine ourselves and see if we are worshipping Him in spirit and in truth. That is what He wants us to do.

THOUGHT: The heavenly Father looks for those who will worship Him in Spirit and in truth.

December 21 -- John 12:23-38
The Hour Is Come

Jesus Christ came into the world to "save that which was lost" (Luke 19:10). The Bible account of His life describes Him as a man with keen insight into the needs of others. He is also portrayed as someone who was able to meet those needs when people would let Him do so.

There were times when the religious leaders of the day questioned Jesus. They were trying to get something against Him so that they might accuse Him before the legal authorities.

There were times when those same religious leaders took up stones to kill Him, and Jesus had to remove Himself from their midst. In spite of this opposition, Jesus continued His ministry. He healed the sick and He cast out devils. He gave sight to the blind and He gave hearing to the deaf. He gave food to the hungry.

There were various times when Jesus told His disciples of His impending death and resurrection. They just did not understand Him, yet Jesus moved steadily toward the appointed hour. He knew that He must give His life so that others might be able to live.

Let us give some real thought to the fact that He had such a great love for us that He would willingly give His life for us. In verse 24 of today's reading He explains, "Except a corn of wheat fall into the ground and die, it abideth alone: but if it die, it bringeth forth much fruit." He "fell into the ground" and He has been bringing forth much fruit since that time.

Through faith in Him, we are the fruit that He brought forth by His death.

THOUGHT: While we all were still sinners, the Lord Jesus Christ died for us.

December 22 -- Romans 6:1-10
Knowing for Sure

These are verses that we need to study very closely. We need to be completely familiar with what they have to say to us. The assurances and joy that we need in order to be a blessing to others will only come as we understand what the Bible says.

There is something in Romans 6:1-13 that will help you to know that you are saved from sin; you are saved for eternity; and you are saved with a message to give to others.

Notice the word "sin" in Romans chapter 6. Sin is mentioned seventeen times in this chapter. In verse 15 it is a verb and it speaks of what we do. In the other sixteen places it is used it is a noun and it speaks of what we are or what we have, which is a sinful nature. Please make sure that you understand one thing. It is the sinful nature that causes us to commit the sins in our life. In order to stop the sinning of verse 15, the old fallen nature--the sinful nature--which is the sin (noun) of the other verses, must be controlled. The only way possible for this to happen is by faith in Jesus Christ.

The reason that Jesus Christ went to the cross to pay the sin debt was to deliver us from sinning. He does this by bringing under control the old fallen nature--the sinful nature--and thereby bringing sin itself under control.

Do you know that you are saved from sin? Do you know that you are saved for eternity? Do you know that you are saved with a message to give to others? Do you have the assurance that the old sinful nature is under control because of the power of the Lord Jesus Christ and Him alone?

THOUGHT: It is our sinful nature that causes us to commit the sins in our life.

December 23 -- Genesis 3:1-5
Satan Is a Deceiver

Today's scripture reading gives an account of Satan's attack upon man through the serpent. In reality, Satan tries to get at God through man. He is the master deceiver. He always tries to make things look good to us so that he can entice us to follow his leading rather than following God's leading.

Peter says that the devil is walking around as a roaring lion seeking whom he may devour. Read I Peter 5:8. There have been many unsuspecting persons who sinned because they had not been properly taught about the tricks of the devil.

We need to be persuaded in our own mind that the devil is real. We need to realize that his whole purpose is to rise above the throne of God. In Isaiah 14 he sets forth his own desires. Because of these desires he has been "cut down." Satan is a real person who has a very strong ambition.

In II Corinthians 11:14-15, we also read, "Satan himself is transformed into an angel of light. Therefore it is no great thing if his ministers also be transformed as the ministers of righteousness."

Satan is a powerful personality and he seeks to turn us away from God. Therefore, it is all the more important that we be aware of his subtlety.

In the next few devotionals I want to share some things that Satan has said to me. I sincerely hope that these studies will be helpful for each of you who are waging war against the enemy of your souls.

THOUGHT: Don't listen to Satan; he is a liar.

December 24 -- Hebrews 2:1-3
Satan Told Me I Need Not Trust Jesus Now

Proverbs 27:1 says, "Boast not thyself of to morrow; for thou knowest not what a day may bring forth." None of us know how much time we have left to live in this world.

When the devil saw that I was going to receive Christ as my Savior, he told me that it was all right to do so. However, he told me to put off accepting Him. He said that there was plenty of time. He tells many people that same thing. Many Christian people put off doing things in service for God. They do this because the devil makes them believe that they have plenty of time.

Paul was brought before Felix the governor to answer charges of being a follower of the teachings of Jesus. Paul gave his testimony of salvation to the governor. Felix trembled and answered Paul by saying, "Go thy way for this time; when I have a convenient season, I will call for thee" (Acts 24:25). Felix made the mistake of putting off his own salvation and we have no record that he was ever saved.

We have known of people taking a loved one to the doctor and being told, "If I could have seen him several months ago, I could have helped him, but it is too late now. There is nothing I can do." Do not be guilty of allowing Satan to cause you to put off your salvation until it is too late.

Christian friend, do not let Satan control your Christian life by persuading you to put off your personal dedication to Christ. Do not neglect the opportunity the Lord has given you for service to Him.

THOUGHT: Procrastination is the devil's tool.

December 25 -- Matthew 2:1-12
Satan Told Me I Need Not Be a Sincere Christian

When I received Christ as my personal Savior, there was nothing that Satan could do about my eternal life, but he knew that he could kill my testimony as a Christian. He has tried to do this. He told me, "Now that you are a Christian, just don't be too sincere. Have yourself a good time."

Our scripture reading for today tells us of a group of men who were sincere in their search for the "king of the Jews." They had a very primitive mode of travel. In their search they traveled in the heat of the desert. They traveled facing the danger of thieves and robbers. They were a long distance from their home. They searched in the light of what little knowledge that they had about the One for whom they sought. They were very sincere in their search.

Today we know that Christ has come. We know that He lived upon this earth and died upon the cross for our sins. We know that He was buried and that He arose from the grave. We also know that He ascended into heaven and that He is coming again someday to receive His own. We have so much more knowledge than these wise men had. Are we as sincere as the wise men were? Are we determined to serve Him at any cost?

The journey of these wise men was long and slow; it was dangerous, hot, and tiring. Yet, our scripture says that they followed the star "till it came and stood over where the young child was." Are we sincerely serving Him today? Do we diligently seek to give to God the best of our abilities? Let us be sincere as we serve Him.

THOUGHT: Sincerity does not save, but it helps us to give a good testimony.

December 26 -- Romans 12:1-8
Satan Told Me I Need Not Live
a Separated Life

Most of you will remember the account given in the first several chapters of Exodus of Moses' appeals to Pharaoh that he let Israel go. You remember Pharaoh's repeated refusals and God's judgments upon Egypt. God had told Moses to go and tell Pharaoh to set Israel free and to let them leave the land of Egypt. Pharaoh said, "Who is the Lord, that I should obey his voice to let Israel go" (Exod. 5:2).

God sent certain judgments upon Egypt and finally Pharaoh began to compromise. At first he said, "Go ye, sacrifice to your God in the land" (Exod. 8:25). This is the approach Satan makes to many people today. He says, "Be a Christian, but live a worldly, pleasure-seeking, and selfish life. Don't miss out on all the fun of the world." The second compromise was, "I will let you go, that ye may sacrifice to the Lord your God in the wilderness; only ye shall not go very far away" (Exod. 8:28). Satan tells us that we don't have to be a truly separated Christian.

Pharaoh then said, "Go now ye that are men, and serve the Lord" (Exod. 10:11). The devil is never pleased when a complete family is sold out to God. It is often the man that is the holdback. Ultimately, Pharaoh said, "Let your flocks and your herds be stayed" (Exod. 10:24). Satan tells us not to sell out completely to God but to keep at least a material interest in the world.

God's way is that we present our bodies and all that we are in order to best serve Him. He wants us to be completely separated from the influence of a sinful world.

THOUGHT: You cannot serve God and serve the lust of the flesh.

December 27 -- Romans 12:1-8
More on the Separated Life

A trucking firm ran an advertisement in the newspaper for a truck driver. Three people applied for the job. The same examination was given to each of the applicants. They were given the following problem. "You are driving a loaded truck of a given weight down a mountain road. There is a curve with a ninety degree turn and there is a precipice with a thousand feet drop below it. How fast can you drive and how close can you come to the precipice without losing control of the truck and going over the edge?"

The three men gave their answers. One man said that he could drive fifty miles per hour and come within one foot of the precipice. Another said that he could drive forty-five miles per hour and come within six inches of the precipice. The third man said that he did not know how fast he could drive or how close he could come to the precipice. However, he said that he would drive as slowly as he needed to and would stay as far away from the precipice as he could. Who do you think ended up getting the job?

Many Christians want to live just as close to the world as they can and still be called Christians. Some of the leaders in our churches love to go to dances and to movie houses. They frequently go on Sunday camping and fishing trips instead of going to church. They partake of alcoholic beverages and gamble and tell dirty jokes. In other words, they live lives just like the people in the world around them. Then they wonder why they have no influence over other people.

May our God help your family and mine to be "holy, acceptable unto God, which is your reasonable service."

THOUGHT: God and sin never agree.

December 28 -- Philippians 4:1-4
Satan Told Me Worldly Life Was More Fun

The Bible says, "By faith, Moses, when he was come to years, refused to be called the son of Pharaoh's daughter; choosing rather to suffer affliction with the people of God, than to enjoy the pleasures of sin for a season" (Heb. 11:24-25).

The devil tells you that there is pleasure in sin, but he does not ever tell you that it is just for a season. He does not ever tell you that, after you have rebelled against God and His will for your life, you will have the chastisement of God upon your life. Hebrews 12:7 says, "If you endure chastening, God dealeth with you as with sons; for what son is he whom the father chasteneth not?"

Some time ago my wife and I were on the way to a Sunday School department social. We saw a man coming out from a house that was in a run down condition. The grass and weeds had not been cut for months. The man was dirty, unshaven, ragged, and showed definite signs of malnutrition. We thought that we also saw the marks left by the use of drugs and alcoholic beverages. His appearance was no evidence of pleasure and joy, but it gave strong evidence of sin and sadness. We went on to the social, where we saw several couples who were clean and well dressed and who were rejoicing in the Lord. These people, unlike the other man we had seen, knew what it was to commit their problems to the Lord and to rejoice in His goodness.

Yes, there may be pleasure in sin for a season, but there is eternal joy in knowing and serving the living God. "Rejoice in the Lord always, and again I say, rejoice."

THOUGHT: The greatest enjoyment one ever has is in serving God.

December 29 -- II Timothy 3:14-17
The Young Christian and Bible Doctrine

One of the greatest perils in the life of a new Christian is wanting to know too much too soon. In other words, it is the lack of patience. There should be, and there will be, a desire to learn about God. The young Christian must be patient. Along with this he must be faithful in prayer, Bible study, and church attendance. In order to help the new Christian, we will present a brief survey of Bible doctrine and several scripture references that he can study.

1. We believe that the Bible is the Word of God. It does not just contain the Word, but it is the Word. It is the revelation of God in print. God has said exactly what He wanted to say. We take it for what it says, as today's scripture lesson tells us.

2. We believe that there is only one God, who is eternally self-existent in the persons of God the Father, God the Son, and God the Holy Spirit. We do not try to understand this; we just believe what God has said about the matter. Read Genesis 1:1; John 10:30; and John 4:24. Many people say that they do not believe what they cannot understand. These same people believe in the use of electricity, although they do not understand what it is and how it works. I know nothing about electricity but I use it just the same. Neither can I explain how a black cow can eat green grass and give white milk from which comes yellow butter. Nevertheless I drink the milk and eat the butter.

3. We believe in the deity of Christ. Yes, He is God. Read John 10:33; Matthew 1:23; and Isaiah 7:14. We may not understand how these things can be. However, many of God's doings are not understood by us but we still believe them.

THOUGHT: Feed on the milk until you can eat the meat of the Word.

December 30 -- Romans 3:19
The Young Christian and Bible Doctrine

We continue with our brief survey of Bible doctrine.

4. We believe that every person who is outside of Christ is by nature lost. For him a regeneration by the Holy Spirit is absolutely essential.

5. We believe that there is a personal devil who is called Satan. We believe that hell is a place of eternal and conscious punishment for all unsaved people. Read John 1:6-7; Matthew 25:46; and Revelation 20:14-15.

6. We believe that God's Holy Spirit convicts one of sin. The Holy Spirit regenerates souls, makes believers children of God by the new birth, assures them of heaven, and lives within them to enable them to live holy lives. Read John 16:8 and I Corinthians 3:16 and 12:3.

7. We believe that saved people are justified by faith in the shed blood of Jesus Christ. Read Acts 13:38-39.

8. We believe that a true New Testament church is an organized group of baptized believers practicing scriptural ordinances. Read about this in Acts 2:41-47 and Matthew 28:19-20.

9. We believe in the eternal security of all believers. Read John 10:28-29.

10. We believe that baptism by immersion is a scriptural ordinance to be administered by the church. Read Acts 8:38-39; Matthew 3:15-16; and Romans 6:3-5.

11. We believe that the Lord's Supper is a scriptural ordinance of the church to be partaken of by obedient Christians. Read I Corinthians 11:23-29.

12. We believe that there will be a resurrection of both the saved and the unsaved. Read John 5:28-29.

THOUGHT: What the Bible says is that which really matters in life.

December 31 -- Romans 6:1-10
Preparing for a New Year

The old year is almost history. There is nothing that you can do after today that will be entered into the ledger book of this year. We are suddenly poised to enter a new year. There are some things that we can do to be better servants of the Lord next year than we have been this past year. People often talk of making New Year's resolutions as they begin a new year. However, most people freely admit that the resolve is usually not strong enough and the resolutions are broken before the new year is very old.

There are many Christians who have no real assurance of their salvation. Having no real assurance of salvation, they have no lasting peace in their soul. Having no real lasting peace in their soul, they have no excitement and joy in serving God. This is a tragic thing. Yet, this is the experience of many people. Perhaps it is the experience of some of you who are reading these words now. The assurance of salvation, which will bring a peace of soul and which will bring joy in serving God, can be found in the Bible. Wouldn't it be great if all Christians could have the joy of this assurance?

To prepare the way for a new year and to get the most from our meditations, each of us needs to do certain things. Ask yourself these questions and give honest answers. Am I saved? If I died today, would I go to heaven? If you answered no, then you need to be saved (see "Do You Need to Be Saved?" on the next page). If you answered yes, do you have real peace in your soul? Is there a joy in serving God?

Have you made any resolutions for the new year? Why don't you resolve to make it a practice of studying the Bible every day of the coming year and then do it?

THOUGHT: The new year brings to us the need for making new decisions.

Do You Need to Be Saved?

Throughout the pages of these devotionals you will find the fact emphasized that every person in the world needs to come to Jesus Christ for His salvation. You may not fully understand why this is true. You may not know the facts that are given to us in the Bible and because of this lack of knowledge you may still be unsaved. You may know some or all of the facts but you have not accepted them as applying to you in your situation. You may be confused because of things that you have heard about how feelings relate to salvation. In any event we urge you to read and study the following Bible verses and to make your own personal choice of Jesus Christ as your Savior this very day.

1. All people are lost apart from Christ. Isaiah 53:6 and Romans 3:23.

2. All lost people are condemned in the eyes of God. John 3:18; John 3:36; and Ephesians 2:12.

3. All lost people are facing eternal death. Romans 6:23 and Acts 4:12.

4. All lost people can be saved by turning in faith to Jesus Christ. Ephesians 2:8-9; Acts 3:19; John 3:16; Acts 16:31; and John 1:12.

5. All people who place their faith in Christ should confess Him. Romans 10:9-10 and Matthew 10:32-33.

I, (your name) _____ on (date) _____ do accept God's Son, Jesus Christ, as my own Lord and personal Savior.

Suggestions for Devotions

The following are some suggestions on how to have daily devotions and how to benefit from the use of this daily devotional guide. You may wish to use this guide in your family devotions or you may wish to use it for your personal devotions or in your personal Bible study. Throughout the guide we have included many scripture references that we believe you will want to use in your daily Bible study effort.

It is best to have a particular time set aside each day for devotions. For some people the best time may be in the early morning. For others the best time may be at meal time. Still others may find that just before bedtime is best. You may want to carry the guide with you to work and read it on your break. Or, you may want to put it in your car to read when you are waiting in your car at the mall.

We suggest that your devotions include the reading of the scripture passage for the day and reading the commentary. Reading the scripture references given in the commentary and using a concordance to look up related Bible passages would be helpful in your study. Include a time of prayer for those for whom you are concerned, including missionaries that you or your church support.

If you use the guide for family devotions it would be good for as many members of the family as possible to take part. For example, the father might read the scripture, the mother might read the commentary, and the children might lead in prayer. You could rotate participation so that different members of the family read or pray on different days.

Our prayer is that this daily devotional guide will be used to strengthen your faith as you study the Holy Bible.

TOPICAL INDEX

Abel's Faith Acknowledged Sin, 183
Abel's Faith Admitted His Unworthiness, 185
Abel's Faith Obeyed God, 184
Abraham's Ram, 298
Accepted in Christ, 258
All Ye, Come, 241
Another Lesson on Prayer, 84
Anything Costs Something, 331
Apostle, An, 122
Are You a Maturing Christian? 242
Are You Ashamed? 117
As Simple As This, 365
Assignment or Opportunity, 301
Assurance, 64

Babes in Christ, 186
Be Not Unequally Yoked Together in Marriage, 155
Before and After, 86
Beginning of a Prayer List, The, 221
Besetting Sin, The, 227
Blessing God, 87
Blessings of the Blood, 181
Built-in Desire, A, 9

Called of God, 341
Calling, 103
Certain Things God Wants Us to Know, 367
Cheer of Salvation, A, 193
Chosen of God, 352
Christ Must Go through Samaria, 143
Christ Presented to the Colossians, 176
Christ Seen in Personalities, 174
Christ Seen in Praise, 175
Christ We Serve, The, 240
Christian Giving, 15
Christian Joy, 82
Christian Life Is Positive, The, 47
Christian's Relationship to the World, The, 362
Christians Do Sin, 189
Church at Corinth, The, 131
Church Attendance, 274
Cleansing, 374
Come and See, 350
Commit Thy Way unto the Lord, 329
Commitment, 105
Committed to a Task, 199
Committed to God, 200

Companions, 192
Cricket in the Spider Web, The, 74
Cross and God's Love, The, 250
Cross of Christ Is Necessary, The, 287
Cure for Anxiety, A, 234

Daily Guidance, 114
Danger of Careless Living, The, 188
Daniel's Decision Was a Hard One, 212
Desire for Missions, The, 275
Devil Is Real, The, 246
Devil Works Evil, The, 164
Devil's Attempt at Cover-up, The, 312
Directions for Godly Living, 369
Discipleship Calls for Self-denial, 360
Divine Wrestling, 219
Do You Have a Favorite Verse? 20
Do You Remember When You Were Saved? 243
Doing It Now, 309
Doing or Being, 361
Dying on Third Base, 215

Eating the Word, 111
Evangelism, 163
Everybody Needs Salvation, 54
Expectancy, The, 65

Fact of God's Love, The, 285
Faith, 79
Faith of Abel, 182
Fate of the Sabbath, The, 310
Favor with God and Man, 95
Fellowship, 375
Five Evidences of the New Birth, 366
Folding at the Foundation, 259
Following Jesus, 260
Forgiving Sins, 333
Foundation, 62
Foundation, The, 57
"Fraidy" Cats, 339
From Darkness to Light, 161

Gethsemane, 216
Getting the Spirit to Build, 355
Gift of God's Love, The, 278
Giving Sight to the Blind, 371
God Answers Prayer, 230
God Is Not Mocked, 191
God-Man, The, 173
God Wants to Bless His Own, 194
God Will if You Will, 116

God Will Provide, 334
God's Courtroom, 125
God's People Consecrated, 269
Gone Forever, 323
Good Health for a Holy Life, 115
Good News from God, 263
Good Question to Consider, A, 284
Gospel Attracts, The, 139
Gospel of Salvation, The, 42
Gospel Repels, The, 140
Grace and Peace, 104
Gravity, 170
Great Appearance, A, 204, 313
Great Claim, A, 205, 314
Great Commission, A, 206, 315
Great Promise, A, 207, 316
Greatest, The, 245
Growing as a Christian, 343, 344, 345
    346, 347, 348, 349

Hallelujah Chorus, 13
Happy Decisions, 214
Have You Seen What Isaiah Saw? 370
Healing the Sick, 335
Heaven, 209
Heaven Is a Big Place, 35
Heaven Is a Place, 49
Heaven Is a Place of Comfort, 32, 195
Heaven Is a Place of Eternity, 30, 203
Heaven Is a Place of Joy, 33, 198
Heaven Is Really a Place, 208
Help When Needed, 262
Holy Decision, A, 213
Holy Ground, 340
Holy Spirit Is Our Teacher, The, 223
Home, The, 152
Hopeless Sinners Can Be Saved, 364
Hour Is Come, The, 378
How Excellent Is His Name, 317
How Much Is Enough? 327
How the Zeal of Jesus Affects Me, 129
How to Become Strong Christians, 368
How to Get Rid of Fear, 138
How to Get to Heaven, 56
How to Grow as a Christian, 43, 45, 46, 48
How to Have Fullness of Joy, 372
How to Prevent Unhappiness in the Home, 153
Human Wisdom Cannot Know the Things
    of God, 210
Humility, 282
Humility of Jesus, The, 249

I Am Confident, 22
I Am Convinced, 23

I Am Glad That God Knows, 318
I Have Concluded, 25
I Sat at the Trial, 201
Illustrations of Knowing One in
    His Person, 290
Inner Desire Will Turn Us to God, 237
Instructions to Timothy, 123
Is Heaven All? 358
It Is Confirmed, 24
It Is True, 319

Jesus and the Storm, 332
Jesus at Calvary, 167
Jesus at Work, 162
Jesus Gives When We Ask, 231
Jesus Himself Is Coming, 50
Jesus Knows All, 353
Job Was a Man of Principle, 134
Job Was a Man of Propriety, 135
Job Was a Man of Prudence, 136
Job Was Protected, 137
John The Baptist, 107

Kind of Fears That Beset People,
    The, 151
King Asa, 236
Knowing for Sure, 379
Knowing Him and Doing His Will, 289
Knowing Jesus in His Person, 233

Last Message in the Bible, The, 235
Light of the World, The, 373
Living in Darkness, 322
Living Word, The, 52
Long Life for Loyalty, 94
Look Up and Rejoice, 239
Looking at Revival, 264
Love of God, The, 21
Love the Brethren, 100
Love the Lost, 99

Man as He Is, 224
Man Will Be Judged According to
    His Works, 128
Man Will Be Judged According to
    Performance and Not Knowledge, 92
Man Will Be Judged According to
    Reality and Not Profession, 89
Man Will Be Judged According to
    Truth, 126
Man Will Be Judged by Accumulated
    Wrath, 127
Man Will Be Judged by the Secrets
    of the Heart, 90

Man with a Concerned Heart, A, 354
Message of Missions, The, 267
Message of the Cross Meets Human Needs, The, 286
More about Instructions, 124
More on John the Baptist, 108
More on the Separated Life, 384
More on Unhappiness in the Home, 156

Need in America, The, 271
Never Give Up, 330
New Birth, The, 97
Nicodemus, 96
Normal Christian Life, 34
Not by Good Works, 326

Obeying the Word, 159
Object of God's Love, The, 272
Occupy Till I Come, 31
Only One Way, 226
Open Door, 338
Our Giving Ought to Be Personal, 17
Our Giving Ought to Be Proportional, 19
Our Giving Ought to Be Provisional, 16
Our Giving Ought to Be Punctual, 14
Our Giving Ought to Be with Pleasure, 18
Our Great God, 257
Our Responsibility, 61
Our Shepherd, 63
Out of Place, 217

Pardon, 130
Pardon by Blood, 58
Patched-up Religion, 55
Peace of God, The, 157
Peace with God, 158
People in Despair, 72
Perfect Peace, 295
Peril of Asceticism, The, 180
Peril of Ceremonialism, The, 178
Peril of Mysticism, The, 179
Peril of Rationalism, The, 177
Person of the Gospel, The, 118, 297
Peter Was Committed, 85
Power of His Resurrection, The, 266
Power of the Gospel, The, 120, 296
Power over the Devil, 336
Prayer, 270, 281, 342
Prayer for Missions, 41
Prayer without Repentance, 238
Preaching against Sin, 38
Precious Faith, 106
Preparing for the New Year, 388
Program of the Gospel, The, 121

Promises, 93
Provision Enough for the World, 244
Purpose of God's Gift, The, 276
Purpose of the Gospel, The, 119
Put to Death, 60

Real or Unreal, 328
Reasons Why, 44
Reckon, 306
Redemption Completed, 171
Regulate, 308
Reign, 307
Remember, 305
Renewed Prayer Life, A, 81
Renewed Service, A, 83
Repentance, 37
Resurrection, The, 51, 311
Revival in Elijah's Day, 251
Risen with Christ, 168
Rules for a Happy Home, 154

Sad Condition, 144
Safe with the Lord, 256
Satan Is a Deceiver, 380
Satan Told Me I Need Not Be a Sincere Christian, 382
Satan Told Me I Need Not Live a Separated Life, 383
Satan Told Me I Need Not Trust Jesus Now, 381
Satan Told Me I Was Good Enough, 68
Satan Told Me Worldly Life Was More Fun, 385
Satisfaction, 88
Seeing Single, 337
Seeking, 169, 302
Service, 376
Serving God, 202
Seven Arguments against Anxiety, 145
Should I, or Should I Not? 187
Simon Peter, 102
Sin Always Finds One Out, 359
Sin Is a Disease, 73
Sin of Not Praying, The, 228
Skeptic Saved, A, 351
Slums and Ghettos, 29
Smile of God's Countenance, The, 8
Some Astounding Things, 98
Source of Spiritual Knowledge, The, 220
Spiritual Awakening, 299
Spiritual Growth, 225
Steadfastly, 12
Sterilizing the Tongue, 320

Stop-Look-Listen, 28
Strange Sayings, 53
Study, 109
Study Daily, 112
Substitute, 27

Thanks, 172
There Is Just One Way, 324
There Is No Respect of Persons with God, 91
There Is No Substitute for Personal Contact, 80
There Is Power in the Blood, 166
Three Things about the Church, 26

Understanding, 110
Unity in Purpose, 273
Urgency of Missions, The, 268
Urgency of Winning the Lost Now, The, 363

Valuables, 190
Visitation at Work, 146
Visitation Evangelism, 147

Walking with God, 141
Watchful Eye of Our Lord, The, 248
We Are Given the Mind of Christ, 222
We Need a Refuge from the Power of Sin, 247
We Need a Vision of God, 304
We Need Preaching about Judgment and Hell, 36
We Should Recognize His Presence, 113
Welcome of Grace, 300
What a Christian Can Do about Sin in His Life, 75
What about the Future, Young Person? 254
What Can I do with Jesus? 283
What Christ's Resurrection Did for Me, 265
What Does It Mean to Know Jesus in His Person, 232
What Fear Does to Us, 150

What Is the Problem with Youth? 255
What It Will Be Like When Jesus Comes, 66
What Kind of Example Are You? 77
What Paul Said about God's Gift, 277
What Revival Will Do, 71
What Sin Does in the Life of a Christian, 78
What the Resurrection Life Will Do for Us, 288
What Will Your Day Be? 321
When Decisions Should Be Made, 40
When Is Revival Needed? 67
When Will We Have Revival? 70
Who Decides What I Will Do with Jesus? 280
Who Knows about Sin? 76
Why Be Concerned? 148
Why Is Everybody Talking about Jesus? 303
Why Is It Important to Receive Jesus as Savior? 279
Why Prayers Are Not Answered, 218
Wives in Submission, 291
Woman in God's Work, The, 294
Words about a Soulwinner, 149
Work of the Pastor, 160
Worship, 377
Wrong to Be Gone, 142

Young Christian and Bible Doctrine, The, 386, 387
Young Christian and Stewardship, The, 10, 11
Young Man Who Made His Decision, A, 211
Young People Today, 252
Your Members upon Earth, 59
Your Soul Is Valuable, 253

How to Order Additional Books

To order additional copies of WALKING *by* FAITH, photo-copy this page and complete the information below:

Ship to: (please print)
Name _____
Address _____
City, State, Zip _____
Day phone _____

_____ copies of WALKING *by* FAITH
@ $14.95 each $_____
Postage and handling @ $2.25 per book $_____

Total taxable $_____
NC residents add 6% sales tax $_____

Total amount enclosed $_____

Make checks payable to: Avalon Valley Press

Send your order to:

    Avalon Valley Press
    P. O. Box 1186
    Graham, NC 27253-1186